LIBRARY LIT. 6 - The Best of 1975

edited by

BILL KATZ

The Scarecrow Press, Inc.
Metuchen, N.J. 1976

ISBN 0-8108-0923-0
Library of Congress Catalog Card Number 78-154842

Printed in the United States of America

CONTENTS

INTRODUCTION

Here we are again--the 30 best articles published between November 1974 and November 1975. In last year's introduction my stand-in, Professor Robert Burgess, asked: "What purpose does this yearly anthology serve?" Well, for the compiler it is a way of checking off the years. Growing reader acceptance threatens to carry the series well into that uncertain future. The sometimes secret hope that perhaps next year there will not be enough entries for consideration is somehow never realized. Actually, articles seem to improve in ratio to their volume. If anything, judging becomes increasingly more difficult.

The librarian's intellectual odyssey, at least as represented by these and past selections, is indeed encouraging. The writing here is quite up to anything to be found in other professions, is often superior in both style and thought. If nothing else, this annual collection seems to document that not all library literature is intolerable boredom. In fact, those who invented the silly convention that librarians can't write need only check out one or two of this year's entries.

How does one decide which is the "best"? Pure subjective choice, based upon some experience and a feeling for the traditional quality of good writing, is the only answer. That's my reply, although other judges in other years profess a more detached objective method, often helped along by argumentation which is so threatening that the more balanced members of the jury simply give up before the onslaught.

I note all of this to reassure the skeptical that our jury meetings are not quite governed by the standards set by normal committee gatherings so familiar to those who populate the American Library Association gatherings, or, for that matter, the sacred and profound assemblies of librarians who discuss baffling administrative problems. No, the jury tends to be somewhat more relaxed, certain their role is to come up with decisions more definite than a schedule for another meeting. They deliver the 30 best articles, lift a glass to the winners, and forget the whole business for another year.

Having revealed the mysteries of the inner circle, let it be noted that contributions for consideration by the meistersingers are always welcome. To date this request for candidates has resulted in about ten or fifteen suggestions a year, often by authors who rightfully suggest they deserve more recognition than that afforded by loving relatives. Sometimes they are right. More detached magazine editors are helpful, too. Still too little heard from: the individual reader who simply enjoys an article and wishes it brought to the attention of others. If you are out there, write me!

William A. Katz
SUNY-Albany
Albany, N.Y.
December, 1975

ACKNOWLEDGMENTS

The 1975 Jury

The jurors who selected the 30 best articles this year were: Anne Roberts, Associate Librarian, State University of New York at Albany; William R. Eshelman, editor, Wilson Library Bulletin; Cavan McCarthy, Teaching Assistant, School of Library and Information Science, SUNY Albany; Eric Moon, President, Scarecrow Press; and the perennial editor of this volume, Bill Katz.

Thank you, Ms. Nichols

The particular thanks of the editor goes to Barbara Nichols, graduate assistant, whose quite superior talents made this volume possible.

PART I

LIBRARIES AND LIBRARIANS

THE PART-TIME LIBRARIAN: A SUMMARY OF SUPPORT*

Laura Arksey

The idea of a less than forty-hour work week for some librarians is gaining a grudging acceptance in the profession, although considerable library talent is wasted because of a continued scarcity of part-time jobs. The attitude that has prevailed in most of the profession until recently has been "fulltime or nothing." An incident which occurred at a large regional library meeting five years ago is illustrative. During a discussion on trends in library education and employment a woman raised the question of part-time employment of professional librarians. It was apparent that the speaker at first misunderstood the question, answering somewhat vaguely in terms of typists, file clerks, etc. When the questioner made clear that she was talking about fully qualified librarians, like herself, who were seeking part-time employment, her question was met with a bass rumble of chuckles and asides from the group, while the speaker moved on to the next question.

Yet a change in the attitude toward part-time employment is being thrust on the library profession as a result of several trends:

1. Pressure from women librarians with families and limited mobility who, as the situation now stands, must choose between full-time employment or unemployment.
2. Budget cut-backs in many public and academic libraries necessitating the choice between laying off a a few full-time employees altogether or a larger number of them to less than full-time status.
3. The slowly growing demand in business and industry

*Reprinted by permission of the author and the publisher from PNLA Quarterly, Spring 1975, pp. 4-9.

for the special librarian and the recognition that for the same amount of money a part-time librarian with special subject competence is a better "buy" than a full-time secretary inappropriately assigned to library or research tasks.

4. The desire of some retired librarians to go on using their skills and experience in a part-time capacity.
5. The growing emphasis in our society on the value of personal fulfillment through leisure as well as work.

In spite of these pressures, a reluctance to consider employing part-time librarians persists in some quarters and the explicit reasons offered are well known by now: expense connected with breaking in to the job, payroll, etc., administrative problems of scheduling hours and dealing with a larger number of people, and a possible lack of continuity in the work. Hopefully, evidence presented in this article will show that the advantages of hiring an increased number of part-time people may far outweigh those disadvantages. However, there is probably also at work something more subtle and hard to budge than these explicit reasons for insisting on full-time work. One possibility lies in the continuing insecurity and self-consciousness among some librarians about professionalism.

There is apt to be the suspicion upon the part of the "dedicated" full-time career librarian that someone who seeks a part-time job cannot have a truly professional attitude. The guardians of our professional image have long cast nervous glances at law and medicine for clues as to professional behavior. If they do so in this case, they do not see at present an abundance of part-time doctors or lawyers. Yet if they were to look a little "lower" on society's scale of professions, at teaching or nursing, for example, they would see an increasing number of part-time professionals working to the mutual satisfaction of employer and employee. Finally, when librarians are willing to take an open-minded look not only at evidence from within their own and other professions but at business and industry, the advantages of employing a larger number of part-time workers become inescapably apparent.

Another subtle factor in the resistance to hiring part-time professionals may lie in the continuing domination of the administrative levels of our profession by men and the tendency of male administrators, consciously or unconsciously, to perpetuate that situation. (At a regional academic library committee meeting recently, at which I was the only woman, one of the men commented that the library directorship at X College was vacant and "They are looking for a top man for the job." There is no reason to assume he was using "man" in the generic sense.) Yet an administrator might argue legitimately that to specify a position as part-time would be virtually to exclude male applicants, for the way our society is currently constituted, educated men work full-time, while educated women work full-time, part-time, or not at all. Yet there is no axiomatic reason why a man could not apply for a part-time job. In an article in an issue of Protean devoted entirely to "The Professional Woman," the question was asked, "Should the library ... make it easier for parents of both sexes to shift when necessary from full-time to half-time and back without penalizing their professional development?" (Robson, p. 28). One respondent, Page Ackerman, Associate University Librarian, UCLA, replied:

> In my own library, at least one large public service unit has more half-time librarians than full-time librarians, primarily because, though many of them started out full-time, family responsibilities made it desirable for them to shift. Most of these staff members are women and these changes were made under a woman department head. Now there is a male department head who argues enthusiastically for half-time assignments because it gives the unit flexibility and because each of the staff members if a superior performer. Here I think the key words are responsibility and performance. (p. 29)

These conditions could apply as well to men as to women and may increasingly in the future as fathers begin to share more in the pleasures and responsibilities of child rearing. However, for the present, far more women than men seek part-time employment in libraries, and in the instance cited above, the arrangement is working out well. Furthermore, in answer to the charge that part-time employment may discriminate against males, there seems little reason yet to worry about unemployment among qualified and capable male librarians. Unemployment among librarians seems to be predominantly a female problem, and an increase of part-time positions would be one practical way of distributing the job opportunities more equitably between the sexes without categorically excluding anyone.

A suspicion on the part of full-time professionals that part-timers are akin to "scab labor" may also be a factor. To some extent this attitude may be justified. When the total salary and fringe benefit package of two half-time librarians does not equal that of a full-time person of similar qualifications, doing the same kind of work, then both the institution and the part-time librarians are contributing to this charge. The justification for hiring two half-time people should not be that they can be had for less, but that for the same price their services equal or may even surpass those of one full-time person. There may be instances when an administrator decides that the combination of one part-time professional and one full-time clerical is more sensible for the same amount of money than hiring a full-time professional with little or no clerical help. The half-time librarian is a scab only if he or she agrees to work for less than the going rate for such a position. (Unfortunately, it may be impossible for part-time librarians in academic libraries to avoid the scab problem entirely until there are corrections of the inequities experienced by part-time faculty in general.)

In trying to substantiate a case for increased hiring of part-time professionals, I have discovered support from three sources: librarianship itself, other professions, and business. The main contributions of the library literature have been to demonstrate the plight of the woman who is both a librarian and a homemaker and who is faced with the choice of working full-time or not at all, and to suggest benefits to libraries of taking more advantage of this source of "manpower." In fact, we are indebted mainly to the equal employment activist within the library profession for dealing with this question at all, even though they usually do so in the context of the employment and advancement of women librarians in general, and the question should not be regarded exclusively as a women's concern. Such advocates as Anita Schiller, Janet Freedman, and Helen Tuttle have done much to raise the consciousness of our profession regarding the "disadvantaged majority" within its ranks. However, one of the most emphatic cases for the part-time employment of family women was made by Eric Bow, Coordinator of Technical Services, Ontario Provincial Library, who asserts that more part-time positions are needed in librarianship "to provide opportunity for librarians who are mothers to continue to climb the career ladder and keep in touch with their field" (Bow, p. 77). He especially recommends that library administrators hire some part-time people as bibliographers, subject specialists, catalogers, children's librarians, and reference librarians, claiming that "various studies show that two librarians working twenty hours per week contribute more to the job than one full-time person; they usually work harder, are more enthusiastic and are less costly" (p. 78). Although he does not cite these studies specifically, common sense and evidence from professions and business, to be discussed later, would tend to support them. His strongest argument, though, is that an interrupted career is a waste not only to the individual but to the profession and that libraries should do everything possible to keep people of known ability in the profession, rather than to let them go because new family responsibilities necessitate a reduction in the work hours.

There are also librarians like myself who entered the profession on a part-time basis and there are many more who would do so if more part-time jobs were available. A creative proposal for team employment was offered by Linda Brass and Thelma Sameth who, upon their completion of graduate work in librarianship, sought a full-time position in children's work, to be shared between them. They suggested the following advantages of hiring such a team:

> A wide variety of skills and interests would bring freshness of approach. Alternating work schedules would prevent tediousness. The responsibility for necessary procedures could be divided to great advantage. For instance, by sharing the constant reevaluation of the collection and dividing it by subject interest and knowledge, two points of view would be presented. A team would be able to advise and consult each other in areas of special competency. Thus, there would be an opportunity for better service through reinforcement of mutual strengths.... By dividing the job, each would be able to spend more time doing outside reading than one person ... could possibly do. Another advantage would be the availability of one partner in the illness of the other. One full-time professional has more limited time and energy to provide innovative children's programs than two part-time professional librarians would have (Brass, p. 2853).

The waste to the profession is obvious if one or both of these young women were denied the opportunity to use her skills and training in librarianship for a number of years because of a scarcity of part-time jobs. Yet there are currently examples of successful team or shared jobs. At a recent conference in Seattle sponsored by Focus on Part-time Careers, two effective discussion leaders were half-time school librarians Vicki Merrill and Maimu Truitt, who share a full-time elementary library job in the Bellevue Public Schools. In addition, Rhoda Sandler and Judith Platt of the Montgomery County Community College Library give a detailed description in Library Journal of their successful job-sharing experience in audiovisual services (Sandler, p. 3234-5).

Although these and other testimonials from within the library profession would seem to justify an increase in part-time employment, articles from other professions and business provide even more support. The Catalyst organization, a national, non-profit group devoted to helping family women use their education and talents in part-time employment, has amassed considerable data on the subject. Catalyst reports that a number of companies are "impressed with the caliber and retention rate offered by women who want to work part-time on a schedule that fits their family life-style" and with the productivity of such workers. In an experiment in the field of social work, twenty-five full-time jobs were divided among fifty workers. Results indicated that the part-time people "out-performed their counterparts on the full-time staff in calls, client contacts, and number of cases carried." Furthermore, "their attrition rate was only one-third that of the full-time staff." In a case of shared teaching jobs, one principal reported that "each partner gave him the equivalent of two-thirds of a teacher at half the price" (Daly, p. 6).

Gail Bronson, writing in the Wall Street Journal, summarizes a number of cases in which the employment of part-time women has proved beneficial to firms or organizations and quotes satisfied employers in various fields; for example, Peter Powers, General Counsel for the Smithsonian Institution, who asserts, "The woman with a professional background but who can't work full-time because of home responsibilities often works out better than regular employees," and Allen Kulen, Vice-president of United Publishing, who prefers "working with part-time women. The mind doesn't have to be in an office 40 hours a week in order to be creative, and a lot of women seem to put in a lot more thinking time about their jobs than the hours they get paid for it." Jim Malaro, a physicist with the Atomic Energy Commission, who works with a half-time woman physicist and whose wife is a half-time attorney, is an enthusiastic supporter of part-time employment for women. Finally, Peter Lewis, President of Progressive Insurance Co., Cleveland, is quoted as being so impressed with part-time employees on the clerical level that he intends to hire some within "the entire gamut of managerial positions" (Bronson, p. 28).

Further support for the notion of part-time employment even at managerial levels comes from Carol S. Greenwald, business economist at the Federal Reserve Bank of Boston. In a speech she gave at the Annual Conference of the National Association of Business Economists, September 8, 1972, she contended that "employers should be expanding part-time work opportunities in order to attract women of exceptional ability, reduce absenteeism, cut overtime costs and increase efficiency" (Greenwald, p. 13). She began her career as a full-time economist, rising to the supervisory level. When she became a mother, she was allowed to keep her supervisory job, sharing it with another economist, but reducing her hours to twenty per week. At the time of her address to the Annual Conference, she had been under that arrangement for a year and a half. Ms. Greenwald is interesting as an example of a part-time worker functioning in a team-supervisory capacity, yet she cites benefits of part-time employment to the organization at all levels of work. They are: 1) a higher quality, more competitive labor pool from which to draw, because the option for part-time work will draw applications from highly educated, talented women who would otherwise be unable to consider working; 2) lower unit costs, due to "rapid and dramatic decreases in absenteeism, turnover, recruitment activity, and overtime pay"; and 3) a rise in productivity because "one can keep up a much faster work pace for four hours a day than one can for eight hours" (Greenwald, p. 21). Obviously such advantages could apply as easily to libraries as to federal reserve banks.

Finally, my own job situation may be of interest as an example of part-time employment which seems to be working out to the mutual satisfaction of the employee and the institution. For five years I was a half-time cataloger and for the past year have been a half-time bibliographic specialist in the humanities in a college library which presently has a professional staff of four full-time and three part-time librarians. My part-time status and scheduling of hours enable me to give the freshest, most productive hours of the work day to my job and still have time to do justice to my husband and three children in pursuing personal interests. Also, I have time to do a good deal of job-related reading and thinking at home. (Lest this sound like a Geritol ad, I am not the youthful, glamorous wonder woman whose teen-age daughter asks, "Mom, how do you do it?") But as a librarian and homemaker, I am very happy with the present arrangement and am convinced, on the basis of my own experience and reading on the subject, that part-time employment is not only advantageous to me but makes a substantial contribution to the profession. The benefits of part-time employment could and should be enjoyed by a larger number of librarians and libraries.

Bibliography

Bow, E. "Interrupted Careers: the Married Woman as Librarian," Ontario Library Review 56:76-8 (June, 1972).

Bronson, Gail. "Part-time Professionals: More Well-Educated Women Find Firms Willing to Hire Them for Less Than Full-time Employment," Wall Street Journal 180:28 (January, 1970).

Daly, Margaret. "Flexible Work Plan for Married Women," Better Homes and Gardens 52:6 (January, 1974).

"Flexible Personnel for Flexible Workloads," Personnel Journal 49:61-2 (January, 1970).

Freedman, J. "Liberated Librarian?" Library Journal 95:1709-11 (May 1, 1970).

Greenwald, Carol. "Part-time Workers Can Bring Higher Productivity," Harvard Business Review 51:20 (September, 1973).

________. "Working Mothers: the Need for More Part-time Jobs," New England Economic Review 13-22 (September/October, 1972).

Janjii, M. "Part-time Work in the Public Service," International Labour Review 105:335-49 (April, 1972).

Robson, L. (editor). "The Professional Woman," Protean (December, 1971), entire issue.

Sandler, R. "Job Sharing in Montgomery County," Library Journal 98:3234-5 (November 1, 1973).

Schiller, A. R. "Women Employed in Libraries: the Disadvantaged Majority," American Libraries 1:345-9 (April, 1970).

Snape, W. H. "Part-time in Norway," New Library World 146-8 (July, 1973).

Tuttle, H. M. "Women in Academic Libraries." Library Journal 96:2594-6 (September 1, 1971).

AN ARCHIVISTS' COOPERATIVE*

L. Bell

The general proposition that I wish to put before you is that in the era of mass-production in which we live the rather peculiar needs of archivists will increasingly fail to be met unless we join together in expressing those needs and, equally, unless we join forces we may not be able to exploit to the full for archival ends the technology which is the hallmark of our era. Essentially, these are two ways of looking at the one thing, for the exploitation of technology in archives is a matter of achieving high, if not properly mass, production. I shall exemplify this proposition in three areas and show how, in my view, greater cooperation can lead to satisfactory conclusions in those areas and in what form cooperation might be embodied. It should not be supposed that I am starting with a self-evident general proposition and, in the course of casting around for deductions to draw from it, have lit upon these examples. On the contrary, the problems have come my way while engaged upon quite separate activities, solutions have suggested themselves quite specifically in relation to these difficulties, and only later has it occurred to me that these possible solutions are all aspects of the generalization with which I opened my remarks. It is, of course, fortunate that they have this in common because a single embodiment, a single organisation for cooperation may, within reason, serve for them all.

The first case I wish to consider is that of materials used by record offices in conservation. We have first of all in this area a problem of suppliers. The materials and tools that repairers use, whether blued steel pins for seal repair or water soluble Topane for treatment of mildew,

---

*Reprinted by permission of the author and publisher from Journal of the Society of Archivists, Vol. 5, No. 3, April 1975, pp. 149-157.

cannot be bought by going along the High Street. Much effort has therefore been devoted by repair shops to compiling lists of suppliers and from this has naturally followed central compilation by the Conservation Section of the Society. One must also point to the use made of the Technical Committee to provide answers to questions about suppliers. It is not my view that the existence of these difficulties across the whole range of conservation supplies suggests as a solution centralised provision of goods rather than centralised provision of information, which is what we have at the moment. The information network, however, does exemplify the value of cooperation and shows how archivists and repairers have for some time expected to receive assistance from a central source.

It is a short step from questions about availability of materials to questions about their suitability. We have all of us learnt, in relatively recent times, of the importance of the chemical and physical constitution of the materials with which we juxtapose our archives. We have learnt, in particular, about acidity and schooled ourselves in something of the mysteries of pH and indicator dyes. We have, therefore, a new range of problems in preparing specifications of materials for particular archival purposes and in carrying out tests to check whether materials meet specifications. The Technical Committee of the Society has for some time been considering the implications of a Technical Advisory Service which would be capable of dealing with a wider range of more complex problems than those I have mentioned and I have no wish to preempt any proposals which that Committee may wish eventually to make to the Society's Council. Nevertheless, the problem of the quality of the materials ordinarily bought by record offices is one aspect of the issues which I wish to explore. For such materials it should not be extraordinarily difficult, given goodwill, to agree on quality specifications. Such specifications should take the form of minimum results under standard tests, whether these are of pH values or of fold endurance. The tests could be applied at the request of purchasers, who may or may not have used the specifications when placing orders, or at the request of manufacturers or materials suppliers. In the latter case the suppliers would be entitled to advertise that their materials conformed to the Society's specification, as long as they were prepared to submit to spot checks, and in both cases the Society should charge at least sufficient to cover all its costs. The tests might be carried out by public analysts or by the laboratories with whom contact has been made in this field over the years. At all events there will be costs to be met and they must be passed to the eventual consumers, those requesting the work. The existence of such a service would not, of course, rule out the testing of materials by purchasers, a practice which repairers are steadily expanding. In such cases laboratory testing to a specification would be available as a reinforcement for complaints. Nor could a set of specifications be expected to be unchanging or complete, in the sense of covering the whole range of materials in use at any time. There will always be some materials being used in techniques under development for which it will not be possible to lay down a specification in the form, "If the material conforms to the following tests it is satisfactory." This is probably the case with laminating tissue at the present time. In such instances, however, it should nevertheless be possible to devise ad hoc tests which could eventually grow up to become standard specifications.

I now turn from questions of quality to those of quantity. This is a particular aspect of the supplies problem with which I began my remarks about conservation materials. It takes the form of the materials being available provided a sufficiently large order is placed and may apply to any type of material, whether boxes for documents or tissue for mechanical lamination. In some cases the order size is beyond even relatively large buyers, such as the Public Record Office. I said earlier that it was not my view that centralised buying was the solution to the general supply problem over the whole range of conservation materials, but I suggest that it may be the solution in instances where size of order is a barrier. It is worth pointing out that the number of such instances may be increased by the imposition of quality standards and this leads me to a point which is central to this whole problem. If proposals for cooperative buying are to work the profession must face up to the need to adopt standards of size, type and colour, for example, as well as quality. We should no longer be able to indulge our little quirks as to the way our boxes are fitted together or the colour patterns on the buckram of our file-cases. Co-operative purchasing can proceed only to the extent that prospective purchasers are able to commit themselves to having exactly the same materials as their neighbours and there will doubtless be cases in which this would be bad policy for particular record offices, for example because of shelf sizes which they cannot change or because of the existence of a useful colour coding scheme. Such difficulties must be left to be investigated as part of the market research into individual products and I should like to consider now certain other difficulties which present themselves.

It is sometimes supposed that a central buying agency can take only one form and the form usually envisaged is that of a full-blown commercial enterprise carrying out the complete range of purchasing, warehousing, distributing and invoicing functions. This is not the case. There are at least two other ways in which the Society could achieve the objective of ensuring supplies of materials for record offices. One is simply to act as guarantor, to offer to be the purchaser of last resort. This, of course, is to take up a particular commercial position and one would not do it except with the same degree of consideration as in making an actual purchase. No one should suppose that I am suggesting any reckless underwriting of a small and uncertain market. The second possibility is to undertake the purchase but employ an agent to carry out all or some of the commercial functions, whether the original supplier or another wholesaler. There seems to me to be no reason why all of these methods should not be employed at one time for different products. The extent to which any of them is available or suitable for any particular product is not something to be settled at a Society Conference. These questions require detailed investigation and I should like now to turn to certain points affecting such investigations.

The first, and most important, is the need to treat this as a serious commercial enterprise. The size and future prospects of the market for any product must be studied most thoroughly and prices must be set which take fully into account every element of cost, whether it be the cost of hiring space or the cost of hiring money. The order size and the re-order period must be related to the rate of consumption and there must be no hesitation in refusing to purvey a product, however archivally desirable, if it cannot be justified commercially. Nor should there be any hesitation in securing whatever profit the market will bear. Once that profit has been secured, but not before, it can be used to subsidize other desirable, but less rewarding, activities. It goes without saying that the products so marketed will bear the Society's seal of approval as having passed the tests, of either form, described earlier. This increases the captivity of our market and makes our commercial life a little less arduous. By and large our market is ourselves and we can reinforce our position as purchasers if we can point out to our financial masters the value of the Society's tests. I do not, of course, suggest that the seal of approval be given solely to products sold on behalf of the Society but I do not envisage initially any direct competitors. The reason for this is that the Society's activities should in the first place be confined to products which would not otherwise be obtainable. Only after establishing a position in this field should we move into competition, either to lower a price or from some solid reason of convenience. It would not pay us to damage the interests of efficient established suppliers.

There are other aspects of such an organisation which I propose to leave for consideration until the end of my remarks when I shall be drawing together a number of threads, and I turn now to brief consideration of a related problem.

We are all of us aware of the difficulties caused by the rising tide of modern records. Many record offices have installed dry mounting presses for lamination but some have found that it is not suitable work for skilled repairers and that the rate of production is not very high. For some time now much thought has been given to these problems with a view to devising more rapid machinery suitable for operation by relatively unskilled staff. I might say in passing that the production of some types of laminating tissue is dependent upon the existence of a number of machines with large appetites. Two types of machine are under consideration, a Public Record Office type and a British Library type, with rather different characteristics, and the latter has already been delivered. Assuming satisfactory development of either or both of these I suggest an established central buying agency should consider undertaking a lamination service for those many offices which are too small to consider the purchase of an advanced and expensive machine with a very large appetite for materials but have nevertheless a substantial amount of documents to laminate. The traditional bugbear for commercial repair services has always been the question of custody but if the Society of Archivists cannot solve that problem to the satisfaction of its members I doubt whether it is soluble. The provision of a common laminating service could, of course, be achieved in other ways than in conjunction with a central buying agency but that is beyond my present scope.

The second area I wish to explore is that of microfilming. This has some features in common with lamination.

The machinery is expensive and it has to be fed large quantities of work. Some offices have been able to instal microfilm cameras but I submit there is a need for a centralised service. Two conditions that I have already mentioned apply. One is that it must operate on a commercial footing with a soundly investigated market and realistic charges, which will include a sensible amount of profit. The other is that it should overcome the custody difficulties that face any kind of centralised service that deals with actual records. A microfilming operation would deal in the first place with orders placed by the researching public but should not be satisfied with a passive role. If it is to become established it must seek to advertise its wares in conjunction with the offices whose records it films. In so far as this activity brings records into the ken of those who would not otherwise use them it is helping us to achieve one of our basic archival objectives. There is something to be said for centralising all the commercial aspects in the microfilming service so that it retained the title to all the films and had commercial freedom to determine whether to sell the customer the camera negative or a duplicate, and at what price. It would be responsible for advertising the contents of its library and could eventually move into microfilm publishing if desired. All this would, however, considerably increase the initial capital investment and it would therefore be more sensible to adopt the simple solution of a bureau service to record offices who would themselves take the commercial responsibility for sales to customers. Even so, much negotiation would be required before record offices could commit themselves to an operation which involved not merely buying in a service but the sale of the proceeds in a manner which suitably protected the interests of the rate-payer. Without some further incentive it is possible that the business may not be viable but incentive may be found to exist in a solution of the ancient archival problem of distribution.

Differences of opinion about the proper home of some groups of records have always been with us and film has been employed as a solution in a number of cases. There is no need for me to recite examples or to remind you of instances in which it has not yet been used. The main stumbling block is, of course, the cost of supplying the film and there is no way of making this difficulty disappear. What I would suggest, however, is that it may be possible to create a system for spreading these costs to make it easier for offices to acquire films of records that would contribute to their coverage in the areas which they serve.

The first requirement is the existence of a microfilming facility, whether of the kind I have described or in the hands of individual offices. The second must be the willingness of offices seeking to acquire such films to allow any of their own records to be filmed on the same terms. The third is that the terms must be more favourable than a simple full-cost purchase. What I am suggesting is in the first place a small discount on the full cost, which in the case of a centralised service would have to be met by a subsidy from the other orders placed and in the case of facilities operated by individual offices by the expectation of equivalent gains from the scheme. There would thus be an element of exchange in the system and this is something that is often easier to arrange than a purely cash purchase. An office seeking to acquire a film of a particular set of records would be required to declare its interest by purchasing at full cost a copy of the relevant means of reference. The price of this would be low relative to the cost of the film. This means of reference would be placed on its shelves in the usual way. Searchers in that office would be able to order a film of relevant records by using the means of reference and would be expected to pay a proportion of the cost. The film would become the property of the office in which it was made available for use but the searcher for his contribution would have the use of a film reader in a place equipped for the study of records and with relevant reference works available. Such searchers would also generally have the benefit of reduced travelling time and inconvenience. By bringing the searcher into the transaction we should not only reduce the cost to the acquiring office but ensure that the demand for films within the scheme was related to their relevance and to the rate at which they could be used. Orders placed within the scheme would have to be given a high degree of priority if it was to be satisfactory to users but the regulation of demand in the way I have described should allow a priority system to remain workable. I should envisage the searcher's contribution as about one-third of the discounted price and the discount as about ten per cent but these figures must be subject to adjustment to equate supply and demand. In so far as such a scheme was operated by a centralised service it would overcome friction caused by different offices having different full-cost charges because of differences in their circumstances.

It must be recognised that there would be considerable practical difficulties in the way of the introduction of such a scheme by a large number of offices each responsible to its own masters. There would also be a problem in creating a centralised microfilming service because of the investment that would be necessary before it acquired enough business to pay its way. Nevertheless, it offers the prospect of all records being available in all places to the extent to which there is a real demand for them, and that is not something to be lightly put aside.

I come finally to the third area for possible cooperation, the use of computers by record offices. I propose to consider first what applications are suitable and then to examine the organization that would be necessary to implement them. Cooperation is essential here because of the high cost of getting into a computer system, not simply in terms of cash but in terms of effort and enterprise. We have a large number of relatively small offices in this country and though the East Sussex office has very creditably led the way with ARCAIC and PARC and demonstrated that it is possible for an office of this size to go it alone it is not realistic to suppose that more than a handful of offices will have the will or the capacity to do the same. The first requirement of an application therefore is the very obvious one that it should meet a need common to all offices, that it should perform an operation that all perform or would wish to perform. The second requirement is that the application should be as advanced as possible without being experimental. Obviously one is looking for powerful performance but the general run of offices would not be attracted by experiment. Experiment, like exporting, is fun and experiment is necessary but the general need is for the computing to be largely invisible. One wants to put information in and get a useful tool out without having to worry about what happens in between. The third point is not a requirement but a desideratum. Given that cooperation is necessary it is clearly sensible to see whether such cooperation can produce a result which would be beyond the capacity of individual systems.

I assume that suitable applications will consist of the manipulation of information derived from records to serve as means of reference to them. There are other things one can do with computers but they tend to be useful within the confines of a particular office rather than applicable across the board. Such information arises at three levels, that of classes or series, that of pieces within a class and that of individual documents or topics within a piece. At these lower levels one is thinking primarily of indexing. It is possible also to construct lists but major benefits can come only in conjunction with indexing. There is already some interest within the profession in a generalised indexing system, as shown by the existence of the Indexing Committee, but indexing of the necessary quality, involving strict control of terms, is not yet available from computers, though this goal is being sought. Such indexing is still too experimental to be put on general offer. Detailed work of this kind, moreover, presupposes a large quantity of input before it begins to become useful and I imagine that such a project would attract only a limited number of offices. The provision of information about classes of records, on the other hand, should be within the scope of many. What I am talking about is, of course, a guide, and this is something which all offices ought to have. Furthermore, a universalised guide, combining information at this level about the holdings of a number of offices, would be a desirable bonus. The PROSPEC system, with some development, is capable of meeting this requirement (see Journal of the Society of Archivists, Vol. 4, pp. 423-7).

In this system each entry relating to a class has fields for the code of the class, the number of pieces in it, the physical nature of the pieces, the first date, the last date, the class title, the description and the index terms. Fields with predictable contents can be validated by the system to find errors and others contain free text of whatever length is necessary. In an application for a number of offices the code field would consist of letters chosen mnemonically to identify each office and numbers chosen by the individual office to determine the order in which the classes are to appear. It would be desirable to have some standardisation of this order. Control over the choice of mnemonic letters to ensure that offices appeared in a sensible order in a unified guide would equally be helpful. By using the existing main code field in this way we make it necessary to build in another code field to accommodate the class codes now in use within the offices. Input to the system would consist simply of filling up a form (see Fig. 1, p. 23) for each class but it must be emphasized that this stage involves a weighty commitment for the participating offices. It will not be sufficient to present an existing guide. To enter an amendment or correction it is necessary to specify only the main code and the field, or part of a field, concerned.

Output (see Fig. 2, p. 24) is produced in upper and

lower case with the main code in the left margin, followed by the class title, covering dates and number and nature of pieces run on in as many lines as necessary. The full description follows in a separate paragraph. Since the office code field is not yet in existence its place in the output remains to be determined but I suggest that it could appear in round brackets immediately after the class title. Index references (see Fig. 3, p. 24) are, of course, to the main code in the margin, but there is an additional facility to incorporate in the index references to other text, such as an administrative history. This requires, of course, additional input. The output may also be typeset.

To enable unified guides to be produced selectively I would propose building in one further field (14 in Fig. 1) to contain a coded classification. This would make it possible to select for output all classes of Quarter Sessions records, for example, or all classes containing estate records, or all those relating to a particular region. This could be used as an alternative method of arranging a union guide but some additional programming would then become necessary to rewrite the references and clean out redundant entries in the index. This programming should not be undertaken at the first stage. The role of the Society in such a system would be firstly, to purchase the additional programming required at an estimated cost of £500 and, secondly, to manage the use of the system. Offices would send their forms to the Society which would then be responsible for checking, standardizing the indexing and entering the classification code. The forms would then go to a bureau for conversion into machine-readable paper tape. A man-readable version of the paper tape would be available, if required, for correction by the participating office and a paper tape containing only the corrections would be prepared. By reading the two tapes successively the computer would carry out the corrections. Output would be produced at whatever intervals were desired and the Society would have to acquire by agreement the right to publish at any time outputs containing information from more than one office. The benefit of the system consists in having an up-to-date guide at any time required, complete with its index, to which must be added the incentive or discipline required to get offices to compile guides and the facility to have union guides of various forms.

It is estimated that given a reasonable number of participants the cost to offices would be of the order of 45p per class for entry, 20p per amendment and 3p per class output. This includes data preparation, computer processing, use of the basic systems and the Society's charges. This last point requires some development. Obviously the Society would be entitled to recover its capital investment, together with a reasonable profit, but there is more to it than this. The tasks I have outlined are not proper work for honorary officers or for committees. The day-to-day checking, indexing, distribution of material and invoicing constitute a job for which somebody must be paid and revenue must be sufficient to cover this payment. It is not, however, a full-time job once the main body of information has been accumulated or in the initial stages, though there could be a short full-time stage if the scheme is well-supported. Apart from that stage I suggest the most suitable procedure would be to pay an office for the services of a young archivist for whatever time is required. It is clearly preferable for work of this kind to be carried out during normal working hours with the backing of all the usual administrative facilities.

I have now to draw together the threads of my discourse. I have indicated three areas in which archivists by acting cooperatively might obtain objectives not otherwise open to them. In each case there is a need for initiative and enterprise and I have suggested that this should be a Society enterprise. Indeed it is difficult to see whence the initiative for an archivists' cooperative would come if not from the Society. What I am suggesting, therefore, is that the Society should consider going into business and that in doing so it should spend money from its reserves. It should consider additional ways of raising capital and in judging its expenditure it should have regard to what the economists regard as the real cost, the lost opportunity to buy the next best thing. The prime consideration is whether it can make a profit and, given that it would be selling to its own members, who constitute a closely defined market, not only are the prospects of profit at first sight fair, the probability of reducing the uncertainty about the prospects is very high.

To conduct a commercial enterprise it would be necessary for the Society to acquire a limited liability company in whose name the operations would be carried out. For a number of us this could create problems in relation to our own employers and these have yet to be investigated. Apart from that the complications are of the kind that normally attend commerce and whose solution is a matter of routine. Before embarking upon such a course we should have to use the existing organisation to examine the market, to see how many offices would be prepared to use a centralised filming service or a computerised guide service, to determine what materials created supply difficulties, what qualities they should have and at what price they could be supplied.

One thing that is clear is that it would not be sensible to attempt all these things at once. The resources available for investment are limited and these resources are not only money. Even with a considerable element of paid employment--and such employment would be necessary in microfilming and materials supply as well as in the computing context in which I have discussed it--commercial operations would make demands on the time of members and, particularly, officers.

We have, therefore, a problem of resource allocation, a need to establish a system of priorities among the projects I have been discussing. It would not be out of place for me to conclude by giving my views on this point. I begin by placing the microfilming service last in the queue. My reason for this is that it is administratively the most complex. A great deal of negotiation will be necessary to agree terms on which a number of authorities would be prepared to buy and sell cooperatively and it might well become easier to do this after establishing a business relationship in other fields. Between materials supply and computing the choice is more difficult. They are both desirable objectives, but not in comparable ways, and there appears to be little to choose between them administratively. My impression, however, is that a faster turnover and a bigger percentage profit can be got from computing, and on these grounds I would propose making that the first target for commercial operation. Profits will have to be generated by the first project before a second can be undertaken and I think this can happen more quickly with the preparation of guides. Clearly we must begin by studying both markets to see whether this impression is correct and there is no reason to delay implementing any part of the second choice which does not make heavy demands on resources.

I am aware that much of what I have said will seem outlandish and that I should find it difficult to demonstrate precedents at every point. My task has been to provide a basis for discussion and I hope I will be found to have done that.

MAIN CODE		EX_{345}
LOCAL CODE	13	Q/RRp
NO. OF PIECES	02	5
FIRST DATE	03	1717
LAST DATE	04	1786
NATURE OF PIECES	05	rolls
TITLE	06	Papists' Estates
DESCRIPTION	07	These registers (4 rolls) give very detailed legal description of 90 estates (manors, advowsons, farms, cottages and lands, etc.), with names of occupiers, field names and tenants' rents. The fifth roll registers the warrants of attorney, the persons named being either local lawyers or relations or friends of the papists.
INDEX TERMS	08	Religion [papists' estates]; Estates [papists' estates]; Law [warrants of attorney]
CLASSIFICATION	14	A B C D

Fig. 1

EX_{345} Papists' Estates (Q/RRp) 1717 to 1786 5 rolls
These registers (4 rolls) give very detailed legal description of 90 estates (manors, advowsons, farms, cottages and lands etc.), with names of occupiers, field names and tenants' rents. The fifth roll registers the warrants of attorney, the persons named being either local lawyers or relatives or friends of the papists.

Fig. 2

Estates
debtors' estates, EX_{12} EX_{275}
Papists' estates, EX_{345}
sequestration and taxation of Royalists', EX_{38}

Fig. 3

THE FIRST LIBRARIAN OF CONGRESS: JOHN BECKLEY*

Edmund Berkeley and Dorothy Smith Berkeley

The National Intelligencer of Washington for February 5, 1802, announced: "The President of the United States has appointed John Beckley Librarian of the two Houses of Congress." The name was a very familiar one at the time, requiring no identification. Since this is not the case today, some account of his career before 1802 may help to explain Jefferson's choice for the first Librarian. Beckley's librarianship came late in his life, and he is better known by historians as a political figure. His appointment as Librarian was, however, by no means a political appointment. He was undoubtedly the best qualified applicant for the position. Jefferson had a very real interest in and concern for the Library, and he was thoroughly familiar with Beckley's qualifications.

John James Beckley was born in England, August 4, 1757. Little is known of his family or of his early education. Accounts indicating he had attended Eton are not authenticated and are almost certainly erroneous. It is well established that he was sent to Virginia by the mercantile firm of John Norton & Son in response to a request for a scribe. The request had come from the elderly John Clayton, clerk of court for Gloucester County and a botanist well known in European scientific circles. Beckley arrived in Virginia just before his 12th birthday and lived in Clayton's home as a member of his family for the next four years. Clayton was the grandson of one of the founding members of the Royal Society of London. His father had been attorney general of Virginia when the son became clerk of court in 1720. He had inherited his father's library and had added to it extensively. He was extremely well qualified

*Reprinted by permission of the authors from The Quarterly Journal of the Library of Congress, April 1975, pp. 83-110.

to guide the continuing education of young Beckley and did so with enthusiasm.

John Clayton died in late December of 1773. Beckley, who had witnessed his will, proved it on January 6, 1774. Faced with a decision concerning his future, Beckley elected to remain in Virginia rather than return to London. In his close association with Clayton he had become acquainted with many of the more influential members of the colony, and intelligent, well-trained clerks were in short supply. He had no doubt that he could support himself. Soon after Clayton's death he was employed by Thomas Adams, clerk of Henrico County. In February 1775 he became clerk to the Henrico committee of safety. During this pre-Revolutionary period a remarkable number of committees were appointed in Virginia, and Beckley served as clerk to a surprising number of them. An ordinance establishing a committee of safety for the entire colony at Williamsburg was adopted August 24, 1775. Soon thereafter Beckley was assisting the clerk of that committee. On February 7, 1776, he was officially appointed assistant clerk, working with John Tazewell for Edmund Pendleton, president of the committee.

The functions of the committee of safety came to an end with the establishment of state government and the election of Patrick Henry as governor. Beckley was employed to complete the records and journals and to prepare a detailed ledger of the committee's accounts. The establishment of state government meant more committees, and Beckley was soon appointed clerk to the committee of trade and the committee of courts of justice and assistant clerk to the council of state. By November 1777 he had replaced John Pendleton as clerk of the Virginia senate. He was also finding time to study law, which he may well have begun in Clayton's library. It is very probable that he studied in Williamsburg with Edmund Randolph, attorney general of the new state, with whom he was closely associated throughout his life thereafter. Randolph was elected to the Continental Congress and resigned his post as clerk of the Virginia House of Delegates in June 1779. Beckley not only replaced him in this capacity, but also took over his law practice during his absence.

The Phi Beta Kappa Society had its beginning at the College of William and Mary on December 5, 1776, soon after Beckley came to Williamsburg. Since he was not a student at the college, Beckley was not eligible for membership. But on December 10, 1778, the constitution of the society was broadened to permit the election of non-students, and a few months later, on April 10, 1779, Beckley was elected. Within a month, as might have been predicted, he was chosen clerk, or secretary. He became a very active member in spite of his many other commitments. The group, at the time, was a remarkable one, including William Short, later minister to Spain, John Page, later governor of Virginia, and John Brown, later U.S. Senator from Kentucky. Brown and Page remained close friends throughout Beckley's life. Beckley, Brown, and Short formed a committee of three to design a seal for the society. Beckley was also one of a committee of three who prepared resolutions to govern the expansion of the society to other areas, thus giving it its present national character. In his capacity as secretary, he drew up the charters for new chapters at both Harvard and Yale Universities. A few months after his election to Phi Beta Kappa, Beckley was elected to the Williamsburg Lodge of Freemasons. Among the members of the lodge were Edmund Randolph, James Madison, James Monroe, and Henry Tazewell. At about the same time, Beckley became clerk to the high court of chancery and also to the court of appeals.

The year 1779 was an eventful one for Beckley in several other respects. Thomas Jefferson was elected governor in June to succeed Patrick Henry. Beckley may have known him earlier, but certainly knew him well thereafter. In December the general assembly decided to move its meeting place from Williamsburg to Richmond for its next meeting in the spring of 1780. Also in that year his sister, Mary Anne, came to Virginia with Mr. and Mrs. John Baylor, who had recently married in London. Mary Anne later made her home with John in Richmond until she married one of his clerks, Nathaniel Gregory.

The move to Richmond began a new period in Beckley's life in many ways. He rented a house and acquired several slaves. He began to practice law on his own, and he involved himself in city affairs. He had not long been settled at Richmond when the arrival of Gen. Benedict Arnold with a fleet in Chesapeake Bay made it necessary for the general assembly to remove itself and its records briefly from the city. Soon after their return a threat developed from General Cornwallis, and the assembly removed first to Charlottesville and then to Staunton. During these dangerous times Beckley was impressed by the coolness and leadership shown by Governor Jefferson. He later gave strong testimony to this when political opponents accused Jefferson of cowardice.

Richmond was incorporated as a city in May 1782. In June of that year Beckley purchased a lot and thus became eligible to participate in the first city elections in July. Eight hundred freeholders of the city elected 12 councilmen for a term of three years, one of whom was the 25-year-old Beckley. The councilmen then elected Dr. William Foushee as their mayor and Beckley as one of four aldermen. Another of the aldermen was Jacquelin Ambler, father-in-law of John Marshall. (Marshall later served with Beckley as a councilman. He was also a Mason and a member of Phi Beta Kappa, but in spite of all of these associations Beckley and Marshall were never on very cordial terms.) Beckley was soon very much involved in a multitude of problems of a new city government. He performed so effectively that he was elected as the second mayor of the city when he was but 26. He was continuously active in the city government during the nine years he lived in Richmond and three times served as mayor.

While the general assembly was in Staunton, Beckley was able to visit Warm Springs and adjacent areas of western Virginia after the assembly adjourned. He was tremendously impressed by the potential of this little-settled country and began to acquire land grants in the region. He became associated in land speculation with George Clendinen, a member of the assembly. Clendinen had established himself on the present site of Charleston, W. Va., and named the city for his father. Beckley's interest in land and in western Virginia and Kentucky increased, and he was continuously involved with both for the rest of his life though he never lived in that area.

Although Beckley's early life was spent in Virginia, he had his eye on the national scene on which so many of his Virginia friends were playing an active part. His first attempt to become personally involved seems to have been in April 1787, when he accompanied Gov. Edmund Randolph and James Madison to Philadelphia for the revision of the Articles of Confederation. If he hoped to become clerk of that convention, he was disappointed. He did make some useful acquaintances, and the experience whetted his appetite for national service. A year later he was very active in the state convention for ratification of the federal Constitution.

When the elected delegates convened at Richmond in June, they chose Edmund Pendleton president and Beckley secretary. There followed the famous debates between those favoring ratification, led by James Madison, Edmund Randolph, and John Marshall, and the opponents led by George Mason, Patrick Henry, and William Grayson. It was Beckley who prepared the 15 copies of the ratification that were to be delivered to Congress and the various states.

Beckley's urge to participate in the federal government increased and by 1789 had become irresistible. He decided to make a determined effort to be elected first Clerk of the U.S. House of Representatives. With this in mind he obtained letters of recommendation from friends. Edmund Randolph wrote to Caleb Strong, of Massachusetts, and perhaps to others, in glowing terms of Beckley's ability as a clerk. James Madison also promised support. As an official cover for his trip to New York, and perhaps to help with expenses, he agreed to deliver the official report of Virginia's vote for the presidency. He went nearly a month before the vote for the clerkship would be held, hoping to campaign a bit for the office. He was joined in New York by various old friends, including Madison, John Brown, John Page, and Alexander White. It was well that he had support, for he had strong competition. The first vote for the clerkship resulted in a tie, but Beckley won on the second ballot.

Beckley had led an eventful life since coming to Virginia, but now an even more exciting period began. He was at first involved in all of the pomp and ceremony of Washington's inauguration and the absurd arguments over matters of titles and protocol. Following Washington's address to the Congress and his withdrawal from the Senate chamber, it was Beckley who read the manuscript of the address to the members with that clarity of enunciation for which he was to become famous. And then there was the activity of the Congress as soon as the initial formalities had been completed. Matters of critical importance had to be decided, and feelings were very strong about many of them. The most controversial of these were the financial questions involved in funding the new national government and settling the debts incurred during the Revolution, especially veterans' warrants. Unfortunately, the divergent views concerning the best solutions to these problems tended to be somewhat regional in character. What is more, the potential for quick profits attracted speculators in large numbers, and many members of the Congress were involved in speculation. Not surprisingly, feelings became very heated, and the Congress soon became distinctly polarized on these issues. The story is much too long to be dealt with here, and it has been analyzed thoroughly by many writers. It did, however, directly involve Beckley and profoundly influenced the remainder of his life, so it must be discussed in general terms at least.

Alexander Hamilton, as secretary of the treasury, had the direct responsibility for proposing financial measures. Opposition to his proposals was led initially by James Madison. Beckley, having had considerable experience with accounts and financial matters, having served in the Virginia militia as well as the state government, and being closely acquainted with Madison, felt concerned. As Clerk of the House, perhaps he should have maintained a rigid neutrality regarding measures before the Congress, but he never did. His personal involvement was such that Senator Maclay, of Pennsylvania, noting in his diary that he wished to be associated with the southern group in Congress, indicated that the southern leaders were Madison and Beckley. Jefferson was not present during the early skirmishing. He had been in France and expected to return there when he came home in the fall of 1789, but Washington persuaded him to accept the post of secretary of state. Another Beckley friend was a member of the cabinet. Edmund Randolph had become attorney general.

Soon after Jefferson's arrival in New York he permitted Hamilton to persuade him to influence the Virginia group to soften its opposition to his proposed measures and break a deadlock on the funding and assumption bills. A compromise was reached--some said a "deal" was made--whereby Alexander White and Richard Bland Lee, of Virginia, would support Hamilton's measures in return for a promise to locate the permanent seat of government on the Potomac. This is one of the few times that Hamilton and Jefferson were able to reach agreement, and Jefferson had reason to regret it.

For many reasons, social and otherwise, Hamilton was rather closely associated with many of the individuals who were openly speculating in the government debts and who stood to make large sums if they were able to anticipate what measures Hamilton would propose and what would be passed by Congress. There can be no doubt that some of these men were able to obtain information before it reached the general public. Their source, in many instances, was apparently William Duer, appointed assistant secretary by Hamilton. Related to Mrs. Hamilton, Duer had been a member of the old Board of Treasury. He was closely associated with many of the leading financial entrepreneurs, including Robert Morris, William Constable, Andrew Craigie, and Theodosius Fowler. The grave suspicions that many of Hamilton's political opponents had with regard to his office were greatly strengthened later by Duer's disgrace and imprisonment for debt. A distrust of the Treasury Department became widely held, and many, including Beckley, distrusted Hamilton personally. From such early beginnings there gradually evolved the Federalist and Republican Parties, and animosity between them became extremely bitter.

Beckley's intense absorption in political affairs was interrupted for a time when he fell in love. The young lady was Maria Prince, daughter of a retired New York ship captain formerly engaged in trade with Cayenne. After a brief courtship John and Maria were married just before Congress moved from New York to Philadelphia. They lived in Philadelphia from 1791 until 1801. Although Beckley had become acquainted with a number of New York political figures, he was not there long enough to take part in either city or state politics. At Philadelphia he played an active role in both and in national politics as well.

Soon after the move, Beckley quite unintentionally made a major contribution to the party split which was evolving. He had obtained from England the first part of Thomas Paine's Rights of Man and thought that it would, if republished, prove a good antidote to John Adams' Discourses on Davilla. The latter series of essays seemed to advocate monarchy, nobility, and aristocracy and had produced a storm of protest. Beckley persuaded Jonathan Bayard Smith to republish the Rights but first lent it to Madison, who in turn lent it to Jefferson. At Beckley's request Jefferson sent it directly to Smith with an accompanying note expressing his pleasure that it would be reprinted. Smith included Jefferson's comments on the flyleaf of the reprint, and it sold rapidly, as Smith had correctly surmised it might. John Adams and other Federalists were outraged by Jefferson's comments and a great commotion ensued. Jefferson had not intended to make a public attack on his friend John Adams, but all attempts to explain the incident proved futile.

Beckley was particularly delighted by an honor which

came to him in this year (1791). He was elected to membership in the American Philosophical Society. He had long known of the society, since John Clayton had been one of the early members. Political prominence was no assurance of election. Although Jefferson, Randolph, and Hamilton were already members, John Adams was not elected until two years later. Meetings were held twice each month, at which papers were given. Since the society's building was close to the state house, Beckley was probably able to enjoy their fine library at other times. He presented to the society for its collections two specimens of printing. Calligraphy was one of his hobbies.

A new friendship developed for Beckley in 1791 when he joined Madison and Henry Lee in persuading Philip Freneau to come to Philadelphia and start publishing the National Gazette. The dominant Philadelphia paper at the time was John Fenno's Gazette of the United States, and Fenno's views were antagonistic to everything Beckley and his friends espoused. Freneau's paper gave them a much needed public voice for their views, and they supported it not only with their writing but also by obtaining subscriptions in Philadelphia and elsewhere. Beckley maintained a very close association with Freneau.

Soon after coming to Philadelphia Beckley became the close personal friend of Gen. William Irvine, of Carlisle. How the friendship began is not known but the two families became very intimate and exchanged long visits over a period of years, and the two men carried on an extensive correspondence when Irvine was not in Philadelphia. This was an important friendship for Beckley politically, since Irvine was a very active figure in Pennsylvania politics. He soon had Beckley equally involved. Another close personal friendship developed with Dr. Benjamin Rush. Their political views were congenial, and Rush was moderately active in political matters.

More old friends from Virginia arrived in Philadelphia, most importantly Senators James Monroe and Henry Tazewell. The Williamsburg Lodge of Freemasons was now represented at Philadelphia by at least five of its members: Beckley, Madison, Monroe, Randolph, and Tazewell. Monroe and Beckley had long been friends and became even closer. Tazewell made his home with the Beckleys while Congress was in session and died there in 1799. With so many close friends in the Congress and the Cabinet, Beckley would have found it extremely difficult to adopt a nonpartisan position had he been inclined to do so. He had no such inclination. He was ardently Republican in his views and became very active in promoting Republican causes at all levels. Since he maintained a home in Philadelphia while members of Congress were in the city only when Congress was in session, it was natural for him to keep in touch with many of them by correspondence in their absence. He thus became a sort of clearinghouse for information of concern to Republicans from all parts of the country and assumed the unofficial role of party chairman.

Beckley was also a voluminous writer. He became a frequent contributor to Freneau's Gazette under a variety of pseudonyms, including "Mercator," "The Calm Observer," and "Timon." As "Mercator" he challenged the Treasury Department's claim that it had reduced the public debt by almost two million dollars. He used his ability with figures and accounts to demonstrate that the debt had actually increased by almost the same amount. His attacks drew replies from Hamilton, writing as "Civis." Monroe and Beckley jointly published a pamphlet (long incorrectly attributed to John Taylor of Caroline) entitled An Examination of the Late Proceedings in Congress Respecting the Official Conduct of the Secretary of the Treasury. When Monroe replaced Gouverneur Morris as minister to France, Beckley wrote to him at length concerning political affairs at home. Monroe reciprocated with long letters to Beckley, copies of which went also to Jefferson, Burr, George Logan, and Robert R. Livingston. He suggested that Beckley and Logan publish these letters anonymously as an antidote to European news screened by the British before reaching the United States. These were published and had political repercussions.

Before Monroe's departure for France he became involved in an investigation of alleged speculation by Alexander Hamilton. The apparent evidence had been brought to the attention of Congressman F. A. C. Muhlenberg, who asked the assistance of Monroe and Congressman Abraham Venable. The three men conducted a quiet investigation and, finding the charges serious, sought an explanation from Hamilton. The evidence was all admitted to be true by Hamilton, but he explained the whole series of remarkable events by admitting he was being blackmailed by one James Reynolds with whose wife he had had an affair. The three investigators were reasonably convinced and, having had one of Beckley's more confidential clerks prepare copies of all papers involved, as requested by Hamilton, they asked Beckley to keep the findings secret. The details of the probe into the "Reynolds Affair" are confusing and lengthy and cannot be dealt with here. But more will be said about Beckley's connection with it later.

Beckley's antipathy for Federalists and Federalist causes was greatly intensified by their treatment of Edmund Randolph. Randolph, who had served briefly as an aide-de-camp to Washington during the Revolution and had played a very active part in the early planning of the new government, came to Washington's cabinet at considerable financial sacrifice. Intensely loyal to Washington, he was almost the only prominent Virginian in the government who maintained a genuine neutrality between Republican and Federalist commitment and thereby endeared himself to neither group. Republicans regarded him as something of a "trimmer," although none questioned his integrity. The Federalists found him difficult to manipulate and did not like his influence on Washington. When he advised Washington against signing the Jay Treaty without further concessions by the British, the Federalists and their British friends determined to destroy his influence with Washington. They found a means of doing so when the British conveniently furnished Timothy Pickering with papers seeming to indicate that Randolph had accepted money from the French, or had expressed a willingness to do so. Pickering and Oliver Wolcott managed to convince the President of Randolph's guilt. Incredible as it may seem, Washington signed the treaty without even discussing with Randolph the charges against him and then demanded an explanation from Randolph in a full cabinet meeting. Guilty of nothing other than devotion to Washington and to the best interests of his country, Randolph promptly resigned and set about trying to vindicate himself. It was very difficult to do, and historians have been all too slow to recognize that he was totally innocent of any wrongdoing.

In spite of divergent political views at times, Beckley and Randolph were devoted friends. He was infuriated when he learned of Randolph's treatment. He had known Washington a long time and had always referred to him in respectful terms. He was now completely disillusioned and convinced that Washington had become the head of a pro-British faction in this country. He had been strongly opposed to the Jay Treaty and had campaigned vigorously against its passage. Beckley retaliated by attacking Oliver Wolcott under the pseudonym of "The Calm Observer." He accused Wolcott of overpaying Washington's salary and drew Wolcott and Hamilton into a prolonged rebuttal of his charges. In spite of Wolcott's indignant denials, Beckley was able to demonstrate conclusively that Washington had repeatedly overdrawn his allowance by Congress. Many were shocked by such an attack on Washington but it had the effect of embarrassing the Federalists in a number of ways.

Beckley's disposition was not improved when he learned that the Federalists in the cabinet had persuaded Washington to recall Monroe from Paris in August 1796. It was evident that Republicans were to be ousted from any position of prominence which the Federalists could attack. He was inspired to assume a leadership role in the forthcoming national elections. Washington's Farewell Address was published in mid-September, and the campaigning to choose his successor began at once. This would be the first contested presidential election. The eventual candidates were John Adams and Thomas Pinckney for the Federalists and Jefferson and Aaron Burr for the Republicans. It was apparent that most of the votes of the northern states would go to Adams and that most southern votes would go to Jefferson. This made clear the importance of the middle states, especially New York and Pennsylvania. Beckley was convinced that the Pennsylvania vote could be won by the Republicans, and he dedicated himself to that end. He was a member of a five-man committee directing political strategy for the state, and he acquired a reputation as a vigorous campaign manager. So effective were his methods of organization at the grassroots level that the final vote was Jefferson 14, Burr 13, Pinckney 2, and Adams only 1. The national vote went to Adams by the narrow margin of 71 to Jefferson's 68. Pinckney received 59 and Burr 30. The delivery of the Pennsylvania vote assured Jefferson of the vice-presidency, and Beckley had played an important role in its delivery.

The Federalists were well aware of how narrowly they had averted the disaster of a Republican administration. The behind-the-scenes maneuvering which had destroyed the political influence of Randolph and Monroe had been successful and could now be directed to strengthening their control of government and the weakening of the Republican position wherever possible. Thus began the era of the Alien and Sedition Acts and all that went with them. Republicans were embarrassed and harassed in many ways, and British influence was strong. Even Vice President Jefferson was subjected to social ostracism. It is not surprising that Beckley was high on the list of politically active Republicans the Federalists would like to depose. Since he held elective office, he was clearly vulnerable. He was, obviously, aware of this, but since he had been consistently reelected by large margins, he had felt comparatively secure. He should have known better. Many of his most active supporters in Congress were prone to arrive at the last minute for the beginning of a session. This now provided a method for attacking Beckley. A Federalist caucus was called, and it was agreed to demand an early vote for the clerkship and to vote for a young law student named Jonathan Williams Condy. In spite of many protests in the House they were successful in demanding an immediate vote and Condy won by 41-40.

Republican outrage and Federalist glee were widely expressed in public and in private. Beckley's abilities as a clerk were generally recognized, and the purely political basis for his removal was beyond question. Beckley could derive small comfort from the indignation of his friends. His financial situation, which had been precarious, was suddenly critical. Many people were wholly or partially dependent upon him. His wife, her mother, and her younger brother were members of his household. His parents and an afflicted brother in England, his sister and her children in Virginia, another brother-in-law and his family all looked to him for help. He had invested all of his savings in land at various locations, primarily in western Virginia and Kentucky. His holdings were both extensive and potentially very valuable, but his efforts to sell any of the land had been frustrating. He had not developed a law practice in Philadelphia and to do so would be difficult. He had also been foolish enough to endorse notes for friends and relatives. The threat of debtors' prison was both real and frightening.

There followed for Beckley the most difficult period of his life. Desperate attempts to solve financial problems were just successful enough to avoid debtors' prison. He was humiliated at having to borrow money from friends, including Jefferson and Rush, not knowing when he could return it. His health had always been delicate, and his constant worry did nothing to improve it. None of this was alleviated by the arrogant jeers of the Federalist press and their almost complete dominance of the political scene. There seemed, for a time, no way in which he could strike back at his tormentors, but one means finally suggested itself. At the time of the Reynolds affair, Monroe had asked him to keep the records of the matter, but to keep them secret. He had made no commitment to do so but had honored the request. Now Beckley believed it was Hamilton who was directing the actions of Wolcott, Pickering, and others to bring about not only his, Randolph's, and Monroe's political destruction, but that of the whole Republican cause as well. Although Hamilton was no longer in the cabinet he was still the symbol of Federalism, and Beckley felt he was fully justified in letting the country know what manner of man was behind Federalist activity. Monroe was returning from France at the time and could not be consulted. Beckley alone made the decision to publish the full account of the Reynolds affair.

Beckley persuaded James Thomson Callender to edit the papers relating to the Reynolds affair as a supplement to his History of the United States for 1796, published by Snowden & McCorkle. It reached the public just as Monroe arrived from France in late June 1797 and had even more impact than Beckley could have anticipated. Hamilton refused to believe that Monroe was not involved in the release of the papers, an error of which many historians have been guilty ever since, and a duel was narrowly averted by the diplomacy of Aaron Burr. Monroe's conduct throughout the entire Reynolds affair was meticulously honorable, many historians to the contrary notwithstanding. Hamilton, to the consternation of his friends, published a defense. He left the public, as he had left Monroe, Muhlenberg, and Venable, with a choice of either accepting his account that he had repeatedly paid blackmail to a man because of threatened exposure of having carried on an affair with his wife or of suspecting that he had concocted the tale as a cover for having actually been guilty of speculations. Mrs. Reynolds steadfastly denied the story, contending that it had been fabricated by Hamilton and her husband. She promptly had Burr obtain a divorce for her.

Hamilton's friends condemned the publication of the Reynolds affair as mean and base, with little concern for the justification in doing so. They were, however, completely aghast when they read his published defense. Friend and foe alike were amazed that he had confirmed the authenticity of Callender's account by taking any notice of it. Many agreed that he had effectively put an end to his political ambitions, which were widely believed to include the

Presidency. Beckley had indeed scored a direct hit on the Federalist leadership.

Federalist domination of the political scene continued for several years, and Beckley failed in his attempts to regain his clerkship. His financial affairs continued to be critical, and he gave serious thought to returning to Richmond or moving to Kentucky. Somehow he managed to survive in Philadelphia, and finally a break came in 1800. He worked hard for the election of Thomas McKean as governor and he was elected. Soon after his election he appointed Beckley clerk of the mayor's court for the city of Philadelphia and clerk of the orphans' court for the county. This was indeed just retribution. The man removed from office was Joseph Hopkinson, McKean's nephew (and, incidentally, author of the words to "Hail Columbia"), whose wife was Emily Mifflin, daughter of the former governor, and whose sister had married Jonathan Williams Condy, Beckley's replacement as Clerk of the House. The combined salaries of the two posts approximated Beckley's former salary as Clerk, of which McKean felt that he had been unjustly deprived.

From Beckley's point of view the tide was at last beginning to turn. Although he was seriously ill at the time, he must have been immeasurably cheered by the political news. John Adams had finally had more than enough of Hamilton's satellites in his cabinet and had disposed of both James McHenry and Timothy Pickering. There remained only Oliver Wolcott, and the opportunity for Beckley to help attack him again soon presented itself. Anthony Campbell, a clerk in the Auditor's Office of the Treasury Department, informed Israel Israel, sheriff of Philadelphia, that he had evidence of misuse of public monies on a large scale. He produced copies of the accounts of Pickering, Jonathan Dayton, Speaker of the House, and others, showing large sums due to the government. He insisted that these should be made public. Israel sought the advice of Beckley and William Duane, who had succeeded Benjamin Franklin Bache as editor of the Aurora. The men were intrigued but they were cautious. They wanted to see the actual records from which Campbell had obtained his information. They must be sure of the facts before giving the matter any publicity. Campbell then agreed to take the risk of "borrowing" the actual records on a Sunday morning for them to examine. He did so, and the group spent the day poring over them and recording the facts. They had Campbell return the books. Duane, with assistance from Beckley, then began a campaign of heckling Wolcott with pertinent questions about monies owed to the government, which Wolcott found very difficult to answer. This was continued throughout the summer. Wolcott soon realized that Duane had inside information and, as Campbell fully expected, he lost his job. So, too, did his friend William P. Gardner, who had aided him. In spite of Wolcott's defenses it was all too apparent that some rather dubious accounting practices had been followed in the Treasury Department and that considerable favoritism had been shown in the collection of monies due. Papers in other parts of the country naturally picked up this material from the Aurora and added their own commentary. Someone even suggested that a fire in the Treasury Department offices might be very convenient. Since the attacks had also involved Wolcott's predecessor in office, Hamilton considered suing Duane, but thought better of it. The attack achieved its objective when Wolcott submitted his resignation to take effect December 31.

This was, of course, an election year, and the Republicans were delighted by any ammunition they could use against the Federalists. Beckley, who was always inclined to take an optimistic view, began to see hope of a Republican victory in November and determined to do everything within his power to help bring it about. He dug out an essay he had written in 1795 dealing with Federalist attempts to establish a standing army and sent it to his friend Ephraim Kirby, in Connecticut, to be republished as a pamphlet. He worked closely with Mathew Carey, Tench Coxe, and others in giving wide distribution to Republican propaganda. He devoted many hours to writing a 32-page _Address to the Citizens of the United States_, signed "Americanus," in which he attacked the record of the Federalists and refuted each charge they had made against Jefferson. He included a seven-page biography of Jefferson, the first ever published. Mathew Carey printed 2,000 copies of the first edition, and there were later editions published elsewhere. In spite of the personal tragedy of the death of his small daughter, Mary, his own child, he undertook a series of essay in the _Aurora_, defending Jefferson from the attacks of the clergy.

Beckley's efforts toward party organization at the grassroots level were so effective that Federalists accused the Republicans of establishing presses in every town and county in the country. Beckley would have been happy were it true. In October he somehow managed to obtain a copy of a pamphlet written by Hamilton, viciously attacking Adams and promoting Pinckney. It had been intended for secret distribution to certain key Federalists. Even before many of them had received their copies, Duane was publishing choice excerpts in the Aurora. Adams and his many supporters were furious, and even Hamilton's friends were once more astonished. The effect was quite as sensational as Duane and Beckley had hoped. Once again Beckley had thwarted the political plans of Hamilton, to his intense satisfaction. He wrote to a friend that Hamilton's attempts to replace Washington had failed permanently. Many a Federalist sadly agreed.

The long-planned move of the federal government from Philadelphia to Washington was occurring during the fall of 1800, with all of the confusion and problems which might have been expected. Records and papers were stored in temporary quarters at Washington, pending completion of permanent depositories. On November 12th a fire occurred in the quarters of the War Department. Duane and others of the Republican press immediately suggested that it conveniently prevented scrutiny of the records by the Republican administration which would be coming in. They were not really as optimistic as they attempted to sound. There were strong indications that the election would be close. Beckley and his friends had felt sure that they could deliver all 15 Pennsylvania votes for Jefferson, but they were outmaneuvered by the state senate and had to settle for eight. The national vote ended in a 73-73 tie between Burr and Jefferson, with 65 for Adams, 64 for Pinckney, and one for Jay. Republicans of Philadelphia were summoned by Beckley to a meeting on December 19th to plan a public festival. They held it on January 3d at the "Sign of the Green Tree."

The tie vote between Jefferson and Burr could not be resolved until Congress officially recorded the vote in February. On January 20th a second fire broke out, this time in the house rented by the Treasury Department. Any doubt which many Republicans had about the earlier fire at the War Department was fully erased by the second, and the Republican press loudly proclaimed that both fires had been set. A few of the more moderate Republicans were still prepared to give the Federalists the benefit of the doubt, but Beckley was not among them. The House of Representatives appointed a committee to investigate the fires. It reached no definite conclusions about either fire, but it received quite a bit of evidence suggesting that the second one had been set. The fact that Samuel Dexter, secretary of war, was temporarily in charge of the Treasury Department complicated matters. Wolcott's resignation had become effective, but he was present at the fire and was accused of trying to save only his own papers. Dexter was eventually sued by the owner of the house, who implied that Wolcott had set the fire. Wolcott returned to Washington from Albany for the trial and made a convincing defense against all charges.

Congress met on February 11 to decide the tie between Burr and Jefferson. Seven days later Jefferson won on the 36th ballot. It had been a tense and trying week, with talk of naming an interim President and threats of armed resistance to any attempt at usurpation. The reaction to the final decision was wild celebration by Republicans in all parts of the country. They had gone a long time without a major victory, and they had been subjected to every conceivable indignity by the Federalists during the Adams' administration. Few today realize that Republicans regarded this period when the Alien and Sedition Acts were in effect as a "reign of terror" and were genuinely afraid to make critical remarks in public or even in their private correspondence. It is not surprising that they celebrated. At Philadelphia one observer said that the bedlam was so continuous that he could not read a paper for three days. A grand "jubilee" was planned for March 4th, at which the "Ciceronian Beckley" would be the orator.

With the end of the hated Federalist domination, Republicans who had worked hard for their overthrow awaited Jefferson's appointments with interest. Few Republicans had held any public office under the earlier regimes. In fact, Adams had even made a number of last minute appointments before leaving office. Now at last the Republicans would have their turn. Few, if any, had worked harder than Beckley, and few had suffered more from loss of office. Surely he would be among the first to be rewarded. Jefferson was inundated with requests for appointment and letters of recommendation of friends. He was, however, reluctant to make appointments except where vacancies existed. He did remove from office those who had received "midnight appointments" from Adams. By July the outrage in the Republican press became so loud that he modified his stand and conceded that office holding should be equalized between the two parties. Slowly he removed from office any Federalist against whom any serious charges could be maintained. Many people sought Beckley's recommendation for appointment, and he wrote numerous letters for them. He was also consulted by cabinet members and others about the advisability of certain appointments. He made no written application on his own behalf. His friends began to be concerned. Monroe wrote to Jefferson about him. Governor McKean wrote on behalf of both Beckley and Tench Coxe, indicating he had done all he could for them. Jefferson replied that he shared McKean's concern but could see no immediate hope of a place for either of them. In October Jefferson wrote to Beckley that he assumed he would be reelected to his clerkship of the House and asked him to appoint one Samuel Hanson as an engrossing clerk. Beckley has left no written comment concerning Jefferson's treatment of him, but his son wrote many years later that Beckley had told his intimate friends that he thought Jefferson had failed him. [1]

Beckley was again called upon to deliver an oration at the Fourth of July celebration in Philadelphia. Soon afterward Samuel Otis heard a rumor that Beckley was seeking to replace him as Secretary of the Senate, which may or may not have been true. Beckley was busily involved in local Philadelphia politics at the time and with sundry legal matters, but he did visit Washington in November, and William Duane is said to have promised Otis to help him keep his post in return for receiving Senate printing. Be this as it may, Otis did retain his office, and Beckley was reelected Clerk of the House on December 7, 1801.

When the Beckleys first came to Washington to live, they boarded in the home of Louis André Pichon, French chargé d'affaires, but they soon leased a house on Capitol Hill, at Delaware Avenue, between B and C Streets. Life in the newly created city must have seemed a bit strange after New York and Philadelphia, but many old friends had also made the move. Their social activities were rather restricted at first, because John was on crutches, suffering from gout and leg ulcers, and Maria was pregnant. A son, Alfred, was born on May 26, 1802. They had lost several children and only Alfred survived.

On the same day Beckley was reelected as Clerk, the House acted on another matter of concern to him, namely, the question of a congressional library. This was by no means a new idea but had been considered off and on for 20 years. In 1782 the Continental Congress had appointed a committee to study the proposal. Its members included James Madison and Theodoric Bland, of Virginia, Dr. Hugh

Williamson, of North Carolina, and Thomas Mifflin and James Wilson, of Pennsylvania. The committee prepared an impressive list of suggested books. It was a rather complete Americana for the period, with the exception of scientific works, including books by Cadwallader Colden, John Lawson, Robert Beverley, John Brickell, and others. In addition there were volumes on European, Chinese, and ancient history, geography, treaties, international law, and languages, as well as encyclopedias. A formal resolution that Congress establish its own library was presented by Bland, for the committee, but failed to pass. The probable reason for the failure was the availability of the facilities of the Library Company of Philadelphia, which had been founded in 1729 and owned something over 7,000 volumes.

Shortly after the first U.S. Congress convened in New York in 1789, the library question came up again. A committee made up of Elbridge Gerry, of Massachusetts, Alexander White, of Virginia, and Aedanus Burke, of South Carolina was appointed to investigate the subject. They drew up a list of books they considered necessary for the use of the Congress. Ten months later Gerry reported for the committee a recommendation that they make an initial investment of $1,000, to be followed by annual expenditures of $500, to purchase an extensive list of volumes on state laws, laws of European nations, treatises on diplomacy, parliamentary procedure, and other such subjects. Congress passed this resolution but did not implement it. Evidently the fine library of the New York Society proved adequate for their needs during the short time they remained in New York, and when they moved back to Philadelphia, again the Library Company of Philadelphia seems to have provided for them. They did, from time to time, add to their own limited holdings by the purchase of such treatises as Blackstone's _Commentaries_ and Vattel's _The Law of Nature and Nations._ In a more frivolous mood they even acquired Burns' poems. Rush's dissertation on yellow fever was probably purchased in response to the frightful epidemic of that dread disease which took the lives of 4,000 citizens of Philadelphia in 1793. In 1802 Congress owned only 243 volumes, which were in the care of the Secretary of the Senate and the Clerk of the House. Beckley had had experience with this sort of library when he had been responsible for books and documents as clerk of the Virginia senate.

When the long-planned move to Washington became imminent, the Congress could no longer evade the issue of establishing its own library on a larger scale. The Capital City was new and afforded few amenities, and these did not include a library. On April 24, 1800, a bill was passed dealing with various problems connected with the removal from Philadelphia. One of its provisions dealt with the library question. Five thousand dollars was to be expended on books and furnishings to be purchased by the Secretary of the Senate and the Clerk of the House, as ordered by a joint committee. Senate members appointed to the committee were Samuel Dexter, of Massachusetts, William Bingham, of Pennsylvania, and Wilson Cary Nicholas, of Virginia. Qualifications of the House committee members were analyzed by Beckley's friend William Duane, no doubt to the delight of the readers of his Aurora (May 10, 1800): Robert Waln, of Pennsylvania, whose gift, said Duane, was the "study of bills of exchange, invoices and policies of insurance"; Virginia's Thomas Evans, "a heavy plodding attorney who has no doubt had great reading in cases in point"; and Leven Powell, who "has read Fisher's Arithmetic, Starke's Virginia Justice, and such other books as enabled him to fill with becoming dignity the important office of deputy sheriff, of the county of Loudon, in Virginia." In further lese majesty Duane suggested that the Library be decorated with numerous mirrors and paintings of royalty and that its books include 15 volumes by "Porcupine"; "The Bloody Buoy & Cannibal Progress for such members as are troubled with weak nerves"; Swift's "Art of political lying, and his tale of a tub--for the use of Mr. Pickering"; Machiavelli for Dexter "to be occasionally loaned to Liston"; and "The Cuckold's Chronicle for the use of General Hamilton." In spite of Duane's opinion of their abilities, the committee came up with a very respectable list of 152 works, totaling 740 volumes, at an estimated cost of just under £500. These were duly ordered from Cadell & Davies, of London, who had to supply many secondhand books for those out of print. They were shipped on December 9, 1800, and arrived in Baltimore in mid-April. They finally reached Georgetown in early May and were temporarily stored, unopened, in the office of the Secretary of the Senate.

The books had at last arrived, but no regulations had been established for the operation of the Library. It was the appointment of a joint committee to draw up regulations and make other provisions for the operation of the Library that occurred on December 7, 1801, the day of Beckley's reelection as Clerk. The report of the committee, written by John Randolph, was presented two weeks later. It recommended that the room first occupied by the House, but which they had vacated, be converted for the use of the Library. This was a large and airy room, 86 feet long by 35 feet wide, with a 36-foot ceiling, and well lighted with two rows of windows. The report went further into elaborate detail on every facet of Library procedure. It specified that books, carefully numbered and labeled, should be placed "in portable cases with handles to them for the purpose of easy removal, with wire netting doors, and locks." In view of the two recent Washington fires, this would seem to have been a wise precaution. The existing libraries of the House and Senate were to be combined with the newly purchased volumes. The Secretary and the Clerk should oversee all arrangements in placing these, hanging the maps, and in ordering the necessary furniture. They should also have printed catalogs prepared, showing the number of each book and map, and should order book withdrawal slips printed, whose form the report designated. No more than two books could be withdrawn by a member at one time. Folios were to be returned within eight days, octavos and duodecimos in six. The Library would be open daily, except Sunday, from 11 a.m. to 3 p.m. For the time being it would be presided over by the Secretary or the Clerk, or "some proper person for whose conduct they shall be responsible." At the beginning of each session of Congress they would give a report of the state of the library, including expenses and fines collected. In the meantime, the Secretary was directed to sell the hair trunks in which the books had been shipped from London and to render a statement of account.

While the above committee report provided for the Library to be presided over by either the Secretary or the Clerk for the time being, the act, when passed, provided for a permanent Librarian. He was to be paid not over two dollars for each day of attendance, and he would be required to post bond to ensure the safety of the Library furnishings. Randolph moved to strike out one provision of the bill which would have permitted use of the Library by heads of departments, members of the Supreme Court, and foreign ministers. This motion was approved and the bill passed. It was signed by Jefferson on January 26, 1802.

Although the salary specified for the Librarian of Congress was not exactly impressive, there were many applicants for the post. A number of them evidently believed they could use it to supplement income from some other source. On the day following the joint committee's first meeting, John McDonald, "late of Philadelphia," applied. On January 15 Augustus Woodward wrote to Jefferson recommending William O'Neal. On the following day Dr. Richard Dinsmore applied for the position and was recommended by Stevens Thomson Mason. Madison and Gallatin were named as references by Edward Nicholls, a Maryland lawyer serving as a clerk in the Treasury Department. A letter of application from Thomas Claxton makes mention of the large number of applicants. Among the many was a clerk in Beckley's office, Josias Wilson King. When the Federalists replaced Beckley with Condy as Clerk of the House, Condy appointed King as his principal clerk. Somewhat surprisingly, Beckley retained King but appointed his old friend William Lambert as chief clerk. This meant a smaller salary for King, which he hoped to augment with the pay as Librarian. When he had completed enrolling the Library bill on January 21, King wrote to Jefferson, seeking the appointment and stating that he had obtained Beckley's permission to apply. There is no way of knowing whether or not Beckley had also informed him that he had already approached his friend Judge Levi Lincoln, U.S. attorney general, about his own interest in the position. Lincoln had told him that he would speak to Madison about it, but after learning of King's application Beckley wrote to Madison directly.

When Jefferson appointed Beckley Librarian, he added measurably to an already heavy load of duties and responsibilities. It was rather generally recognized that the duties of the Clerk of the House were more burdensome than those of the Secretary of the Senate. This was the reason for the belief of many that Beckley coveted Otis's position. As early as the first session of Congress, Senator Maclay, of Pennsylvania, had noted in his diary that Beckley's goal was to be Secretary of the Senate. From time to time afterwards the word went around that Beckley would try to oust Otis. Many years earlier Beckley had replied to charges that he was overpaid as clerk of the Virginia house with a detailed description of those duties. They read like a very full-time job, indeed, and were certainly no less so in the U.S. House. As Librarian he would not be much concerned with the checking in and out of books, although he might do some. This part of the work would be done primarily by one of his many clerks. There would be a variety of time-consuming collateral duties, including lengthy meetings with congressional committees. One of the first such duties came when the committee asked him to determine how much of the original appropriation remained unspent, so that they might order additional books. When he investigated this, he discovered that there had been no statement of account rendered covering the books ordered from England.

Knowing Jefferson's deep interest in the Library, Senator Abraham Baldwin, a member of the joint congressional library committee, asked his advice concerning the purchase of additional books. On April 14, 1802, Jefferson replied:

> I have prepared a catalogue for the Library of Congress in conformity with your ideas that books of entertainment are not within the scope of it, and that books in other languages, where there are not translations of them, are to be admitted freely. I have confined the catalogue to those branches of science which belong to the deliberations of the members as statesmen, and in these have omitted those desirable books, ancient and modern, which gentlemen generally have in their private libraries, but which cannot properly claim a place in a collection made merely for the purposes of reference.
>
> In history I have confined the histories to the chronological works which give facts and dates with a minuteness not to be found in narrations composed for agreeable reading. Under the laws of nature and nations I have put down everything I know of worth possessing, because this is a branch of science often under the discussion of Congress, and the books written on it not to be found in private libraries. In law I set down only general treatises for the purpose of reference. The discussions under this head in Congress are rarely so minute as to require or admit that reports and special treatises should be introduced. The Parliamentary section I have imagined should be complete. It is only by having a law of proceeding, and by every member having the means of understanding it for himself and appealing to it, that he can be protected against caprice and despotism in the chair. The two great encyclopedias form a complete supplement for the sciences omitted in the general collection, should occasion happen to arise for recurring to them. I have added a set of dictionaries in the different languages, which may be

> often wanting. This catalogue, combined with what you may approve in those offered by others, will enable you to form your general plan and to select from it every year to the amount of the annual fund of those most wanting.... [2]

Early in July, Beckley was able to sent a statement of the unexpended appropriation ($2, 480. 83) to Jefferson and to the committee. In his letter to Jefferson he suggested that the works of naturalists Georges Buffon and Mark Catesby be added to the Library. Surprisingly, he referred to Catesby as an American author. As Clayton's former scribe he should certainly have known that Catesby was English since Clayton had frequently sent specimens to Catesby in London. Beckley's servant, who brought the letter to Jefferson, also presented him with the House journals he had requested for Caesar Augustus Rodney. The latter, a Delaware Republican, was challenging James A. Bayard for his congressional seat. Beckley also wrote Jefferson that when Rodney came to the city he would make all of the newspaper files and printed documents available to him. On July 16th Jefferson notified Beckley that he had ordered 700 volumes approved by the committee for the Library. Six new presses, each four feet wide, would be needed to accommodate them.

Throughout the summer Beckley's ill health continued unabated. By late August he decided that only a cure at Virginia's sulfur springs could help him. Jefferson invited him to visit at Monticello for as long as he cared to stay, thinking he was going to the Augusta springs. He went instead to Berkeley Springs, near Martinsburg, a much easier trip. He spent September and October there during the congressional recess, returning home almost completely recovered. There he found that his old friend and family doctor, Benjamin Rush, had sent copies of six of his lectures. In thanking him he started what amounted to a new Library policy. He wrote that he hoped Rush would send him copies of all his publications "that I may place them, where they so deservedly merit to be, on the first shelf appropriated, in our Congressional Library to works of Ethics and Philosophy."[3] From this time on he lost few opportunities to encourage authors to donate their writings to the Library. Some months later, on February 13, 1803, his friend Samuel Harrison Smith, editor of the National Intelligencer, noted that the Library "already embraces near fifteen hundred volumes of the most rare and valuable works in different languages. We observe with pleasure that authors and editors of books, maps, and charts begin to find that, by placing a copy of their works on the shelves of this institution, they do more to diffuse a knowledge of them than is generally accomplished by catalogues and advertisements."

Some years later Beckley evidently prompted Smith to repeat this advice for, on April 11, 1806, he again wrote in the Intelligencer:

> It is worthy of the consideration of the authors and publishers of books in the United States, whether it would not be well worth their while to send copies to the keeper of the Congressional Library; By depositing their works in that collection, they will be seen and perused by gentlemen of distinction from all parts of the United States. The fame and emolument of the writers and proprietors of printed books can perhaps be promoted in no manner more effectually than by placing copies of them in this growing collection. It will be a publication of them to all the states and territories, in some respects more effectually than by advertisements in the newspapers, and by the distribution of catalogues. Gentlemen desirous of having their publications exhibited in this public and conspicuous place, may forward them, to Mr. Beckley the librarian, who will thankfully receive, and carefully preserve them, for the use of the Representative Bodies of the American nation.

One of the first Library matters to concern Beckley was the publication of a catalog of Library holdings as directed by the Congress. He prepared one and had it printed by William Duane in April 1802. It gave the number assigned to the work, the title, the number of volumes, the dollar value of the set "as near as can be estimated" and that of the individual book. There were 212 folios, 164 quartos, 581 octavos, and 7 duodecimos, making a total of 964 volumes. There were also nine maps and charts. A 2-1/2-page supplement was published in October 1803, printed by James B. Westcott. A second catalog, 13-1/2 pages long, appeared in 1804, with no printer's name mentioned. The "Record of Books Drawn--1800-1802," in manuscript, is still preserved in the Library.

Library accounts continued to pose a problem for some

time. When Jefferson placed the second order for books, he requested George W. Erving, U.S. consul at London, to assist an agent of William Duane in purchasing the books. He did so because he thought that Cadell & Davies had been far too high on the first order. He advised Erving (July 16, 1802) to look for "neat bindings, not splendid ones," and smaller volumes rather than the expensive folios--"good editions, not pompous ones." Robert R. Livingston, U.S. minister to France, was asked to supervise the selection of books ordered from Pougers, Paris booksellers. Erving reported that the English books had cost £68 but no statement was received from Livingston. Jefferson decided to wait for his return to this country to inquire about the cost. When finally he was able to talk to Livingston, the minister could furnish no figures. He had supposed that the bankers involved had furnished him figures. On January 10, 1806, Jefferson wrote to Gallatin asking if the bankers had sent him an accounting. He suggested that if they had not done so, that he, Jefferson, and Beckley could work out an approximation.

By March Jefferson had solved the problem. He wrote Beckley that when he had written to Pougers placing the order for books, he had also ordered some volumes of an encyclopedia for himself. He had specifically warned Pougers not to confuse the two orders and to be careful to pack and address them separately. In spite of these instructions, Pougers had packed his books with those for the Library. Livingston had paid them $1,866 for the Library's books, and $535 for Jefferson's books. Packaging and shipping costs to Le Havre had been charged to the Library account. Matters were further complicated by the addition of two hampers of wine for Jefferson, who had paid transportation costs of everything from Le Havre to Georgetown. The confusion was ended by Jefferson's sending Beckley a check for $39.94, which he had decided he should pay. This, with Jefferson's explanatory letter, was presented by Beckley to the Vice President and the Speaker of the House for "their approbation, pursuant to law."

Among the Librarian's duties was that of acting as host to dignitaries visiting the Library. The new Capitol began to attract visitors, and the Library was becoming one of the sights. This was certainly one of Beckley's more pleasant duties. In June 1804, Charles Willson Peale, Dr. Fothergill, of Bath, and other distinguished gentlemen accompanied the famous German naturalist Baron Alexander von Humboldt on a visit. They admired the Senate chamber, the view from the top of the Capitol, and Pennsylvania Avenue, with its four rows of trees. Peale recorded in his diary: 'We first went to the Library, where Mr. Beckley received us with politeness, and also accompanied us through the other apartments. The Library is a spacious and handsome Room, and although lately organized, already contained a number of valuable books in the best taste of binding."[4]

There were personnel problems to worry Beckley. The most serious of these involved Josias King, the Federalist clerk whom he had inherited from Condy in the Clerk's office. Since King had sought the post of Librarian for himself, there was, naturally, resentment toward Beckley. Apparently it was to some degree suppressed for several years, but finally, in December 1805, Beckley fired him. King wasted little time in taking his case to the House. He prepared a memorial that made two major accusations against Beckley. The first was that Beckley had appointed him assistant librarian "to label, arrange and take charge of the books in the library" and had promised to divide the Librarian's salary with him but had failed to do so. For a number of reasons it seems most unlikely that Beckley had made such an agreement. In the first place he needed money desperately himself. Secondly, King was already fully employed in the Clerk's office and could easily have been assigned to library work instead. Furthermore, if Beckley had been making such an arrangement it would seem far more likely that he would have picked one of the clerks who had worked for him for years, such as Lambert. It also seems strange that King continued to work for several years without receiving the promised compensation. Evidently the committee of accounts, assigned by the House to investigate his charges, agreed, for they found no basis for this charge. The second charge involved a grant of additional compensation made by the House to certain employees for extra services rendered, March 27, 1804. This grant of $1,700 included $200 for King and was to be paid out of the contingency fund of the House. King did not receive his money at that time and borrowed it from a Washington bank and, of course, paid interest to the bank. He now asked that he be reimbursed for the interest paid. At the time the House made the grant, the contingency fund had already been overspent by $192.15, and Congress adjourned without replenishing the fund. It was not until the next session of the Congress that an appropriation was made to the contingency fund and King and others could be paid. It would appear that the committee was correct in concluding that the memorialist had no claim against Beckley.[5]

In view of his own sad experience, it seems most unlikely that Beckley would have fired a young man with a family to support at Christmas time without extreme provocation. He would have been well justified in firing King when he was reelected as Clerk but had kept him on for several years. In spite of the fact that the committee of accounts completely exonerated Beckley at the time, historians have tended to cite King's testimony in support of the thesis that Beckley neglected the Library. This cannot be justified.

The Library had other problems besides those of personnel. In 1805 the House took back the impressive room it had assigned to the Library and substituted a former committee room. This was situated in a wing of the building which was already in such bad repair that the floor was shaky and the roof leaked. In addition to these difficulties, the room was too small to accommodate the rapidly growing collections of books and maps. In spite of having moved the Library to inadequate quarters, Congress continued to provide for its growth. In December 1805, the Senate appointed a committee to "inquire into the expediency of purchasing maps and books for the library." The committee chairman, Samuel Latham Mitchill, was an excellent choice. At 28, he had been professor of chemistry, natural history, and agriculture at Columbia University. His erudition was not confined to these subjects, and he was known as the "Stalking Library" by his colleagues.

Mitchill reported to the Senate on January 20 that "Every week of the session causes additional regret that the volumes of literature and science within the reach of the National Legislature, are not more rich and ample." Not only did it lack "geographical illustrations" but it was deficient in works on historical and political subjects. He thought that an untutored government would be no danger provided that "steps be seasonably taken to furnish the library with such materials as will enable statesmen to be correct in their investigations, and, by a becoming display of erudition and research, give a higher dignity and a brighter lustre to truth." The Senate was impressed and his advice resulted in the act of 21 February 1806, which allocated $1,000 per annum for five years for the purchase of books and maps for the Library. It also officially, for the first time, permitted the secretaries of state, war, navy and treasury, as well as the attorney general, to use the Library. There had already been times when these gentlemen had consulted works there and even withdrawn them. The previous November Samuel S. Hamilton, acting for "John Beckley Librarian," had sent a notice to the secretary of state: "Mr. Madison borrowed of the Library of Congress: The Annual Register for the Years 1758, 1759, 1778, 1779-1784 and 1797. Grotius Puffendorf and Sir William Temple's Works--Which he is respectfully requested to return before the meeting of Congress." Another new feature of the act was authorization for the purchase of books published in the United States. Of the $1,000 appropriated for 1806, Mitchill, Joseph Clay, and John Quincy Adams were each allowed to spend $494 for books bought in New York, Philadelphia, and Boston. This idea may have been initiated by Col. William Tatham, who recommended purchasing Americana--perhaps exhibiting a personal interest since he offered to sell the Library his own collection.

The liveliest accounts of the Library come from the pen of Federalist Senator William Plumer, of New Hampshire. During Beckley's five years as Librarian, the two men continued a running feud. Plumer wrote in his Memorandum of Proceedings in the United States Senate, 1803-1807: "It has been the practice of Congress to print the journals of their proceedings, the messages of the president, the reports of the heads of departments--of committees--board of commissioners of the Sinking fund--&c&c&c. Of each of these there has always been printed supernumerary numbers, that is, more than one for the President, Vice President, each senator & representative & head of departments, who are regularly furnished with them. These spare copies, & such copies as the members leave in their drawers at the end of the session, are in the recess carried up in the large lumber room over the senate chamber. When I came here in Dec. 1802, I was informed that each member of Congress was entitled to each document if he would take the trouble of selecting them. I accordingly began--selected & removed a considerable number when I received a message indirectly from John Beckly [sic] clerk of the House of Representatives, in whose custody the key of the chamber was, that those documents were the property of the United States & that members of Congress had no right to them. A few days after I found one of his favorites: a member of the House selecting a number of those papers. I then renewed my search & in the course of the session procured a trunk of them, which I sent home."[6]

Plumer continued his collections and four years later possessed all copies of the Congressional Journal from 1774 to 1806, as well as many documents, the whole amounting to more than 70 volumes, although they did not constitute a complete set. Finding that Otis would have the journals bound and charge the cost to the government, Plumer had between 40 and 50 done (the Clerk of the House maintained no such practice). During December 1806 he spent two hours daily, with the exception of Sundays, collecting. Towards the end of the month, Beckley withheld the key from the librarian on duty. Approached by Plumer, he was reluctant to give it to him but finally consented to do so. Plumer realized that his time was limited: "I was aware that my spending so much time in this business would induce other gentlemen to procure documents--& that the doors would soon be shut against us all--I therefore pursued & closed my search as soon as time would admit. I have procured a large box of these documents for the Massachusetts historical Society--& a large trunk of them for my inquisitive friend Ichabod Tucker, Esq. of Salem.... Neither of these two collections of documents are half so large & extensive as mine...." It was well that Plumer made his collections, for many of these documents were housed in the lumber room for want of any other place of storage. Here was kept the glass for window replacements, which meant a continual parade of workmen, unmindful of where they stepped. The floor, where many of the documents lay for want of shelves, was filthy with plaster and rubbish and a leaking roof dripped water over them.

By the end of 1806 Plumer reported approximately 2,000 volumes in the Library he considered a great boon to "this desert-city." Mr. Kearney, the acting librarian appointed by Beckley, told Plumer that the Speaker of the House, Nathaniel Macon, considered the Library "a useless expence" and would like to repeal the law establishing it. Kearney said he had never known Macon to borrow a book. Plumer noted that Mitchill was one of those who had purchased books with the 1806 appropriation, among which was The Secret History of the Court and Cabinet of St. Cloud (Philadelphia: John Watts, 1806), an anonymous publication derogatory of Napoleon and his court. Plumer considered it a most improper book for the Library, particularly since Napoleon had complained to the British concerning a similar book. Bristling, Plumer immediately approached Kearney and "asked him if that book belonged to the library. He answered that it did not. I told him I had seen it on the written additional catalogue. He replied, it once belonged to the library--but Dr. Mitchel had withdrawn it. I answered, I approve of that. He said, no book in the library was in so much demand. It was constantly out--& in the Course of a week it was several times read--The number who took it for the week, read it, & lent it to others. Such a currency has scandal, especially when its shafts are directed against a great man." When Plumer questioned Mitchill, he was told that the bookseller had mistakenly included it in the order. Acidly, Plumer noted in his memorandum, "How unwilling we are to own our errors, & how natural to charge them upon others."[7]

Beckley could not long suppress his love of city political affairs. He was soon involved in Washington city government, as he had been in Richmond and in Philadelphia. He was fourth in the number of votes received among nine men elected to the Second Chamber in June 1805, and he was soon acting as President pro tem of that body on numerous occasions. It is remarkable that he should have undertaken any of this, for he was entangled in serious legal problems concerning his land holdings in western Virginia, was desperately pressed financially, and was in extremely poor health. Although his health improved briefly from time to time, it continued to deteriorate, and he died on April 8, 1807.

Like many great institutions, the Library of Congress began in a small way, beset by many problems. The first librarianship was a part-time appointment for an already very busy man. He held the office for only a few years and died before the Library was given much opportunity by Congress for rapid growth. There is, however, good reason to believe that Beckley took his duties seriously and that he foresaw future greatness for the Library. In his brief term as Librarian he established it as a well-organized and rapidly growing entity, enjoying the confidence of the Congress and the admiration of the public. On this firm foundation others have been able to build.

Postscript:

Beckley's death left his entire life savings tied up in a lawsuit which continued for the next 28 years. His wife, Maria, her mother, and his son, Alfred, were left without funds in a rather desperate situation. Even worse, there was the embarrassment of debts owed to Jefferson, Rush, and others who had rescued Beckley from the threat of debtors' prison during the "reign of terror," and whom he had never been able to completely repay. After various attempts to support herself, Maria found it necessary to make her home with Senator Brown's family and, later, the family of John Fowler in Kentucky. She died in Lexington in 1833. At the suggestion of Gen. William Henry Harrison, James Monroe appointed Alfred to West Point, from which he graduated in 1823. He had served at various military posts when the final settlement of his father's legal entanglement made him the sole heir to a very large and very valuable tract of unsettled land in what today is West Virginia. He resigned from the army and built the first house on what ultimately became the city of Beckley, which he named for his father.

Notes

1. "Autobiography" of Alfred Beckley, Paxton Davis Papers (made available by Prof. Paxton Davis, Washington and Lee University, who is a descendant of John Beckley).
2. Andrew A. Lipscomb, ed., *The Writings of Thomas Jefferson*, 20 vols. (Washington: Thomas Jefferson Memorial Association of the United States, 1902), 19:128-29.
3. Beckley to Benjamin Rush, 8 November, 1802, B1-2, pp. 96-97, Library Company of Philadelphia, Historical Society of Pennsylvania.
4. Herman R. Friis, "Baron Alexander von Humboldt's Visit to Washington, D. C., June 1 through June 3, 1804," *Columbia Historical Society Records*, 1960-1962, p. 16.
5. Joseph Gales, ed. *Debates and Proceedings in the Congress of the United States, 1789-1824*, 9th Congress, 1st Session, 19th February 1806 and 3 February 1806, p. 429.
6. Everett Somerville Brown, ed., *William Plumer's Memorandum of Proceedings in the United States Senate 1803-1807* (New York: Macmillan Company, 1923), pp. 537-39.
7. *Ibid.*, p. 559.

AUSTERITY, TECHNOLOGY, AND RESOURCE SHARING: RESEARCH LIBRARIES FACE THE FUTURE*

Richard De Gennaro

During the last two decades academic libraries, in parallel with their parent institutions, experienced the greatest period of growth and affluence that they have ever known. The watchword was "more"--more money, more books and journals, more staff, more space, and more technology. Many new research libraries were created, and those that already existed experienced unprecedented growth. Although libraries got more of everything during those years, they still could not keep pace with the growth of new fields of research, new doctoral programs, and the increasing production of books and journals. Two decades of affluence not only failed to help solve the many problems that were brought on by exponential growth--they exacerbated them.

This extraordinary period peaked around 1970. A decline began which was further accentuated in 1974 by declining enrollments, reduced budgets, rising costs, and the energy crisis. Recent demographic forecasts point to a further leveling off or even an absolute decline in undergraduate and graduate student enrollments in the 1980s.[1] Undoubtedly the cycle will turn up again; cycles always do, but it is unlikely that those of us who lived through that period of affluence and growth will ever live another comparable one. It almost seems that the normal condition of libraries is austerity. That is the way it was up to the 1950s, and that is the way it is again now that the boom is over. The last two affluent decades may well have been a temporary aberration or perhaps the glorious end of an era in the history of the growth of research libraries.

---

*Reprinted by permission of the author and publisher from Library Journal, May 15, 1975, pp. 917-923.

Faltering Growth

The significance of the changes that have taken place in the library economy in the last five years should not be underestimated. There is mounting evidence that the long-accepted exponential growth rate of research libraries which has been causing them to double in size every 16 years or less has begun to level off and even decline. In the 1971-72 (ninth) issue of the standard statistical study of 58 academic research libraries compiled at Purdue University, the projections in the key indicator of volumes added showed a distinct faltering by the year 1971-72.[2] There was a positive decline when the 1973-74 volumes added category in the Association of Research Libraries (ARL) annual statistics are compared with those of 1971-72.[3] Out of 58 libraries compared, 36 showed a decline between 1971-72 and 1973-74. The total volumes added in the 58 libraries was about 6, 114, 000 in 1971-72, and 5, 538, 000 in 1973-74, a decline of 476, 000 volumes or 7. 8 per cent for the two-year period. The current acute budget crisis which is affecting many of these libraries will accelerate this trend and cause a turn-down in other indicators such as the size of staff and total expenditures. Obviously, further statistical evidence is required before definitive conclusions can be reached, but it seems reasonable to suggest that these signs foreshadow a basic change in research library growth patterns rather than an insignificant cyclical decline.

The Numbers Game

Even during those affluent decades, librarians continued to talk poor and be poor. No matter how rapidly their budgets increased, the demands made on them and the commitments they assumed always exceeded the available resources, and it was taken for granted that this should be so. One of the main reasons for this chronic fiscal crisis in libraries--this chronic imbalance between resources and commitments--is that librarians have all been caught up in a kind of involuntary numbers game where success, progress, and achievement are measured by comparing their vital statistics with those of other academic libraries. Since no valid measures of quality are available, prestige and recognition go to those libraries with the largest numbers. Membership in the prestigious Association of Research Libraries is awarded on the basis of various measures of size.

These statistics are extremely important in many ways, but they do not tell us how good a library is or how well it is satisfying the real needs of its various user groups. There is frequently a significant difference between what library users say they want and what they actually need and use--between their real needs as opposed to their expressed needs. (They are not unlike people who insist on living near a large city for its cultural benefits but then seldom go into town to take advantage of them.) Moreover, the presence of a few great libraries like Harvard and Yale and a few growth leaders like Toronto and Texas at the top of the annual ARL statistical listings has set an impossible standard and caused an unhealthy competition among academic libraries. Unfortunately, even these leaders are now having serious difficulties maintaining their previous commitments and roles.

It should be clear by now that the goal of self-sufficiency or even comprehensiveness is unrealistic and unattainable. Librarians must act on that knowledge and begin to put an end to the numbers and growth game. Instead of trying to keep up with the Harvards and the Torontos and sustain the extraordinary growth of the last two affluent decades, we should be searching for ways to achieve a new kind of orderly and healthy growth pattern which is more commensurate with the resources and needs of our own institutions and in tune with contemporary economic realities. A basic change in attitude about growth and numbers is needed in research libraries as in other spheres of our lives. The natural tendency to equate high expenditures, high growth rates, and large collections with library effectiveness should be resisted.

The Promise of Technology

One of the principal reasons why we have not yet begun to end the numbers game and to accept the new economic reality is that we have had the hope, or the illusion, that new technology would somehow save us, or that it would at least permit us to sustain our traditional growth and development patterns for an additional period of time. We thought that computers would help control processing costs and that microforms would permit filling the gaps in library collections *en bloc* at reasonable costs. It is now apparent that the cost-effectiveness of the localized type of library automation that characterized the 1960s was marginal or even nonexistent for some applications, and that micropublishing is merely creating a whole new class of little-used research materials which librarians are pressured to purchase from their already inadequate book budgets.

The era of localized library automation is passing. Experience has shown that it is not economically feasible for any but the very largest libraries to afford the heavy costs of developing, maintaining, and operating complex local computer-based systems. Many libraries are abandoning this approach in favor of joining cooperative networks such as OCLC and its affiliates, or purchasing turn-key minicomputer systems for specific local applications from commercial vendors. It is becoming acceptable even for major libraries to have no in-house automation program or staff. In-house systems staffs are not essential to implement the local interfaces to these centralized networks or to install and operate the package systems.

Although these new approaches to library automation promise to be much more effective and produce greater savings, particularly in cataloging and processing operations, these savings will be rapidly offset by inflation and diminishing budgets, and libraries will still be left with serious long-term fiscal problems. This is because these problems originate in over-ambitious acquisitions policies and are only exacerbated by costly traditional processing routines. Computer technology will have its greatest payoff for libraries as it is more widely used as a tool to assist librarians in developing and operating networks and other new mechanisms for sharing research resources on a national and international scale. The growing use of the OCLC data base and network of interlibrary loan location purposes foreshadows the high potential of this approach.

There are still some technologists who continue to predict that research libraries as we know them will soon be superseded by rapidly developing large-scale on-line, interactive data and textual access systems based on computers and telefacsimile systems, but such views no longer enjoy the vogue they once did. The lesson that has been learned after ten or 15 years of experimentation and development is that technology alone is not going to save us, nor permit us to continue to build library collections as before, nor solve our problems by putting us out of business. Technology will help in time and in very significant ways, but we should not allow its promise and glamor to keep us from coming to grips with the immediate and critical problems of exponential growth. The solution to these problems lies in the adoption of more realistic acquisitions policies and the development of more effective means of resource sharing, not only through computerized networks but also through the creation of new and improved national resource centers.

Realism in Acquisitions

Long before libraries receive the relief and benefits that the increasingly effective use of technology promises, librarians will be forced to learn the harsh truth that the current economic recession in higher education is teaching us--namely, that no matter how good a case we make for it, the money we will need to continue to build and maintain the comprehensive research collections in the old image of Harvard and Yale is simply not going to be forthcoming. Our institutions do not have the money, and our society cannot or will not provide it.

Moreover, it is time for a serious questioning of the need for building and maintaining the rapidly growing number of multimillion-volume research collections all across the land. In 1951, for example, there were only 14 academic research libraries in the United States and Canada with collections exceeding 1, 000, 000 volumes, three with 2, 000, 000 or more, and two with over 3, 000, 000. By the end of the year 1973-74, there were 76 libraries with over 1, 000, 000 volumes, 25 with over 2, 000, 000, and 14 with over 3, 000, 000. The growth rates in collections such as these range between three and six per cent compounded annually, which causes a doubling in size every 12-24 years and requires steadily increasing investment in material, processing, and space costs. Even with this investment, libraries cannot keep up with the estimated 5-15 per cent annual growth rates in the world's output of publications and the 10-20 per cent annual increase in book and journal costs, nor is there any way they can hope to fill in the retrospective gaps in their collections.[4]

Unfortunately, many of these recently created research libraries serve better to satisfy the prestige needs of their universities and the status needs of certain academic departments and faculty members than the actual research needs of the scholars who use them. The two categories of research materials that are most frequently acquired to satisfy these prestige and status needs are foreign language and microform collections.

There is an increasing awareness among librarians of the great disparity that exists between the money and manpower that are expended to acquire and process foreign language materials and the actual amount of use that is made of them. Large academic research libraries typically spend at least half of their book and journal budgets for foreign language publications, and these are the most troublesome and expensive materials for a library to acquire and process. Harvard estimates that 60 per cent of its acquisitions are in languages other than English. [5] At the University of Pennsylvania Library foreign language materials account for less than 15 per cent of the total use, and half of this is in language and literature classes with French and German predominating. Studies of titles requested on interlibrary loan in the U.S. show that a median of 86 per cent are for materials in English. [6] The British Lending Library reports that over 95 per cent of the items requested are in English. This merely confirms what everyone knows quite well, namely, that English-speaking people generally do not read foreign languages. This is not to minimize the importance of and need for foreign language research materials in U.S. libraries but merely to point out that they are not heavily used and could be shared to a much greater extent than they are now.

During the last two affluent decades some libraries--particularly those in the newly created or rapidly expanding universities--spent significant sums of money purchasing and processing collections of research materials in various types of microform in an effort to catch up and compete with the older and more established institutions. Experience has shown that many of these collections are seldom used, and we now see that their purchase by individual libraries was frequently unwarranted. In recent years librarians have become more selective in their purchases of microform collections and are relying increasingly on the Center for Research Libraries for the loan of specific titles or collections upon request by a user. Even with the rapid expansion of its membership in recent years, the Center receives surprisingly few requests for its microform holdings.

The scholars who need to make use of extensive collections of research materials in any form can rarely be satisfied by the holdings of any one library--even including the largest ones. This is more true today than every before, despite the continued growth of collections, as the following statement by the Harvard Librarian so aptly attests: "Research interests have become so broad and the quantity of printed materials useful to research has increased so greatly that the Harvard Library today, with its 7,000,000 volumes, is more frequently reminded of its inadequacies than it was 60 years ago when it had only 1,000,000. It is less nearly adequate now than it was then to meet all the demands of Harvard professors and students."[7] That statement was made in 1963; since then 2,000,000 additional volumes have been added and Harvard has fallen farther behind.

From Holdings to Access

It is becoming increasingly clear that the long-term solution to the chronic fiscal, staff, space, and other problems besetting research libraries lies in setting aside the old models of Harvard and Yale and developing new and more realistic sets of goals, including especially more selective acquisitions policies designed to meet the actual needs of particular institutions and their library users. These old established libraries with extraordinary collections should serve as resources for other libraries, not models. The traditional emphasis on developing large local research collections must be shifted toward developing excellent local working collections and truly effective means of gaining access to needed research materials wherever they may be. Since a substantial percentage of all library costs ultimately stem from acquisitions, this reordering of priorities will have beneficial effects throughout the library. The ordering and processing backlogs which plague most libraries could be reduced or eliminated, storage areas could be cleared, space problems alleviated, and library staffs could begin to enjoy the feeling that comes from knowing that they can cope with their workloads as they shift their emphasis from processing materials to serving readers--from holdings to access.

Such a drastic change in goals would not have been politically feasible before because senior faculty members and administrators, most of whom were trained at the few leading research universities whose libraries we use as our models, are just as committed to the traditional concept of research libraries as are librarians. However, two new factors have emerged which will permit and even force librarians to adopt new goals and new models. One is a change in attitude on the part of administrators and faculty members brought on by the new climate of austerity, and the other is the growing awareness that viable and acceptable alternatives are or may soon be available as a result of advances in resource sharing concepts and capabilities.

To make it politically and practically feasible for academic research libraries to abandon finally the traditional models and the chimeric goal of self-sufficiency while at the same time improving their ability to fulfill their research functions, an effective national library network will have to be created. An excellent design for such a network, complete with a national resource system, a national bibliographic system, and a network communication system, has already been submitted to the National Commission on Libraries and Information Science.[8] However, this is a complex undertaking from political, organizational, and technical points of view, and its implementation, if approved, will necessarily be in stages over a period of years. In the meantime, there is one element in the proposed national resource system which is of such paramount importance to all libraries that it should be singled out for priority implementation. This is the concept of a national library resources center, which has been an important ARL concern in recent years.[9] Modeled after the British Library Lending Division, this center would assume responsibility for acquiring and making available to libraries, through loan and photocopying, a comprehensive collection of periodicals and monographs in all subjects except medicine. It could start with periodicals and later be expanded to include monographs. The existence of such a center would extend the resource base of all libraries by permitting them to be more selective and to expend their resources on materials which are of particular interest in the local environment. We will return to this concept again in the discussion of strategies for resource sharing which follows.

Strategies for Resource Sharing

Two highly successful models for effective resource sharing already exist--the Center for Research Libraries (CRL) in Chicago and the British Library Lending Division (BLL) in Boston Spa, England.

The Center for Research Libraries is a nonprofit libraries' library with over 100 members and a collection of over 3,000,000 volumes of research materials. The Center is to its member libraries what a local library is to the individual scholar. Just as the scholar tries to acquire for his personal library the materials he uses regularly and can afford, and depends on the university library for the materials he uses less frequently or cannot afford, so the individual member library draws on the Center for little-used and expensive collections of research materials which extend and supplement its own local resources.[10]

Unlike other libraries, the CRL has no local constituency to serve and is therefore able to provide assured and rapid access to its materials to all of its members on an equal basis. Its effectiveness is measured not only against the relatively modest amount of material that its members borrow each year, but also, and more importantly, by the savings they make by being able to forego the purchase and storage of those materials which they would otherwise be called upon to acquire.

Unfortunately, the Center for Research Libraries is filled to capacity and requires substantial new funding to expand its space and functions. Founded in 1949 by a group of ten midwestern universities and with the assistance of foundation grants, it has reached a critical stage in its existence, and the nature and direction of its future development are undergoing a thorough review by its board of directors.

The British Library Lending Division, formerly the National Lending Library for Science and Technology, has also achieved remarkable success in building an organization to provide a national and even international lending and copying service for libraries. In contrast to the Center for Research Libraries, which started with the concept of providing access to little-used research materials, the BLL started with the concept of providing rapid and assured access to a corpus of the most useful and frequently requested periodicals, first in science and technology, then expanding to the social sciences and humanities and including monographs as well as periodicals. It now receives some 44,000 periodicals and 60,000 monographs a year in all subjects and languages, but its main strength is still largely in science and technology.

The government-funded BLL's sole mission is to provide these extramural services, and since its founding in

1962 it has been increasingly successful in meeting the interlibrary loan and copying needs of libraries of all kinds in the United Kingdom by pioneering new and more effective methods of acquiring materials and handling and expediting orders. In fact, the BLL has been so successful in Britain and Europe that it recently instituted a new Overseas Photocopying Service for journal articles. BLL officials suggest that the BLL may be capable of handling the overseas need for certain categories of low demand materials on a cost and time competitive basis with traditional internal interlibrary loan services and that it may be unnecessary for the U.S. and other countries to replicate these collections and services. A survey has shown that the BLL's services to foreign countries compare favorably for speed with any national system that is not based on a central loan collection.[11]

A single facility in Britain is probably not a viable long-term solution to our resource sharing needs. Nevertheless, a number of U.S. libraries are beginning to make use of the BLL's services, and their experience, if successful, could stimulate interest in the creation of a similar government-supported and nationally oriented, centralized facility to support library resource sharing in the U.S.

The University of Pennsylvania Library recently became one of the first U.S. libraries to make regular use of the BLL's Overseas Photocopying Service. In an effort to maintain the total periodical resources available to its users in the face of continuing inflation in book and journal prices and a declining budget, the Penn Library adopted a policy of offering free photocopies of articles from journals that are not available in its libraries. By absorbing the costs, rather than passing them on to the users, the library encourages the use of the service and avoids the expense and difficulties inherent in billing and collecting small sums of money. While it still continues to use neighboring libraries and the Center for Research Libraries as sources, the BLL serves as the prime source for science and technology, in which its chief strength lies. Requests are sent by teletype to the BLL and orders are promptly filled and dispatched by air mail. The charges, which amount to about $1.50 for each ten pages, are billed to a Pennsylvania account and paid for from a special library fund. The goal is to provide easy access to the specific articles that users need in the infrequently used periodicals that the Library can no longer afford to acquire.

The British Strategy

The key to the success of the BLL is that it started as a completely new entity in 1962, building its specialized collections and services on a centralized basis independent of the British Museum and the great university libraries. Thus it had no other conflicting mission, commitments, goals, or traditions and was free to develop new services in new ways. Moreover, it relied entirely on simple and available communication technology--mail and telegraph.

In contrast, we in the U.S. are committed to the seemingly logical idea that an effective national resource sharing system must take maximum advantage of and be based squarely on our existing great research libraries, and that it requires the prior development of a complex computer-based telecommunications network to make it function. Paradoxically, it is our insistence on these points that has most inhibited the development of an effective resource sharing system in the U.S. while the British built a parallel structure without complex technology and succeeded to a point where they are serving an international market.

The reasons for this divergence are clear. In the first place, the development of our computer-based bibliographical system and telecommunications network, despite the excellent progress that is being made, will require considerable additional time and resources. In the second place, the strength of the great research libraries lies in their retrospective holdings, and it is precisely the weight and legacy of these holdings that will keep them from becoming efficient resource libraries for the vast and increasing quantity of contemporary materials that are in the greatest demand. These libraries, like great department stores, were designed to serve patrons on their premises; what we urgently need now are more facilities like the CRL and the BLL which resemble warehouses and which are designed to serve other libraries in the manner of mail order merchandise distribution centers. The great research libraries can also draw on the recent materials in these new facilities; they in turn can serve, with compensation, as sources for needed retrospective titles which cannot and should not be duplicated.

U.S. Strategy

The present approach to resource sharing and

interlibrary loan in the U.S. (apart from the CRL) has been oriented theoretically in a hierarchical system extending from locality to state and region, with a handful of the largest research libraries at the apex serving as the collections of last resort. In practice, borrowing libraries, in an effort to save time, commonly bypass the system and send their requests directly to the larger libraries which they hope and expect will have the needed titles. Since these major resource libraries are expected to provide interlibrary loan service in a spirit of noblesse oblige and without compensation of any kind, they have never had any incentive to give priority to this costly and difficult activity. Indeed, the more efficient one of these libraries becomes at filling requests the more requests it will attract, until its service again deteriorates to a point where further traffic is discouraged. It is a no-win situation. Filling free interlibrary loan requests has always been treated by the large netlenders as a troublesome extra, and this, along with the cumbersome nature of the decentralized system, accounts to a large extent for the relative slowness and inefficiency of this activity in the U.S.

With the promise of federal aid as an incentive, there is increasing acceptance of the concept of decentralized sharing and state-oriented systems of compensated interlibrary lending. This concept has worked rather well for certain states such as New York, Illinois, and others which have substantial bibliographical resources, but for many states it will only result in a pooling of poverty until an effective national library network becomes a reality.

If we continue to put our faith in building and improving hierarchical interlibrary loan systems with existing resource libraries at the apex, it is because we have not yet assimilated the findings of recent interlibrary loan studies and the lessons that have been learned by the National Library of Medicine and the BLL. The evidence shows that more than half the requests are for items purchased in the previous ten years; many are for items already owned by but not available in the requesting library for a variety of reasons; 85-95 per cent are in English; and more than half the requests to academic libraries are for serials. These findings suggest that such requests can be more easily satisfied from a centralized and specialized facility such as the British Library Lending Division whose sole function is to serve this need. Contrary to library folklore, exotic and obscure retrospective materials are not what are most commonly requested on interlibrary loan. Requests for such items constitute a small percentage of the total and could be easily handled by the existing large research libraries if they were freed from having to cope with routine requests and if they were adequately compensated for it--preferably by a federal subsidy of some kind.

The Case for an NLRC

The traditional hierarchical system for sharing retrospective resources by interlibrary loan, even after it is forged into a national system and improved (as it should be) by adding a compensation feature to it, may still fall short of filling the need that research libraries have for an effective system for gaining access to recent and current materials and particularly periodicals. The time appears to be ripe for a melding of the Center for Research Libraries' experience with little-used materials and the British Library Lending Division's success and experience with interlibrary lending and copying of the most-used materials. These two functions are essential, and ideally they should be in the same organization so they can better complement each other. There is an urgent need for the Center for Research Libraries to expand its functions to include a national library resources lending facility along the lines of the BLL but with initial emphasis on periodicals. In order to do this, the Center will require a new source of funding and substantial new space. The obvious solution which has been suggested is that the Center be made into a federally funded component of the national library system. If this proves to be an unfeasible line of development for the Center, then a completely new beginning could be made as it was in Britain. Perhaps a surplus military or other government facility could be pressed into service to meet this urgent need.

It would be difficult to overestimate the importance of creating a national library resources center. Consider the following factors:

> Serials subscriptions consume more than half of library expenditures for materials, and the percentage is rising at an alarming rate as journal prices continue to rise at a faster rate than monograph prices. Some departmental libraries in science and technology are now expending 80-100 per cent of their book funds for subscriptions, leaving little or nothing for the purchase of

monographs. Serials are not only expensive to buy, but they require substantial additional expenditures for cataloging, check-in of issues, binding, and storage.

Bibliographical identification and location tools are more advanced and more effective for serials than for monographs, and they make it easier to fill requests. Since we have the Union List of Serials, New Serials Titles, and countless computer-produced published lists of the serials holdings of libraries of all types, the need for a computerized data base and telecommunications system for interlibrary loan of serials is less pressing than for monographs.

Over half of all interlibrary loan requests are for periodical materials, ranging from a third in public libraries to 85 per cent in governmental and special libraries. About 85 per cent of periodical requests are filled by photocopies of articles.[12]

The designers of the proposed national library program estimate that within a period of less than ten years a national periodicals resources system could provide a substantial proportion of the article photocopies which make up a high percentage of all interlibrary loan requests.[13]

The BLL estimates that it is now handling about three-quarters of all interlibrary loan traffic in the United Kingdom and that 83 per cent of the requests are satisfied from stock, with a further eight per cent from other libraries, including some abroad.[14]

In view of these factors, it is hard to escape the conclusion that the creation of a national library resources center modeled after the British Library Lending Division should be a prime objective of U.S. library planners. It provides an efficient and immediate way to increase the total resources available to all libraries and would be an indispensible element in the national library network that is rapidly emerging. Unfortunately, no mention is made of this concept in the second draft (September 15, 1974) of the NCLIS program document,[15] nor does it appear in the list of priorities at the conclusion of the proposed design of a national library system that was prepared for the Commission by Westat, Inc.[16]

Copyright

The growing concern that publishers and copyright

holders have about this kind of library resource sharing will have to be allayed in some way. The Westat report just cited suggests that concentrating copying service at a single national center might facilitate a resolution of this problem. Perhaps the British experience could again serve as a model. Britain revised its copyright law in 1956 permitting libraries limited fair use privileges, and the BLL has been operating completely within its provisions with little apparent adverse effect on publishers. Libraries continue to purchase those books and journals most in demand by their readers. The BLL serves only a backup function, and if it did not exist borrowers would simply have to do without since much of the material requested has gone out of print or is otherwise unobtainable in the book trade.

Publishers have the idea that if they can discourage interlibrary loan and photocopying, libraries will be forced to spend more money to buy books and journals. The fact is that with or without effective sharing mechanisms, and with rising prices and declining budgets, libraries simply will not have the money to maintain their previous acquisitions levels. Publishers may suffer some losses. Some publications may go under, others will never be published because it will be foreseen that there would be insufficient demand for them. In the end, it may not be a bad thing if the tremendous number of journal titles currently being published were to decrease significantly. This could occur without a serious loss to scholarship since many of them were created to exploit the library market in the affluent sixties.[17] The idea that library budgets should support commercial publishing is a product of the last two affluent decades and is no longer viable, if it ever was. Library sales have contributed to the support of some scholarly publications, but it is becoming clear that if subsidies are needed, more effective and reliable mechanisms than library book budgets will have to be found.

Conclusion

Academic libraries--and perhaps all libraries--have entered a new era of austerity in which the financial resources available will not be enough to enable them to continue to build their collections and operate as they did during the last two affluent decades. There is evidence that the exponential growth rates of library collections and budgets are declining and the time has come to shift emphasis away from holdings and size to access and service. More realistic concepts of collection building will have to be adopted, and new patterns of service will have to be devised.

The urgent task of developing effective means of library resource sharing has two major components of equal importance. One is to increase the total library resources available, and the other is to improve the organizational and technical mechanisms for gaining access to them. To increase the total resources available involves not only strengthening existing libraries but also creating an essential missing element: a national ibrary resources center modeled after and combining the best features of the Center for Research Libraries and the British Library Lending Division. To improve the mechanisms for gaining access to these resources involves building a national library network supported by a computer-based national bibliographical and communications system. These two major components must go forward together. We should not allow the more glamorous and exciting technological elements to overshadow the more prosaic but equally important resource building elements.

References

1. Fiske, Edward B. "Education Feeling No-Growth Pains," New York Times, p. 57, 88, January 15, 1975.
2. Dunn, Oliver C., et al. The Past and Likely Future of 58 Research Libraries, 1951-1980; a Statistical Study of Growth and Change. Instructional Media Research Unit, University Libraries and Audiovisual Center, Purdue University, West Lafayette, Ind. 1971-72 (Ninth) Issue, 1973.
3. Academic Library Statistics 1973-1974. Washington, D.C., Assn. of Research Libraries, 1974.
4. Fussler, Herman H. Research Libraries and Technology. Univ. of Chicago Pr., 1973. p. 34.
5. Buck, Paul. Libraries and Universities. Harvard Univ. Pr., 1964. p. 72.
6. Stevens, Rolland E. "A Study of Interlibrary Loan," College and Research Libraries, September 1974, p. 336-343.
7. Bryant, Douglas W. "A University Librarian Looks Ahead," 1963. 48p. (Mimeographed)
8. Resources and Bibliographic Support for a Nationwide Library Program. Final Report to the National Commission for Libraries and Information Science.

August 1974. (WESTAT, Inc., Rockville, Md.)

9. For the original expanded version of this concept see: Palmour, Vernon E., et al. Access to Periodical Resources, a National Plan. For the Assn. of Research Libraries, Washington, D.C., WESTAT, Inc., February 1974. (NSF Grant GN 35571)
10. This was paraphrased from the Introduction, Handbook, the Center for Research Libraries, 1973. Chicago, Ill.
11. The British Library First Annual Report 1973-74, p. 7.
12. Resources and Bibliographic Support ... op. cit., p. 107.
13. Loc. cit.
14. The British Library, op. cit., p. 7.
15. A National Program for Library and Information Services, 2nd Draft. (Rev.) Prepared by the National Commission on Libraries and Information Science. September 15, 1974. Washington, D.C.
16. Resources and Bibliographic Support ... op. cit., p. 147-48.
17. This point is nicely underscored by a letter addressed to Chemical & Engineering News (December 10, 1973) and signed by 11 distinguished chemists from Europe, Britain, and the U.S. urging librarians to refrain from purchasing "unnecessary" chemistry journals. It was reprinted in College & Research Libraries, July 1974, p. 268-69, under the title "Too Many Chemistry Journals."

A LEGEND IN HIS OWN TIME

From the Investigative Legacy of Elsie Dinsmore*

David Peele

WLB Editor's note: Biographies of librarians, as typified by library school theses or even published works, follow a depressingly repetitious pattern. They are written only about the great and well known figures in the field, and there is always praise for the librarian and the seminal thinking done by her or him on pressing problems. Frequently an appreciation of the librarian is offered by colleagues who have studied under her; been influenced by him, etc. There may even be a festschrift put together by these colleagues with a lengthy laudatory essay at its beginning.

The editors of Wilson Library Bulletin have long believed, however, that librarianship should not be defined by the good examples only. Where are the biographies of those who stunk up the profession; whose presence in it was an unmitigated disaster; whose activities set back its development by years? We had long been aware of the presence of one such person here in New York, and while we despair of ever obtaining a complete study, our quest for information about him has been at least partially met by Elsie Dinsmore.

We must pause here to pay tribute. We regret to report that Ms. Dinsmore, whose editorial talent was so brilliantly exorcised on "Was Melvil Dewey a Whig?" (WLB, April 1972, p. 727-732), has gone--gone to join the biggest binder of them all in that great golden bookstack in the sky. Her timely demise--yes, timely, we're all pretty happy about it here--has deprived the world of the squashed fruit of the scholarship to which she referred in her letter to the editor in the June 1972 issue of WLB, p. 886.

---

*Reprinted by permission of the author and publisher from Wilson Library Bulletin, April 1975, pp. 561-564.

For reasons unknown to the sane, she persisted in spending her declining years writing about--or rather, spent her writing years declining about--David Peele, an obscure drudge whose contributions to library science were rated by an impartial panel of experts as minus 17 on a 100-point scale. (A partial panel of experts--all the unfortunates who worked with him--revised that figure to minus 258.)

On her death the New York City Department of Sanitation and the staff of WLB had an unfriendly contest to see at whose disposal Ms. Dinsmore's literary remains would be placed, and we regret to report that we lost. We went over and had a goose[1] at Elsie's effluvia. Most of it was unreadable and most of what was readable was unprintable, but we did discover two coherent fragments of what undoubtedly would have been her minum opus. We feel the unearthing of these bits is a discovery ranking with the invention of the dribble glass in the history of human achievement and only regret that Ms. Dinsmore did not live to complete her studies of the person who, in the words of one of his colleagues, was "the greatest living argument against permanent faculty tenure for librarians."

* * *

Fragment one. As the previous pages have testified, the early life of David Peele showed few of the qualities we associate with librarianship, but virtually all of those we connect with stupidity. That such a person was accepted at Swarthmore College speaks ill for the admissions standards of the day, and one becomes sick when one learns what he did there.

An early instance of the deceit that characterized his entire life occurred in the library of that institution, where he was employed to work in the stacks as a shelver. What he would actually do, though, was filch the date-due stamp and pad from the circulation desk, go into the stacks and find the most obscure, little-used books, write his name on the book card, and then stamp it and the date-due slip as if the volume had been charged out. He envisioned future weeders inspecting all these volumes, finding his name

---

1. We are aware that the customary phrase used here is "had a gander." The Wilson Library Bulletin, however, does not play sexual favorites.

everywhere, and marvelling, "This David Peele--what a tremendous reader he must have been." He expected to go down in history as the college's greatest reader.

He did indeed go down in history, as well as most of the other subjects he was enrolled in. (It is believed he was the only person in the annals of the college to flunk Physical Education on intellectual grounds--he was too embarrassed to read the hygiene text.) And so, though his name is all over book cards in the stacks, the only volume he was ever known to have actually read was George Day's _Productive Swine Husbandry_. (With good reason he despaired of ever having a normal marital relationship.)

To find him at Case Western Reserve School of Library Science a year later is a piece that passeth all understanding, and since the record he compiled at the school has been lost (or more probably, burned) we shall never know the full story of what happened.

Schools the country over name buildings after distinguished alumni, and the David A. Peele Women's Locker Room now gracing the Case WRU campus commemorates the spot where our hero spent most of his time. There are those who claim it was the screams of co-eds [_sic_] he assaulted at that location that led to his expulsion, but those of his former teachers who are able to speak of him without retching stand fast in their belief that "we flunked him out first."

Fragment two. Students approaching the reference desk at Staten Island Community College library soon changed their minds about seeking information when they glimpsed the hideously contorted, repulsive, scowling face glaring at them. This was, of course, our biographee, whose reputation as the crossest reference on the staff was well merited; it is alleged that the only time he ever smiled was when making one of his frequent long distance obscene phone calls.

The proposals he made for public service are still spoken of in hushed whispers at library conventions. His principal peeves and their solutions were:

1) _Theft of magazines problem_. Peele found, as had many before him, that the most filched periodical titles appeared in the areas of education and psychology. In short, the future teachers and psychiatrists of America were

learning to be rip-off artists at an early stage in their careers. "If they rip us off, we'll rip them off," said Peele--and by "them" he meant the front covers of all periodicals in those subject disciplines. He felt this would not only discourage theft but would have the added educational value of forcing the students to search hundreds of titles before finding the one looked for, thus familiarizing themselves with the enormity of the library's periodical holdings.

2) The library instruction problem. At Staten Island Community College, as at other educational institutions, there existed a hard core of teachers who felt that library instruction was worthless. Gentle attempts at persuasion had been the usual solution to this problem; only Peele could have conceived the idea of hiring a good squad of teachers denied tenure. Such persons were angry at the system anyway, and Peele would walk the halls with his disgruntled pedagogues, plunging into classrooms of those teachers who had been reluctant to have instruction. While his squad went to work on the teacher, Peele would deliver a library lecture to the enthralled class.

Other proposals similar to the above soon convinced Peele's superiors to move him backstage into technical services, where they hoped he would do less harm. They were mistaken. He began by insisting that the acquisitions librarian accept and pay for the complete collection of the writings of David A. Peele, beginning with second grade spelling tests. That librarian, after inspecting the proferred material, stated that the second grade tests were the only writings the library could accept; everything written from the third grade on being soft-core pornography.

From this high point, the relationship between the two men went downhill until it reached the low level previously established between Peele and his chief cataloger. His statement, "If the library is the heart of the college, the catalog section is the small intestine," was not one calculated to establish endearing friendship between the two.

The two proposals he made after being on the job for one hour--1) to put all the library's indexes on one continuous role of microfilm in random order, 2) to abandon standard subject headings and, instead, carry Sanford Berman's prose poem on Cataloging Philosophy (LJ, Sept. 1, 1974) to its extreme by putting headings in the card catalog for all types of users, e.g., "If a black racist comes to our library I want him to find material in the catalog under 'Honkies'; if a white racist enters he should find what he needs under 'Uppity Nigras'; the cop hater needs a heading under 'Pigs,' which of course will not be confused with material already under 'Swine'...."--did not convince the cataloging chief that he had a sound grasp of technical service principles. He was also made directly responsible for binding, and his decision to send out 500 items from the vertical file for Class A Library Binding at his uncle's company, which was on the Library Binding Institute's boycott list, did not occasion much joy among those responsible for the library budget.

During the years at SICC he constantly applied--and was constantly rejected--for promotion; college records indicate he was the only person ever demoted from Instructor to Adjunct Part Time Lecturer. Primarily this was because he used one written but never published book review as evidence of scholarly productivity. He had submitted his name to Choice as an expert in the fields of peanut-butter and goat-cheese sandwiches, snakes, and all aspects of library science. Taking his last statement as gospel, the book review editor sent him in 1971 a report on ANACONDA for comment. Our man naturally assumed this to be a volume on herpetology, and reviewed it as such. The results were not printed, and he was not again asked to review....

Final [WLB] editors' note: The words above conclude the Dinsmore writings. The title we have used is the one she apparently was planning for her completed book. The evidence would seem to indicate, though, that it might better have been called, "A Legend on His Company's Time."

NAPOLEON'S GREAT LIBRARIANS*

Antonia Dobi

In contrast to the dictators of our century, Napoleon had a fine humanistic education. An avid reader all his life, as soon as he had an independent income he started to collect books. In Valence, his first garrison, he soon became friends with his neighbor, Aurel, a bookseller. He went to see him every morning to read the newspapers and to browse among the books. Soon Aurel's store yielded up no new treasures and Napoleon started a correspondence with Borde, a bookdealer in Geneva, asking him to sent everything by and about Rousseau. After the arrest of the king, the young officer joined the Society of the Friends of the Constitution, and, because of his love of books, he was elected librarian of the society.[1]

A Librarian who Traveled with the Army...

Besides gathering laurels in the campaigns of Italy, the disciple of Rousseau and the romantics acquired the financial means to buy Malmaison, his first chateau, and there he organized his first library. Louis-Madeleine Ripault, the well known orientalist and historian, was his personal librarian. Ripault accompanied the French army to Egypt and became a member and librarian of the Egypt Institute. Not surprisingly, Napoleon's soldiers did not like the scholars that the young general valued so much. The joke circulated that in case of an attack, the soldiers were to form a square and put the donkeys and the scholars in the middle in order to defend them.

In the course of time, Napoleon established libraries

---

*Reprinted by permission of the author and publisher from Wilson Library Bulletin, November 1974, pp. 229-233.

in all his residences. Ripault organized those of the Tuileries, Laeken, Malmaison, Saint-Cloud, Fontainebleau, Rambouillet, and the small libraries of Napoleon's bureaus in the palaces. All the libraries contained about the same books, shelved everywhere in the same order, so that Napoleon could find any work in a minute.

Ripault was also the Consul's reference librarian. His job was to analyze the non-political periodicals, books, brochures, pamphlets, and acts of literary meetings. It was usually during breakfast that Ripault informed Napoleon of the latest literary events.

And One with Nothing to Do

Napoleon nominated Giacomo-Maria-Carlo Denina, Frederick II's former librarian, as associate librarian to Ripault. Denina had no definite duties; Napoleon simply collected him, as he collected all Frederick's belongings--Frederick's alarm clock accompanied him even to St. Helena. Ripault, an admirer of Marcus Aurelius, never liked Napoleon. Some sarcastic remarks concerning Napoleon's quick and superficial reading habits are to be found in letters Ripault wrote to Ménéval, Napoleon's secretary. [2]

In 1807 Ripault retired and was replaced by Antoine-Alexander Barbier, world-famous bibliographer, author of *Dictionnaire des ouvrages anonymes et pseudonymes* and the *Nouvelle bibliothèque d'un homme de goût*, to mention only two of his most important bibliographical works. Barbier was one of the great librarians who succeeded in rescuing hundreds of thousands of books and manuscripts that had been confiscated during the revolution. He discovered invaluable treasures crowded in depôts such as the complete collection of Fénelon's manuscripts. Barbier continued Ripault's work, organized and developed Napoleon's libraries in the residences, in the Tuileries, Trianon, Campiègne, Rambouillet, St. Cloud, Fontainebleau and the libraries of the two Empresses. He had the characteristics of a rare book librarian, buying such treasures as Bidpai's *Fables* in Persian, published in Calcutta in 1805, a Bodini *Iliad*, and the *Jerusalem delivrée*, translated by Prince Lebrun.

The Emperor's Bookmobile

In 1808 the Emperor asked Barbier to set up the plan

for a portable library, or shall we say a personal bookmobile. He indicated the following composition: forty volumes on religion (the Bible, the Koran, a church history), forty epic poems (Homer, Lucanus, Tasso, La Henriade), forty tragedies (Corneille, Racine, Voltaire), and one hundred novels (Rousseau, Richardson). The rest was made up of philosophical and historical works. In that same year, going to Wagram, Napoleon took the first boxes of his portable library with him. The boxes were covered with leather and lined with green velvet and each could accommodate about sixty volumes in two rows. A catalog made it possible to find any book immediately.

In a letter written from the castle of Schoenbrunn, Napoleon asked Barbier to publish for him a pocket edition of about three thousand volumes of the most important classics and reference works. They were to be edited by the best scholars, to be of uniform size and printed on very thin paper with very little margin. The diligent Barbier composed the catalog of this edition and asked six years and a half a million francs for its execution. This portable library was burned in Russia.[3]

If Thy Book Offend Thee...

Besides the portable library, Barbier sent all the new works to Napoleon by a regular courier service--even as far as Moscow. Napoleon's traveling coach was organized as a study and was always well furnished with books. While riding in his coach, when the Emperor did not like a book, he threw it out the window; in his residences, Napoleon flung such books into the fireplace.

With Barbier as a reference librarian Napoleon could be at peace. There was no book of any importance he did not know, no question he could not answer.

The faithful Barbier served Napoleon in the sad task of forming his last two libraries, his little collections of exile. While in Fontainebleau, the Emperor chose his favorite authors to accompany him to the island of Elba, among them Virgil, Ariosto, Caesar, Sallust, Tacitus, Thucydides, Plutarch, Rollin, and Tasso. He added to them reference works needed for writing the history of his reign and campaigns: the _Moniteur_, the _Bulletin des Lois_, the _Codes_, the _Recueil des traités de paix_, the _Comptes du Ministère des Finances et du Trésor Public_, for example. Napoleon ordered Barbier to send him regularly all new publications of interest from Paris to Porto-Ferrajo.

> These are some of the reference questions asked by Napoleon of his librarian Barbier between 1810 and 1814:
>
> A dissertation on the tiara and its origin;
>
> The protocol for the crowning of the heir presumptive;
>
> Examples in history of emperors who dethroned popes;
>
> Works on quarrels between popes and monarchs;
>
> Books on the topography of Russia and Lithuania;
>
> Detailed works in French on Charles XII in Poland and Russia.

Galleries Pillaged, but Books Returned

Back from the island of Elba, Napoleon returned all the books to the library of Fontainebleau. In this respect he was scrupulous. On his way to Russia, he borrowed some books from the royal library of Dresden which were burned during the retreat. In Paris he promptly ordered Barbier to get new copies of them at any price and send them to Dresden. This is a curious trait of his character, for he pillaged all the museums, galleries of art and castles systematically, in fact scientifically: he was accompanied and advised in these transactions by the great art scholar, Denon. After Waterloo, Napoleon hoped to be able to flee to the New World and asked Barbier to have his entire library of Trianon sent to America. He asked him his last reference questions--a list of works on America and a list of all the books written on himself and his campaigns. He also wanted a complete set of the *Moniteur* and the best encyclopedias and dictionaries.

On the 29th of June, 1815, Barbier wrote to the provisory government to give permission for Napoleon to take his library at Trianon, composed of about 2,200 volumes. into exile with him. As soon as Bluecher heard of the books being packed, he sent his soldiers to Trianon. They arrived when the first few boxes were gone and stopped the packing of the rest. [4] (According to Guillois, the 588 bound volumes in St. Helena came from Trianon, but Barbier, in a letter to Pridel dated December 27, 1815, affirmed that the library of Trianon was in good condition and intact, so that the 588 volumes of St. Helena could not have been sent from there. [5])

The First Paraprofessional

Napoleon's last personal librarian was far from being a world-famous scholar: he had only a primary education. Louis-Etienne Saint-Denis became Napoleon's footman in 1806. He accompanied him on his campaigns carrying his master's spy-glass and silver flask of brandy. He followed the Emperor to St. Helena, where he was entrusted with charge of the library. It is a satisfaction to learn that the most beautiful chambermaid on the island, Betsy Hall, chose him for her husband from among all the eligible prisoners. The proof that Saint-Denis was a lover of books is that he gave to the library of Sens the book that he inherited from Napoleon. [6]

Napoleon was a patron of the great scholars and librarians of his age who were products of the Catholic educational system and carried on a tradition of scholarship that would have been a disaster for France and for the world to lose. No personal sympathy influenced Napoleon in his choice of scholars, most of whom were republicans and viewed with horror the mass murders of the Napoleonic wars. After the victory of Marengo, Napoleon invited Daunou, one of the greatest scholars in France, to the Tuileries to dinner and offered him a place in the State Council. Napoleon's charm and prestige had no effect on Daunou; he refused. Napoleon in a fury told him that he was influenced by no personal sympathy in offering him this position, for he only loved two or three people in the world. "And I," replied Daunou, "love only the republic." In 1807 Fouché asked Napoleon whether he could trust Daunou with an important task. Napoleon answered from Warsaw: "Monsieur Daunou has the gift to do well whatever he is entrusted to do."[7]

Scholar-librarian

Jean-Claude-Francois Daunou was a formal orator and throughout his life always kept the studious habits of a monk. At four every morning he sat down at his desk to work. The list of his publications is given by Thallandier in his Documents biographiques sur Daunou (Paris, 1847, pp. 363-379). He took part in the production of two important reference books, l'Histoire littéraire de France and la Biographie universelle. Like most intellectuals, Daunou was an ardent republican and became a member of the Convention. The Terror put him into prison and he was liberated only after Robespierre's death. In 1800 Napoleon nominated him librarian for life of the Panthéon, and in 1804 archivist of the Empire. In 1811 Daunou was entrusted with the transportation of the pontifical archives to Paris.

Librarian vs. Pope and Russia

Whenever Napoleon asked Daunou a reference question, he replied with a book. When the Emperor suppressed the pontifical government, he ordered Daunou to research the motives that would justify him in public opinion. The result of this research was Daunou's Essai historique de la puissance temporelle des papes. When Napoleon wanted to unveil Russia's plans to menace Europe, Daunou revised, completed and published Rulhiers' Histoire de l'anarchie de Pologne.

Ups and Downs of Napoleon's Library Corps

Both Champollions, Jacques-Joseph and his brother, Jean-François, who was the first to decipher the hieroglyphs, were followers of Napoleon. Jacques-Joseph was an archeologist and took part in the expedition to Egypt. Back in France, Napoleon named him chief librarian of the Grenoble library. He was also professor of Greek at the University of Grenoble and was nominated dean by Napoleon. His greatest scholarly achievement was probably the extraordinary education he gave to his brother, Jean-François, eleven years his junior. Napoleon nominated the great Champollion full professor of history at Grenoble University at the age of twenty-two. Besides his professorship and research work, he had a part-time job as associate librarian at the Municipal Library. After Napoleon's downfall both Champollions lost their posts as professors and librarians and had to flee from Grenoble. In 1828 Jacques-Joseph became curator of the manuscripts in the Bibliothèque Nationale, but during the revolution of 1848 he was deprived of his position again. In 1849 he became curator of the Library of Fontainebleau.[8]

It is interesting to note that the Greek text on the Rosetta stone was translated by another great librarian of the Empire, Ameilhon. Napoleon nominated him chief librarian for life of the Arsenal library, although Ameilhon was a staunch republican.

Librarian's Fringe Benefit--a Baronetcy

Louis-Albert-Ghillain de Bacle-Dalbe was the only librarian who was given a baronetcy by the Emperor. He was Napoleon's topographer and map librarian. As a young man he spent seven years in the Alps, painting the mountains and making maps of them. From the Italian campaign on, the great geographer accompanied Napoleon, and his services were indispensable in setting up a military plan. He was infallible in interpreting maps and would figure out every line and every undulation of a field where Napoleon intended to wage a battle.[9]

Library Power

Napoleon almost added Chateaubriand to the galaxy of great librarians of the Empire--he decided to nominate him head of all French libraries with an ambassador's salary. No personal sympathy influenced him in this decision; he never enjoyed Chateaubriand's art and called the *Génie du Christianisme* a stew (galimatias).[10] This position was offered to Chateaubriand as a sinecure that would allow him to consecrate his time to literature and would induce him to sing the praises of the Emperor. Chateaubriand, however, took the offer seriously and demanded such extraordinary powers that Napoleon abandoned the idea.

Proposes Bibliography Course

The Emperor recognized the importance of bibliography. He proposed that in a special school of history a bibliography course should be taught, so that students would not lose time with inadequate and unreliable books and would get better instruction more quickly and easily.[11] During his reign, the Bibliographie de la France was founded by an imperial decree in October 1811 and some of the greatest French bibliographers lived during the Empire. Brunet's Manuel du libraire et de l'amateur des livres was published in 1810. Peignot published Rêpertoire bibliographique universel in 1812. Achard's Cours elementaire de bibliographie 1806-1807, was the first textbook of bibliography for high school students and undergraduates. The great bibliographical movement in France in the beginning of the 19th century was interrupted by the downfall of Napoleon and the ensuing ups and downs of political life. Germany then assumed the leading role in the bibliographical sciences.

From Patron to Beggar

After being a founder and organizer of libraries, and a patron of writers, scholars and librarians, Napoleon became a beggar of books. On the "Northumberland" the generous Admiral Cockburn put his library at the disposal of his prisoner and gave him his set of the Encyclopaedia Britannica as a gift. It was from the Britannica and British newspapers that Napoleon picked up the little English he learned from Las Cases on St. Helena. On the island, Major Hudson gave him the Annual Register from 1793 to 1808, which was very useful in the writing of his Memoirs.

In 1816 Napoleon impatiently awaited the arrival of the new governor, Sir Hudson Lowe, not only because he hoped for better treatment but also because Lowe was to bring him nearly two thousand books. Lady Elizabeth Holland, wife of Lord Holland (the only member of the House of Lords who opposed the legalization of the detention of Napoleon as a prisoner of war), regularly sent packages to the prisoners. They always contained not only dainties, but books. Napoleon in gratitude bequeathed to her a box adorned with a cameo given to him by Pius VI after the treaty of Tolentino. While on St. Helena, Napoleon spent £1, 396 on books that were bought by the English government for him. After his return to Europe, Las Cases did his best to get more books for the prisoner on his rock. In his letters to Gouldburn, the British undersecretary of state, he asked him to send to Napoleon the Minerva française and all the French and English publications of interest.[12]

From many points of view Napoleon was a disaster

for France, having caused the death of at least 1,200,000 Frenchmen. He utterly disregarded human life and individual liberty. Yet he was a great patron of science, literature, art, and scholarship, who valued the intellectual treasures of humanity and the libraries that housed them.

References

1. Paul Bartel, La jeunesse inédite de Napoléon. Paris: Amiot-Dumond, 1954, p. 194.
2. Helène Dufresne, Erudition et esprit public au XVIII siècle, le bibliothécaire Hubert-Pascal Ameilhon. Paris: Nizet, 1962, p. 472.
3. A. Guillois, "Les Bibliothèques particulieres de l'empereur Napoléon," Bulletin du Bibliophile, 1900, p. 176.
4. Ibid., p. 181.
5. Ch. Schmidt, "La bibliothèque de Trianon a-t-elle été transportée a Sainte-Helène?" Le Bibliophile moderne, Paris, 1901, pp. 377-83.
6. Frédéric Masson, Napoleon at St. Helena. Oxford: Pen-in-Hand, 1949, pp. 94-95.
7. Biographie universelle, ancienne et modern. Paris: Michaud frères, 1811-62, p. 171.
8. Dictionnaire de biographie française. Paris: Letouzey et Ané, 1933-59, v. 8, pp. 349-50.
9. Frédéric Masson, Napoléon chez lui. Paris: Albin Michel, n.d., pp. 163-64.
10. Barry Edward O'Meara, Napoleon in exile. London: Simpkin and Marshall, 1822, p. 564.
11. La Grande encyclopédie, inventaire raisoné des sciences, des lettres et des arts. Paris, 1886-1902, v. 6, p. 605.
12. Emmanuel Las Cases, Le mémorial de Sainte Helène. Paris: Gallimard, 1956-57, p. 628.

THE ARCHIVAL EDGE*

F. Gerald Ham

Our most important and intellectually demanding task as archivists is to make an informed selection of information that will provide the future with a representative record of human experience in our time. But why must we do it so badly? Is there any other field of information gathering that has such a broad mandate with a selection process so random, so fragmented, so uncoordinated, and even so often accidental? Some archivists will admit the process is a bit out of kilter. They say a simple formula of more cooperation, less competition, increased governmental largess, and bigger and better records surveys--a logistical device we often mistake for an acquisitions strategy--should be sufficient to produce a national mosaic that will bequeath to the future an eminently useable past.

A handful of critics, however, have suggested that something is fundamentally wrong: our methods are inadequate to achieve our objective, and our passivity and perceptions produce a biased and distorted archival record. In 1970, Howard Zinn told an SAA audience that the archival record in the United States is biased towards the rich and powerful elements in our society--government, business, and the military--while the poor and the impotent remain in archival obscurity. To correct this, the chief spokesman for history's new Left urged archivists "to compile a whole new world of documentary material about the lives, desires and needs of ordinary people."[1] How this task was to be done he shrewdly left to the archivists. In 1971 Sam Bass Warner, a noted historian of urban life, urged us to make our archives more useful. Like Zinn, Warner subscribed to Carl Becker's notion that history should help people to understand the world they live in. To do this Warner asked

*Reprinted by permission of the author and publisher from *The American Archivist*, January 1975, pp. 5-13.

archivists "so far as it is humanly possible" to "abandon the pursuit of the classic subjects of American history" and turn instead to the collection of data that would yield a "historical explanation of the major issues of our own time."[2] Warner had specific notions of how this should be done which were dismissed as the half-baked product of an archivally uninformed mind.

Even earlier there were rumblings in Columbus, Ohio, where a young and untamed archivist suggested that his colleagues' concern with quantity and competition inhibited discussion of advantages of quality and cooperation; that many, if not most, archival institutions operated "as introspective units justifying their existence solely on their own accomplishments rather than in terms of their role in the overall historical collection process"; and if this "egocentric attitude" was not abandoned competing archival programs would become so proliferated that the possibility of inter-institutional cooperation would be jeopardized.[3]

But the most sweeping indictment in what was emerging as a radical critique of the way archivists go about documenting history and culture came from the Cornell University historian and archivist, Gould P. Colman. Colman, in the American Archivist "Forum," charged that lack of concern about acquisition guidelines had produced possibly "the most serious problem facing archivists...; the politicalization of our profession," politicalization in the sense of "skewing the study of culture by the studied preservation of unrepresentative indicators of that culture." For example governments, particularly the one in Washington, preserved documents out of all proportion to government's impact on culture while other important institutions, such as the family, are poorly documented. Shouldn't archivists, Colman asked, have a responsibility to redress this balance? Documentation was biased further by our propensity to collect what is most easily accessible and by limiting oral history resources primarily to those relatively well-documented aspects of culture which could pay the expensive oral history piper.[4]

The empirical evidence--from published accession notes, from NUCMC, from recently issued guides, from anywhere an archivist keeps a record of what he collects--validates these charges. But the evidence reveals more than a biased record; it reveals incredible gaps in the documentation of even traditional concerns. Take the case of a midwestern state known both for its production and consumption of fermented beverages. Neither brewing nor the brewing industry is mentioned in any of the state's archival finding aids. It is possible that 1000 years from now some researcher will conclude that in a city known as Milwaukee the brewer's art was unknown. The evidence also showed that many archivists waste time and space preserving random bits and pieces, as well as large accessions, of the most dubious value.

But the real cause for concern is that there doesn't seem to be any concern. With a few notable exceptions, there is no realization that our present data gathering methods are inadequate or that our fundamental problem is the lack of imaginative acquisition guidelines or comprehensive collecting strategies at all levels of archival activity. You search archival literature in vain to find something more helpful than a "how we did it here" article on a particular collecting program or an essentially "nuts and bolts" piece on the mechanics of collecting. Equally barren are the annual reports of the SAA committees dealing with identification and acquisition of archives. Further, an examination of the works on historical methodology and social science research indicate that our clients do not think the matter deserves much attention either.[5] For the archivist, the area of acquisition strategies remains a vacuum.

These criticisms, even if correct, are irrelevant for some archivists. To them the archival endeavor is primarily a custodial one. And the so-called dean of Canadian bookmen, Bernard Amtmann, would agree with them. In the May issue of the Canadian Archivist he stated, "archivists are by definition custodians of the material in their possession and their professional training and qualifications do not exactly encompass the ... historical evaluation of material." This evaluation, he said, "must surely be the responsibility of the historian."[6] Whether it was arrogance or ignorance, Bernard Amtmann was only echoing archivists. In 1969 as reported in the New York Times the archivist of New York City was asked what he saved. "Aside from the mayors' papers," he answered, "we try to keep only things which will protect the city against a suit or help it to document a suit against somebody else." He went on to suggest that "some of the historical societies" might be interested in examining the records he was destroying. "You never can tell," he said, "when you're going to come across something valuable."[7] And, in an uninformed way, he was only practicing what Hilary Jenkinson and others have preached.

Small wonder the custodial image is still widely held by our allies in the research community. Indeed, the persistence of the custodial tradition has not only been a major factor in the archivist's failure to deal with acquisition policy on a coherent and comprehensive basis, but has resulted in an obsession--with the "nuts and bolts" or craft aspects of our work.

Reinforcing the custodial tradition is a parallel tradition, that of the researcher as data gatherer. We all know that many of the great manuscript collections--those of Belknap, Draper, and H. H. Bancroft come easily to mind--were brought together in this fashion. The American Historical Association through its committees on source material perpetuated this tradition and even today there are archival programs where the history faculty are the collectors while the archivists are the "keepers of the past."[8]

This tradition, of course, leaves the archivist too closely tied to the vogue of the academic marketplace. For example, only after historians rediscovered the importance of the city in American history did a few so-called urban archives come into existence. Similar efforts, often initiated by the action of concerned historians, were developed to meet the needs for documentation on the black community; on ethnic groups and immigrants; on social welfare; on architecture; on popular culture; the history of science; and so forth. These responses to changing patterns in the pursuit of history, and to the increase of other studies once considered outside the proper use of archives, are a temporary corrective. There is a dilemma here. Most researchers are caught in their own concerns and do not worry about all the history that needs to be written; yet in terms of documentary preservation this is precisely what the archivist must do. Small wonder, then, that archival holdings too often reflected narrow research interests rather than the broad spectrum of human experience. If we cannot transcend these obstacles, then the archivist will remain at best nothing more than a weathervane moved by the changing winds of historiography.

Turning from those traditions which have prevented the archivist from developing a larger acquisition design, let's consider five interrelated developments that are forcing him into a more active and perhaps more creative role.

The first is structural change in society. The process of institutionalizing and nationalizing decision-making, for example, has had a profound impact on documentation, making the archives of associations, pressure groups, protest organizations, and institutions of all sorts relatively more important than the papers of individuals and families. Accession data in the American Archivist reflect this change. Thirty years ago personal and family archives accounted for 38 per cent of all reported accessions; but they account for only 14 per cent today. In this same period, records of labor, of social and political protest, and of social welfare increased from less than 1 per cent to nearly one-fourth of all accessions. Unlike family papers these archives usually do not fall unsolicited into the hands of a waiting archivist, and their percentage rise on the accession charts is partly the result of the sensitivity and hard work of many archivists. Further, as the government has become the primary instrument of social and economic policy the records of its dealings, especially with non-elite population groups, have become more important. But archival holdings do not reflect this change. One reason is the disorganization of state, county, and municipal records; another is the narrow appraisal criteria used by many public record archivists. The result has been the destruction of vast quantities of important social and economic data.

Closely related to institutionalized decision-making and increased governmental activity, is a second and more prosaic factor: bulk. With records increasing at an exponential rate, it is utopian to believe that society could ever afford the resources for us to preserve everything of possible value; for it to do so would be irresponsible. We must realize that when we preserve one body of data it probably means that something else won't be preserved. But I do not think we have adequate methodological tools to make these critical choices. In fact, we might be better off if we forget what we have been taught. It is irresponsible and unrealistic to argue for the integrity of a file of gubernatorial papers that fills up 1500 document cases of which 80 per cent is either duplicate or of marginal worth.

If the volume of documentation has greatly increased, the quality of the information has greatly decreased. Arthur Schlesinger, commenting in the Atlantic Monthly on this third problem--missing data--wrote: "In the last three quarters of a century, the rise of the typewriter [and to this we should add modern quick copy machines of all sorts] has vastly increased the flow of paper, while the rise of the telephone has vastly reduced its importance.... If a contemporary statesman has something of significance to communicate, if speed and secrecy are of the essence, he will confide his message, not to a letter, but to the telephone."[9] An examination of files similar to the gubernatorial papers above is proof that there is much more bulk of much less usefulness.

If the archivist is going to fill in the gaps he will have to become, as Warner suggests, "a historical reporter for his own time." He can use any of several techniques: he can create oral history, he can generate a photographic record, and he can collect survey data. As a reporter he can produce oral history, not as a painstakingly edited source for written texts about the Presidents and their men, but rather as documentation of the day to day decisions of lower echelon leaders and of the activities and attitudes of ordinary men and women. He can use photography to supplement the written record and make it more meaningful. But today, though most archival institutions collect photographs, virtually none has an active field program. And he could, if he has the courage and energy, do as one archivist suggests and create his own mail questionnaires and use other survey techniques to establish a base line of social and economic data.

A fourth factor in the making of the active archivist is that of vulnerable records or what we might call "instant archives." It is documentation that has little chance of aging into vintage archives, that is destroyed nearly as fast as it is created, and which must be quickly gathered before it is lost or scattered. At my own institution, for instance, the collections which deal with the major 1960's movements on the left--civil rights, student activism, and the anti-Vietnam War protest--probably would not exist today if we had not initiated contacts before many of the organizations quietly dissolved.

Technology is a fifth development. We are all aware that electronic impulses easily and rapidly disappear from magnetic tape, that photographic images often fade beyond recognition, that files with quick copy documents are literally self-destructing, and that the program documentation to important EDP data sets often disappears long before the archivist is aware the set was ever created. Because of its short life-cycle, we must collect this material on a current basis or not at all.

Taken together, these five factors--institutionalization, bulk, missing data, vulnerable records, and technology--have expanded the universe of potential archival data, have given a contemporaneous character to archival acquisition, and have permanently altered the job of the archivist, forcing him to make choices that he never had to make before. I see three developments on the archival landscape which, in part, are responses to these conditions--the specialized archives, the state archival networks, and an emerging model for urban documentation.

The specialized archives, particularly those built around a subject area--the Archives of Social Welfare at the University of Minnesota is an example--have great appeal. They offer the possibility of well-defined parameters, and exhaustive documentation. They also allow the development of real staff expertise and may be easier to fund. The apotheosis of this type of program was the recent Eugene McCarthy Historical Project, described by its director as the most systematic attempt ever undertaken "to collect and organize all retrievable material of a political campaign for the presidential nomination." The records are voluminous and the project was expensive and the institutional competition for this prize was keen.[10]

But these archives, especially those centered around the life and times of an individual, do not come to grips with acquisition problems. They side-step them. They contribute to the problem without adding to the solution. But they can contribute to the solution by plugging into larger conceptual frameworks, they can build the kind of interinstitutional linkages and coordination they now lack.

The need to link specialization with coordination was stressed by Sam Bass Warner. Speaking of the urban scene he argued that there is insufficient variation among American cities to justify the repetition everywhere of the same sort of collection. He urged historians and archivists to get together and divide up the archival turf. "San Francisco," he suggested, "might establish a business archive, Detroit, a labor archive, Los Angeles, a housing archive ... and so forth."[11] These specialized archives, in turn, would be <u>linked</u> with existing local, state, and federal programs. This was Warner's half-baked product that was dismissed out of hand.

But the concept of linkage is a key to the new

state archival networks such as those in Ohio, Minnesota, Texas, and Wisconsin. The best of these have a coordinated acquisition program which seeks to be representative in subject coverage, inclusive in informational formats, and statewide in competence.[12] In these regards the Ohio network is one of the most advanced, conceptually if not operationally. The eight centers, most of which are part of a university, function as an integrated archives-library program for their assigned geographic area. Overall collection administration is provided by the Ohio Historical Society which supplies field service assistance in both the public and private sector and assumes responsibility for collections of statewide scope. Furthermore, interconnection assures that the activities of the centers are coordinative rather than competitive.[13] The network concept and structure offer not only a means to document society more systematically, but also to utilize better the limited resources of participating archival units.

In a similar fashion the Houston Metropolitan Archives Center hopes to do for one urban area what the networks have done for their states. Not only is the center the most ambitious urban archives program ever launched, it is also the most handsomely funded--a quarter of a million dollar grant from the National Endowment for the Humanities. The project is backed by a consortium of the three major urban universities and the Houston Public Library. In affiliation with the new statewide Regional Historical Research Depositories system, it serves as the public records depository for Houston and Harris County. Manuscript records, printed and non-text material, and oral history are part of its collecting program; and it will provide a fully automated bibliographic control system for all resources regardless of their location in Houston. And two historians--not archivists--using traditional archives-library components, created this comprehensive model for documenting urban life.[14] These approaches can be a beginning. But we must do much more.

<u>First</u>. We must change old habits and attitudes. The view, held by many in our profession that, in collecting, cooperation is synonymous with abdication, must become an anachronism. Given our limited resources, the competition which produces fragmentation and the idiosyncratic proprietary view of archives must yield to integrated cooperative programs which have easily available information on the location of their resources.

Second. We must commit a far greater proportion of our intellectual resources to developing guidelines and strategies for a nationwide system of archival data collecting. And let me say that I am talking about concepts and flexible programs, not rigid structures or uniform procedures. Let me suggest some beginnings. Our subject area committees must give as much attention to appraisal and acquisition criteria and methods as they do to the preparation of technical manuals and directories. Conceptualization must precede collection and, while this methodology is equally applicable to all subject areas, church archives provide a finely drawn example of how this process can be applied. Why couldn't archivists determine the documentation needed to study contemporary religious life, thought, and change and then advise denominations and congregations on how their records selection can contribute to this objective?

We must also develop empirical studies on data selection. For example, why don't college and university archivists compare the documentation produced by institutions of higher learning with the records universities usually preserve, to discover biases and distortions in the selection process and to provide an informed analysis on how archivists should document education and its institutions?

We need more seminars similar to the recent Midwest Archives Conference seminar on state networks to deal with collecting plans and strategies. One on labor documentation would be especially timely. The goal of that seminar might be a consortium of labor archives. Such a cooperative effort would conserve and amplify rather than waste limited resources. Researchers would be better served if the consortium determined weaknesses in labor documentation and then did something about it. And the individual labor archival institutions might even find some workable way to decide who should knock on whose door.

We need to develop methodologies to cope with the important but vast time-series now produced by public and private agencies. Series such as case files of all sorts are so massive that wholesale preservation even on microfilm is impossible. The sample techniques of the various social sciences may offer a solution to the construction of a "representative" sample and suggest the limits and advantages of using one approach rather than another. Similarly, the conceptualization that went into the development of first economic and later social indicators may be transferrable to archival documentation. And the models built by anthropology, economics, sociology, and psychology may give clues to the direction of future research as well as a vision of what constitutes social relevance. The uneasy partnership of the archivist and the historian must be strengthened and expanded to include other students of society.

If our literature is an index to our profession's development, then we need a new body of writings because our old catechisms are either inadequate or irrelevant when they deal with contemporary archives and the theory and practice related to their acquisition. And without needed conceptual and empirical studies, archivists must continue to make their critical choices in intellectual solitary confinement.

Third. We need to reallocate our limited resources for collecting. The critics also present a strong case that far too much effort and money go to document the well documented. In addition, we need archival revenue sharing that will enable the states and localities to meet their archival responsibilities better. The passage of the National Historical Publications and Records Act would be a modest beginning by encouraging statewide planning and providing funds to implement these programs.

Finally, the archivist must realize that he can no longer abdicate his role in this demanding intellectual process of documenting culture. By his training and by his continuing intellectual growth, he must become the research community's Renaissance man. He must know that the scope, quality, and direction of research in an open-ended future depends upon the soundness of his judgment and the keenness of his perceptions about scholarly inquiry. But if he is passive, uninformed, with a limited view of what constitutes the archival record, the collections that he acquires will never hold up a mirror for mankind. And if we are not holding up that mirror, if we are not helping people understand the world they live in, and if this is not what archives is all about, then I do not know what it is we are doing that is all that important.

As archivists we must be in a more exposed position than we have been in the past, one that is more vulnerable. We might well heed the advice of one of Kurt Vonnegut's minor characters, Ed Finnerty, "a chronically malcontent boozer" and the real hero of the novel Player Piano.

When someone suggested he should see a psychiatrist, Ed replied: "He'd pull me back into the center, and I want to stay as close to the edge as I can without going over. Out on the edge you see all kinds of things you can't see from the center.... Big, undreamed-of-things--the people on the edge see them first."[15]

Notes

1. Howard Zinn, "The Archivist and Radical Reform," unpublished manuscript, pp. 12-13, 18.
2. Sam Bass Warner, "The Shame of the Cities: Public Records of the Metropolis," unpublished manuscript, 1971, pp. 2, 3.
3. David R. Larson, "The Ohio Network of American History Research Centers," Ohio History (Winter 1970): 62.
4. "The Forum: Communications from Members," American Archivist 35 (July/October 1972): 483-85.
5. Examples of the historian's superficial approach to acquisition problems are the "Report of Ad Hoc Committee on Manuscripts Set Up by the American Historical Assoc. in December 1948," American Archivist 14 (July 1951): 233; and more recently, Walter Rundell, Jr., In Pursuit of American History: Research and Training in the United States (Norman: University of Oklahoma Press, 1970), pp. 104-07.
6. An abbreviated version of this article by Amtmann, "Historical Manuscripts at Auction," was widely circulated in the United States in the July 22, 1974, issue of the Antiquarian Bookman, pp. 356-57.
7. New York Times, November 23, 1969.
8. See William F. Birdsall, "The American Archivist's Search for Professional Identity, 1909-1936" (Ph.D. dissertation, University of Wisconsin-Madison, 1973), particularly ch. 5.
9. Arthur Schlesinger, Jr., "On the Writing of Contemporary History," Atlantic Monthly (March 1967): p. 71.
10. Werner Peters, "The McCarthy History Project," American Archivist 33 (April 1970): 155.
11. Warner, "Shame of the Cities," p. 4.
12. Richard A. Erney and F. Gerald Ham, "Wisconsin's Area Research Centers," American Libraries (February 1972): 135-40; James E. Fogerty, "Minnesota Regional Research Centers," Minnesota History (Spring 1974): 30-32; Marilyn von Kohl, "New

Program Focuses Attention on Local Records," Texas Libraries (Summer 1972): 90-93.

13. The Ohio Network of American History Research Centers: Charter; Agreement Number One, Administration of Local Ohio Government Records; Agreement Number Two, Ohio Newspapers; and Agreement Number Three, Ohio Manuscripts. Xerox copies.
14. Proposal, "Houston Metropolitan Archives Center," National Endowment for the Humanities, Division of Research Grants.
15. Tim Hildenbrand, "Two or Three Things I Know About Kurt Vonnegut's Imagination," in The Vonnegut Statement, Jerome Klinkowitz and John Somer (eds.) (New York: Delacorte, 1973), p. 121.

DECISIONS! DECISIONS!*

Ellsworth Mason

When you live on Long Island for nine years, a clear day is a rare and wonderful thing. When the heavy, glowering layers over the north Atlantic move out to sea and we find that the sun is still up in the sky, when the air is cleared of moisture and we can see to infinity, when humidity drops and our skin can breathe again, there is a wonderful sense that all is right with the world. All the elements seem to be in harmony, and we at one with them.

The achievement of a condition something like this occasional harmony of irrational forces is one of the prime aims of human administration, and everything in nature conspires against it. Despite the great natural laws (which we continually discover are wrong) chaos is the basic condition of the world. The shirt on my back, being wrought to an order, is uneasy, struggling to return to primal matter; and it will have its way sooner or later, despite Cluett, Peabody and Co. And despite the remarkable achievements of man, especially in this century, we all carry within ourselves infinite potentialities for chaos. Mastering this tendency is a central problem in developing character; managing a multiplicity of people in whom this tendency is not fully mastered is a central problem of administration in organizations.

I have had insights into the dislocations of organizational dynamics in the course of consulting on eighty-odd library buildings. The first thing a consultant must do on a job (and the same is true of the architect) is to find out who are the people who really govern decisions. If you follow the wrong lead horse, a year of careful work can be pulled

---

*Reprinted by permission of the author and publisher from The Journal of Academic Librarianship, Vol. 1, No. 1, March 1975, pp. 4-8.

from under you by a single decision of the man who calls the shots. One of the most effective contributions a consultant can make is to persuade the planning agency to center authority firmly in the hands of a group that is informed and is charged with the responsibility of reconciling the various constituencies present in the organization. Any organization must reconcile competing demands into firm decisions.

This is not always possible to do. There is always that Dean of the School of Geology, a world expert on pisolites, who is in charge of planning the new geology building. He also proceeds to plan the geology library; of course, without consulting the librarian. Since in his list of priorities the library ranks below parking spaces, faculty offices, laboratories, classrooms, and rock specimens, it turns out to be the width of a pipe corridor and to have shelving enough for half of the present collection.[1]

There is that Board of Trustees that calls for final bid plans two months before they can possibly be finished.[2] There is that superintendent of schools who orders only single carrels for library seating, whereas many students hate them. This list could go on indefinitely, and be expanded by examples reported by friends from industry, where major branches are abolished by a remotely issued memo, whereas upgrading one weak manager could have made them profitable. Because of the enormous complexity of most enterprises, men in authority these days are continually required to make decisions in areas where they are completely ignorant. While he would not think of diving from the cliffs at Acapulco without learning to swim, a man whose only experience with construction has been sand castles on the beach at the age of four will take on the planning of fifty million dollars' worth of complex buildings without batting an eyelash. Never before in history have so many had so much opportunity to make such ignorant decisions.

This condition reached its apogee in our times in the American involvement in Vietnam, where the rigid authority of two presidents seemed to many to be so intolerable that the very principle of authority, on which Europe rose for nine-hundred years, seemed intolerable too. That principle had been severely jolted by the First World War, which was the really traumatic event of this century, and in recent times it has been called so violently into question that the use of authority in any human affairs has been denied in government, in the church, in the home, in schools.

One of Dylan Thomas's most eloquent poems protests the disproportion between the man making a decision and the magnitude of its effects in these words:

> The hand that signed the paper felled a city;
> Five sovereign fingers taxed the breath,
> Doubled the globe of dead and halved a country;
> These five kings did a king to death.[3]

This view of authority as a destructive force has run rampant through radical thought of the last ten years, through the student uprisings of the 60s, and through the faculties in the academies. From the faculties, it has spread to the library world.

In a number of library schools, which tend to grow more remote from reality every day (as the split between theory and practice becomes a gulf), there were foam-flecked courses bristling with fury at the idea of anyone telling anyone to do anything for any reason. Chanting the creed of Romanticism before the altars of Rousseau, a clump of hairy-chested spewers of library so-called literature issued dicta riddled with the conviction that all administrators are evil, all subordinates fine, pure and oppressed and that in point of fact, all library managers should be shot down like mad dogs.[4] In light of this recent imbalance in the view of the comparative roles of Freedom and Authority in human affairs, it is important to discuss the uses and limits of authority in the decision-making process.

First of all, any decision has to be informed, and since everyone is ignorant, although our areas of ignorance vary (that is to say, what we do not know is infinitely greater than what we do know) any good decision-maker has always sought advice from specialists, and even more has built into his staff strengths and skills other than his own that are required frequently. Information must be gathered from all pertinent sources. By the time decisions are made they are colored and largely formulated by facts, attitudes, needs, and reports from different combinations of administrators, department heads, professional librarians, support staff. The gradual emergence of alternatives for decision is a process of the melding of people and information that cannot be accurately described as an individual decision.

It is immediately apparent that the organizational chart, with its genealogical boxes, and levels, and lines of descent, does nothing more than describe in a simplified way comparative levels of authority. It tells nothing about what happens between the levels. A more accurate graphic representation of the decision process would be a wheel, with the center turning and being turned by the forces at the spokes. Each decision is a new wheel with a different number of different spokes.

The tyrant theory of administration sees a bolt hurled from the top of the organization chart, quivering like lightning down the command line to the second level, which hurls a minor bolt down to the next level, and so on until finally it strikes an enchained slave ironically called a professional librarian, who is expected to carry out the order. This view is infantile in its ignorance of the way things happen in real life. Few decisions are simple enough to involve input by less than three managerial levels, most decisions of consequence involve more, and many are so complex that they require further information from outside specialists. The happiest time for any good manager is when he is presented a problem by a subordinate, who tells him what must be decided, states briefly the factors pertinent to the decision, and adds his recommendation. Anyone who really wants positive response from his superior in an organization will shape problems in this way.

The second fact about decision making is that there are seldom right decisions and wrong decisions, requiring only the obvious skill of telling black from white. Occasionally choices are this simple, but most alternatives embody a number of plusses and a number of minuses; neither route lacks disadvantages. Just think about circulation systems. No system ever devised lacks drawbacks. The one chosen is the one that provides the most advantages for your purposes, and the fewest disadvantages. Making this kind of complex choice requires in addition to the gathering of information a total view of all the library's aims, a broad view of everything that will be affected by the decision, anticipation of any collateral problems that may result, adjustment to the potentials of the people who will put it into action, judgment of whether the end result will approximate the anticipation, and a clear view of ways of following up to see whether in fact that end has resulted.

Because the choice is complex and the process of making the choice complex, it is exactly at this point that misunderstanding among staff members can occur through a simplistic view of the nature of decisions as right or wron This view is strongest among the young and inexperienced, to whom it is often clear that a department head in a neigh boring specialty, about which they know nothing, has established a wrong process, about which they know nothing. This view generally stems from something told them as a fact in library school or in an article.

One of the important things library schools can give students is a realization of the great and wonderful complexity of librarianship, a condition that makes this profession an inexhaustible delight to practice, an endless challenge, and a life full of continuous development. Begin ning librarians seriously underestimate the complex demand of librarianship, and consequently seriously overestimate themselves and their achievements. A while back I interviewed a candidate for a position described in an advertisement as "Reference Librarian," who was upset to learn tha she was not being considered as head of the department. As she said to us, "After all, I've had two years experience." And this in a specialty that takes ten years of wide ranging reading after graduate school and the sharpening of foreign languages before even those of distinctive talent can really work effectively.

So it is possible to reconcile competing demands within an organization, and to gather information through a complex interaction of organizational levels that leads to a sound decision, and still get hung up on simplistic views of the decision. It is impossible through sheer lack of time to explain fully to everyone who would like to know all of the elements that went into the decision, including the alter natives not taken. Nevertheless, if heavily negative reactions prevail, the staff can be the sticking point, since immediately following the decision, management begins.

We can distinguish five levels in the managerial pro ess of achieving action by means of an organization:

1. The establishment of goals.
2. The formulation of policies to attain goals.
3. The translation of policies into effective action.
4. The observation of results, as related to goals.
5. The correction of actions out of line with goals.

The establishment of goals and the formulation of policies are decision-centered areas where the information gathering, multiple input, multi-level consultation processes occur. Translating policies into action, observing the resulting actions, and correcting them are areas of management.

Translating policies into effective action, which is staff-centered, is probably the most difficult step to make work effectively. It requires transmitting instructions through three or four levels of organization, each of which must interpret and reissue them in terms applicable to their own function. There is nothing more difficult than transmitting a simple message accurately through four single bodies. Here we are in the realm of the repeated story, with the astonishing transformation that occurs as it is repeated. This is a simple, but profound, problem in communication between human beings.

In libraries this difficulty is complicated by a series of factors three of which, I think, are intensified in any organization. 1) The overwhelming majority of people in organizations do not like change. People want to do those things they like to do in the way they know best. Even the innovators do not like change: they love to make other people change, but resist changes that originate outside themselves. 2) People in organizations have a tendency to become process-bound. This is especially true in librarianship, where so much effective action depends on regularization and the removal of variations. Our processes are now highly complex and demanding, and we have become ingenious in solving our own problems, without regard to those people out there who use the library, who seem so remote. Triple-split card catalogs are solutions to librarians' problems. Circulation systems that prevent a student from knowing who has a book out and when it is due are solutions to librarians' problems. Our processes convince a large part of our clientele that all librarians are mad, as I argued a few years ago in an article entitled "Unnatural Places and Practices."[5] 3) The users of a library can influence its actions only in minor ways. They are working unorganized outside of the organization, and are helpless when confronted by the power of the organization. This fact can be verified by anyone who studies the so-called chain of command, who will find that decisions of a policy nature are constantly made by anyone of any level of authority on the line, where it actually affects library users.

A kind of heady euphoria settles down on many people

given small amounts of authority, that makes them feel artistic, and although in the head office it is considered very bad form, who has not seen numbers of instances along the following lines? -- The student assistant at the circulation desk makes up rules diametrically opposed to those in the staff manual under his nose, despite weekly training. -- Clerks close branch libraries before posted closing hours. -- Filing clerks, impatient with the rules, file cards by feel, intuitively (this actually happened). -- Professionals refuse to accept interlibrary loan requests unless the citation is verified in blood. -- Department heads suddenly decide to file catalog cards only once every ten weeks.

Needless to say, such continuous free-form creativity is not received by the public with the same applause accorded to Beethoven or Picasso. This kind of thing goes on in all organizations. In architecture one can find sixth-level team members, striplings without an architecture degree, radically re-designing building plans that are nearly finished. This phenomenon, which infiltrates all organizational levels, underscores the supreme importance of immediate, direct supervision, and the ability of the supervisor to make prompt adjustments of disorders.

All of these negative human and organizational factors must be minimized if the library is to be a means of achieving defined ends, and this requires review of actions at all levels. It also requires a responsive professional and suppor staff who are reasonably happy and convinced that someone is willing to listen to them and is looking out for their welfare. In addition, the standing of the library in the university or the community is of the greatest importance to staff response.

If the staff is generally unhappy, action can become completely mired in resistance at the third step of the managerial process. On the other hand, as has been made clear in a number of cases in recent years, it is entirely possible to make the staff extremely comfortable, by raising salaries, extending benefits, upgrading status, and cutting the work week, without improving service to the public in any way. I can lead you to professional librarians sitting on their stenographic spread at $28, 000 a year, who bewail the shortness of their annual six-week vaction, and the length of their 33-hour week. The organization can become an enormous sponge that soaks up increasing resources without letting any trickle through to users.

I find that libraries generally do a reasonably good

job on the first three steps in the managerial process, right down to making the staff reasonably happy, but I find that most of them do a poor job in the last two steps, reviewing and correcting actions to achieve goals, which are exactly the processes that must be strong in order to serve users. To make them strong requires strong leadership in management, and we are in a social and political condition that severely handicaps the emergence of leadership, one of the signal weaknesses of our times. It also requires a condition of accountability at every level, at a time when many at least flirt with the idea that every man should be his own anarch, and when instruments for averting accountability are being imported into all kinds of organizations. We are, in fact, approaching a condition in which libraries may reverse their role as means of achieving ends, and become instead, weapons to exploit those outside for the benefit of those inside.

In recent times, we have been told that the best management theory calls for "participatory democracy" in management. Based on the 18th century doctrine of the perfectibility of man, an idea even untenable by the turn of the century, completely destroyed by the First World War, and weighted down with anchors by the German Nazi movement, this view of human interaction, as it has emerged in librarianship, ignores the fact that theories are ideas and not reality, and that the idea of participatory democracy emerged from industry.

It seems that we must repeatedly be reminded of the fact that industry is permeated with meretricious practices, and that industrial managers leap from one jazzy topic to another in an attempt to stay on top by convincing everyone that they really know what they are doing. The past few years have once again demonstrated what those of us who grew up during the Depression learned thoroughly--that industry seldom knows its ear from a hole in the ground about what it is doing. But it puts up bright-colored smokescreens, and in recent years librarianship has crept after industry as though it were the repository of all wisdom.

Consequently, in defiance of what we know about the nature of people, we have turned to participatory democracy which has proved effective, we are told, in industry. My inquiries among friends in the commercial world have as yet turned up none who has had any contact with it. The first attempt to encourage participatory democracy in a library that I know of took place in a Canadian library that was very well-run, and the head librarian was chagrined at the great difficulty he was having getting any interest in the idea at any level in the organization. The first time I saw anything in action that seemed to be influenced by participatory democracy, it involved a series of twenty overlapping committees involving nearly the entire staff concerning every conceivable subject in the library, and with no clear indication of what impact the committees might have on the areas of the library they were concerned with. Since that time, there have been various declarations of independence uttered vaguely by librarians who proclaim themselves oppressed, but are really power types impatient with serving their apprenticeship. What does this all amount to?

In line with what we think industry is doing, we have set up in at least one library, a board of trustees composed of middle-management and professionals who set goals and policy, which the head librarian is required to execute. In the process of execution, these same middle-managers and professionals pretend that they are subordinates of the head librarian whom they control. Their control is pinned down firmly by an annual statement to the president as to whether or not they approve of the head librarian. Can anyone find the counterpart of this arrangement in industry?

To cast some light on where we might be in this strange social drift, let us turn for a moment to a most remarkable Italian philosopher--Giambattista Vico--who construes the entire course of human societies as a cyclical movement of history involving the gradual shift of authority from the few to the many.[6] Societies, according to Vico, arise from social chaos, when masses of people, confronted by deadly and intolerable external conditions, accept the protection of purposeful, powerful men in exchange for their services. In this first stage of society local oligarchs rule over local slaves.

As their conditions of life ease and their knowledge increases, the slaves revolt to obtain rights. The local oligarchs then unite into a ruling class headed by their most powerful leader, and the second stage of society is reached, in which an autocracy rules over a plebeian class. The autocratic stage of society, marked by continual struggle between the two classes, puts pressure on both of them which results, according to Vico, in the strongest of all social conditions. The autocrats perform heroically to prove their right to rule and the plebeians perform mightily in their own sphere to prove themselves worthy of greater rights.

In the course of time, by the social attrition of rights gradually extended to the plebeians, the power of the autocrats is leveled, and democracy begins as the third stage of society. Quite obviously, all should now be right with the world. Tyranny has been eliminated, autocracy has been absorbed out of existence, and equity has replaced authority. But Vico, who was the first to read history as the result of social dynamics, sees clearly that unbridled individual free-will soon becomes unguided by values, and that self-interest pursued at the expense of the general interest inevitably results in the renewal of chaos, the condition out of which society emerges and into which it inevitably ultimately descends.

Vico describes the human condition as it is poised to plunge once again into chaos:

> These people, like animals, had come to think of nothing but their own selfish interests and given themselves up to extremes of self-indulgence and self-deception, lashing out like animals at the slightest provocation. And so they lived in complete isolation of mind and will like wild beasts. Since each followed his own whimsical inclinations, no two could come together. Because of this condition, through desperate internal dissension and constant wars, they gradually made forests of the cities, and in these forests built lairs, for human beings.[7]

If this sounds prophetic, coming from the first quarter of the eighteenth century, it is because Vico's theory applies rather nicely to human history.[8]

We are in the latter days of the most fatuous fifteen-year period I have ever witnessed. Twice in my lifetime, when this country was under enormous pressures, I have seen what a great nation we Americans are, a truly great nation of people, not for what we had, but for what we were. I am convinced that under our sixteen layers of fat, which are rapidly being stripped off these days, we still are.

We are emerging into a condition of librarianship

that will put this conviction to the test. Every library, public or private, is over-extended beyond its available resources, and in the next decade we will all be making hard choices. In the process, a premium will be placed on good leadership, and also, more than ever before, on good followership. Each must decide what he or she is able to do. There will be authority, more than ever before, and the opportunity to respond to authority. There will be decisions, very difficult decisions, made by a few; and for most of us, including head librarians, there will be the opportunity to help amplify those decisions. And who, in all justice, could ask for a better thing to do?

References

1. This is only a slight caricature of an actual case.
2. This actually happened in planning the Hofstra University Library building in 1964, and resulted in preternaturally large expenses for change orders during construction.
3. The first stanza of one of Thomas's finest (untitled) poems.
4. There still is in the profession a remnant of this mindless antiauthoritariansim that in its irrationality and intensity is the exact equivalent of virulent anti-semitism. It has nothing to do with whether the authority is intolerable or not; it is, rather, a kind of personal therapy.
5. Library Journal 94 (Oct. 1, 1969): 3399-3402.
6. Vico was one of the most remarkable thinkers of Europe. The first twenty pages of my doctoral dissertation, James Joyce's Ulysses and Vico's Cycle (Yale University, 1948) contain a quick summary of Vico's significance and the phases of his historical cycle, which I'd be glad to send any librarian seriously interested in thought.
7. My translation of paragraph 1106 of La Scienza Nuova; see the parallel passage in The New Science of Giambattista Vico; revised translation, by Max H. Fisch and Thomas G. Bergin (Ithaca: Cornell University Press, 1968), p. 424.
8. Vico's theories "have gradually forced themselves on me through circumstances of my own life," as Joyce remarked in a letter to Harriet Weaver dated May 21, 1926: Letters of James Joyce, ed. by Stuart Gilbert (N.Y.: Viking Press, 1957), p. 241.

INTELLECTUAL HISTORY AND THE ORGANIZATION OF KNOWLEDGE*

Robert J. Rubanowice

Among those influences most inimical to the aims of intellectual history I would list the names of Melvil Dewey, Charles A. Cutter, Henry Evelyn Bliss, and a collective villain simply called LC. Should one seek deeper roots, blame could be laid upon remoter sources including Jacques-Charles Brunet and Francis Bacon, the latter as crooked a philosopher as he was a politician.[1] Perpetuating the myopia of these classificationists of knowledge are those contemporary straight-jacketed librarians who unthinkingly give students outmoded advice such as: "History can be found in the 900's."

From the viewpoint of the professional intellectual historian, I offer here some critical remarks on behalf of those dismayed by the inadequacies of present library classification. Motivated by a concern for the library organization of the future, I endorse the sentiment contained in S. R. Ranganathan's remark that "the time has now come for the advance-guard in the field of library classification to go on inventing several new schemes of abstract classification."[2] Mere palliatives are no longer acceptable, as philosophers of librarianship clearly recognize. A radical restructuring is overdue.

Without necessarily proposing what former Librarian of Congress Herbert Putnam might have called "one more crime to the calendar, and further confusion,"[3] I would like to explore this problem as one who has come to realize--as a variant of the experience of Molière's M. Jordain--that I have been "doing" classification throughout my professional life as a historian of ideas. The experience has left me in

*Reprinted by permission of the author and publisher from The Journal of Library History, July 1975, pp. 264-271.

an ambivalent position: with respect and sympathy for classificationists who are agonizing over new maps for accumulated and accumulating knowledge, but also with disappointment and even irritation with those practicing librarians who unquestioningly follow anachronistic rules, thereby perpetuating todays' errors into the next generation. I suspect that my experience is not unlike that of many other academicians in a wide variety of disciplines.

The intellectual historian, or historian of ideas, is interested in everything. Probably his activity is not so much disciplinary as transdisciplinary--with this latter word used not just in contrast to the concept of "disciplinary," but also in contrast to the notion of "interdisciplinary" as well. The intellectual historian rises above traditional academic disciplines, asking any and all questions, using any and all methodologies, borrowing from accepted approaches, modifying and adapting where needed, and creating anew.[4] Intellectual history, although generally operating out of departments of history as from a base, rejects the view of "History" as an autonomous and separate compartment of knowledge. Carried to its fullest, this rejection of the sacrosanct integrity of customary disciplines amounts to the charge that centers of higher education today resemble <u>pluriversities</u> and not universities. In effect, the various departments of academia are prone to ignore the concerns of disciplines other than their own, and even within single departments specialization is frequently carried to gross extremes. The intellectual historian would like to ameliorate this professional deformation or trained incapacity.

I am far from arguing for the priority of "History" either in the university or in its library classification scheme. My complaint lies rather with the very principle of hierarchy itself whereby theories of knowledge mapping have led to debilitating administrative systems and ultimately to the distortion of the very reality being mapped. As Ron Blazek recently remarked in another context: "As a library school instructor, it has become apparent to me that history-type courses have not been among the most popular of electives."[5] I would carry this observation even further, adding the perspective of the intellectual historian, W. Warren Wagar: "History figured very little in school or university curricula before the middle of the nineteenth century. It may shrink to its previous obscurity in the last quarter of our own."[6] From my own viewpoint, I can easily envisage a future time when conventional academic morality might reach the stage for Clio to figure prominently in discussions of suitable subjects for euthenasia.

It seems unfortunate to continue laboring with nineteenth-century residues such as C. A. Cutter's notion that "History included Antiquities, Inscriptions, Numismatics, Chivalry and Knighthood, Heraldry, Peerage."[7] Cutter may well have lost direct influence today but analogues of his approach to history cause one to shudder in recall of those horrible, dry-as-dust history courses where one had to memorize the dates of the six major battles of the Hundred Years' War, or the territorial exchanges of the Treaty of Utrecht, or the fact that in Prussian history Frederick I came after Frederick II because the former was really Frederick III first. To the chagrin of the intellectual historian, Cutter's concept of "History" excludes too much of what the intellectual historian finds relevant--for example, Philosophy and Religion (B), the Social Sciences (H), the Fine Arts (W), and Literature (Y). Library of Congress cataloging shares this same liability.

It seems debilitating to the historian of ideas to take pride "in a library arranged on [the plan whereby] every specialist has his own special library."[8] The sight of a zoologist basking in pigeonhole 594 might warm some hearts, but Melvil Dewey's classificatory principle that "thus all the books on any given subject are found standing together"[9] seems today hopelessly naive in view of the limitless permutations and combinations which ideas possess. Although Dewey did boast of his scheme that it "admits of expansion without limit,"[10] it is now evident that his foundation categories are anachronistic, more suitable to the development of historical studies and accumulated knowledge in the 1870s than in the 1970s.

The intellectual historian regards the greatest blunder of all in current library classificatory practice to be the controlling premise that "History" is a separate compartment distinct from Art, Biography, Communications, Education, Literature, Music, Philosophy, Poetry, Political Science, Psychology, Religion, and Science both Natural and Social--these catagories easily recognizable as standard ones used for review purposes by trade publications such as the Library Journal. These simplistic compartments call to mind the mental processes of a senior colleague who deleted my question on the impact of Freud from a twentieth-century history exam we were jointly preparing because "that's not history." There is virtually nothing that has happened, as well as nothing stored in a major university library, that under one set of conditions or another is not within the proper domain of the intellectual historian.[11]

If, in the process of restructuring venerable though decadent academic pigeonholes, departments of history should crumble, so what? Who needs what has been called "stupid departmentalization" anyway? Apropos to our primary concern here with knowledge mapping, borrowing C. D. Needham's more sophisticated phrasing, who needs library classification systems "reluctant to make major relocations of disciplines"?[12] All seriously outmoded patterns of organization, be they of the structuring of academic departments and divisions, or of the reflected "disciplinary" library classification schemes, should be jettisoned--not necessarily precipitously, but with careful thought and planning.

What must stay, however, is the vision afforded by the transdisciplinary experience of intellectual history. This vision includes the following insights. 1) There are more relations and interconnections among the various bits and facets of accumulated knowledge than is customarily dreamed of by parochial "disciplinary" thinking and classification. 2) The body of accumulated knowledge is clearly not static, fixed, or rigid, but is continually growing and changing. Accordingly, no viable classification scheme (or library) can remain in permanent stasis but must correspondingly grow and change. 3) The structure of this body of accumulating knowledge is probably not really dendritic and hierarchic. The intellectual historian, because of the twentieth-century's debunking of eighteenth-century Enlightenment "Natural Laws," is unsure of the correctness of E. C. Richardson's contention that there is a "natural order" in reality which should be duplicated in classification. The intellectual historian frequently finds the appearance of order, but persists in reserving final judgment regarding the permanency of any perceived structure. 4) The underlying historicist attitude of the intellectual historian makes him suspicious of classificationists who suggest that they have discovered what resemble a priori and invariable "absolute" laws of classification.[13] Historicism regards post-Newtonian science and philosophic existentialism palatable guidelines for mapping reality.

It is crucial to distinguish between three related but separate processes of effective librarianship--namely, the classification, the notation, and the location of materials.

My primary concern here is with classification, with the underlying principles guiding the best structuring or mapping of accumulated knowledge. Discussion of the notation and location of materials are secondary concerns and should follow only after agreement has been reached upon basic classificatory principles. To force classification into a notational scheme, as did Dewey, is putting the cart before the horse and is ultimately self-defeating. It matters little what the specific terms and system of notation might be, so long as the reader or researcher can find any and all of his needed materials.

Likewise, the location, shelf arrangement, or storage of materials can almost be random or arbitrary, in comparison with the importance of proper prior classification. Items might pleasantly be stored by color of binding, or some other such aesthetic arrangement, with over-all room colors coordinated between book jacket covers, shelving, walls, rugs, and other furnishings. Certainly the "one-location-for-each-item" storage principle is unacceptable today. Incidentally, let us not forget the potential uses of computerized hardware in storage and retrival, as well as in notation--such as, for example, the recent use of the IBM 370/135 computer by the University of Connecticut whereby patrons at a centralized library public inquiry terminal can instantly determine the status, location, and availability of 700, 000 items scattered throughout the library's holdings. Anticipated problems in the retrieval of information should not excessively interfere with the mandate for a thorough and radical reexamination of the basic, underlying principles of proper classification.

In conclusion, the probable classification principles most conducive to that thrust and vision of intellectual history which I have been representing will undoubtedly involve exhaustive, analytical, pre-coordinate, facet subject cataloging.

1) The simplest distinction to subject analysis is the author/title approach to organization, this latter being too simplistic for our classification purposes--though it presumably could be retained as an adjunct notational-storage feature of an overall system. Unquestionably, the inadequacy of Cutter's neglect of compound specific subjects and his rejection of classes of "unnamable" subjects is at present indefensible. The current trend in librarianship towards the "concept classification" of subjects seems most promising.

To be especially encouraged is an orientation towards the conceptual vs. the verbal or terminological level of subject cataloging.

2) Without prematurely endorsing the system of Colon Classification as such, I would lend support to Jesse H. Shera's evaluation of Ranganathan that "his great contribution to classification, and the one that is far in advance of the thinking of his contemporaries, is his implicit rejection of the physical book as the constituent unit in classification and his substitution of the thought- or subject-unit."[14] Facet analysis involving the coordination and combining of symbols representing concepts is a radical departure from the traditional, hierarchical emphasis on genus, species, and further, minuter subdivisions. "Instead of trying to construct, from above, one vast tree of knowledge, facet analysis starts from below."[15] Facet analysis enhances the visibility and availability of all dimensions of accumulated knowledge without freezing the bits and pieces of information into permanent place.

3) Analytical cataloging, "a term used to refer to the cataloguing of parts of documents,"[16] follows from the principles of faceted, subject classification. Analytical classification buttresses the primary purpose of a classification-retrieval system, namely, ease of recall of all items of information relevant to a reader/researcher's needs.

4) Although these next two conclusions might not generate as much support as the previous three, I urge that their advantages be fairly considered. A pre-coordinate system has the classifier/cataloger devising compounds and correlations of facets of information in advance of public availability, with the intent of facilitating that very availability itself. Without insulting the capabilities of individual readers/researchers, without eliminating possible ingenious post-coordinate arrangements of information, and without foreclosing the occasional serendipitous discoveries we have all made by simply coming upon information by chance, pre-coordinate cataloging introduces the concept of "programmed serendipity" whereby the readers/researchers' skills and creativity are not dissipated but are efficaciously focused at the outset upon a larger amount of relevant information than otherwise would be available. A pre-coordinate system expects great things from library classifiers and catalogers, but should expectations be any lower for that central group of intellectuals responsible for the custody and sorting of all

knowledge accumulated by the human race? Librarians, after all, have higher responsibilities than merely reshelving books and sending out overdue notices.[17]

5) Finally, exhaustive, rather than selective, limited cataloging is encouraged in principle as a meritorious asset--even though its total implementation might be a thing of the future. The most thorough form of exhaustive, pre-coordinate indexing possible, as C. D. Needham points out, "would result in a catalogue comprising the indexes to all the books in the library."[18] Indices to faceted, subject analyses of the contents of serials, unpublished material, and microdocuments should be created and added to this catalog as well. In light of the dawning of the Age of the Computer, with electronic computer-assisted cataloging, storage, and retrieval imminent, arguments against the expected great bulk and cumbersomeness of an exhaustive, pre-coordinate catalog miss the point--for we are speaking not of 3" x 5" card catalogs nor huge bound folio volumes but of console terminals, micro storage, and push-button retrieval.

Conceptually, we should experiment with classification schemes which transcend the confining conditions of past systems: localized libraries and limited collections. It is incumbent upon us to design systems to classify all knowledge. I anticipate the day when there will be, in effect, only one single centralized or cooperative library in the nation (or in the world, for that matter), where all the accumulated knowledge known to man will be computerized on an exhaustive, analytical, pre-coordinate facet subject basis, and will be available by electronic transmission to anyone anywhere familiar with the classification scheme and pushing the right combination of buttons. We must avoid replication of those "early meetings between 'hardware' men and librarians," as Phyllis A. Richmond has described it, which were "unproductive because the librarians asked 'What can you do?' and the engineers said 'What do you want done?' Neither side understood the answers given by the other."[19] As Richmond suggests further, "after a succession of failures, the realization dawned that input is the major key to successful output."[20] It is the responsibility of each of us concerned with the philosophy of librarianship to help contribute to the development of ever more sophisticated classification systems, parallel to and even in advance of electronic and technological breakthroughs. In this era of experimentation with "alternative life-styles," all I am asking is at least an imaginative flight into future alternative classification systems, suggesting that the basic groundrule simply be: If all the nagging problems of notation, storage, and retrieval with which one has hitherto been plagued were nonexistent, which principles of classification of all accumulated knowledge should be endorsed? The intellectual historian, representing the literate, library-using public, considers the question and its answers of paramount importance.

Notes

1. For Bacon, see Lynn Thorndike, A History of Magic and Experimental Science (New York: Columbia University Press, 1958), 7: 88 and passim Chap. IV.
2. S. R. Ranganathan, "Library Classification as a Discipline," in Proceedings, International Study Conference on Classification for Information Retrieval, Dorking, England, 1957 (London: ASLIB, 1957), p. 12.
3. Quoted by Leo E. LaMontagne, "Historical Background of Classification," in Maurice F. Tauber, ed., The Subject Analysis of Library Materials (New York: Columbia University, School of Library Service, 1953), p. 27.
4. For a sampling of statements on the nature of intellectual history, see, e.g., Arthur O. Lovejoy, "Introduction: The Study of the History of Ideas," in The Great Chain of Being (New York: Harper, 1960), pp. 3-23; Johan Huizinga, "The Task of Cultural History," in Men and Ideas (New York: Meridian Books, 1959), pp. 17-76; and Leonard Krieger, "The Autonomy of Intellectual History," Journal of the History of Ideas, 34 (1973): 499-516.
5. Ron Blazek, "The Place of History in a Library Education," Journal of Library History, 9 (July 1974), p. 193.
6. W. Warren Wagar, Books in World History: A Guide for Teachers and Students (Bloomington and London: Indiana University Press, 1973), p. 4.
7. The phrasing is from W. C. Berwick Sayers, A Manual of Classification for Librarians, 4th ed. (London: André Deutsch, 1967), Table II (The Expansive Classification, 1891-93 of Charles Ammi Cutter), p. 120.
8. Melvil Dewey (1876), reprinted in Ann F. Painter, Reader in Classification and Descriptive Cataloging (Washington, D.C.: NCR, 1972), p. 11.
9. Ibid.
10. Ibid., p. 8.

11. My meaning of an event or happening is broad, endorsing the view that "a thought is as much an event as a battle in a war."
12. C. D. Needham, Organizing Knowledge in Libraries: An Introduction to Information Retrieval, 2nd ed. (London: André Deutsch, 1971), p. 415. Needham eventually argues on behalf of Dewey, as the concluding--cleverly stated, but unacceptable--lines of his book indicated (ibid., p. 424): "Librarians who have to choose between Congress or Dewey are in the dilemma of the proverbial lady facing death or a fate worse than death. If, for the sake of the analogy, we nominate Congress as death, then I think one may well find that the worse fate is not quite so unattractive a proposition after all." Can the classificationist not consider more than merely two alternatives?
13. German and Italian writers have been the best in explaining the phenomenon of historicism, for which see, e.g., Friedrich Meinecke, Die Entstehung des Historismus, Werke, Bd. III (München, 1959): and Karl Heussi, Die Krisis des Historismus (Tübingen: J. C. B. Mohr, 1932).
14. Jesse H. Shera, "Classification: Current Functions and Applications to the Subject Analysis of Materials," in Tauber, Subject Analysis, p. 33.
15. B. C. Vickery, Faceted Classification Schemes (New Brunswick: Rutgers Graduate School of Library Service, 1966), p. 31.
16. Needham, Organizing Knowledge, p. 299.
17. Further on "pre-coordinate" and "post-coordinate," see, e.g., A. C. Foskett, The Subject Approach to Information, 2nd ed. (London: Clive Bingley, 1971), passim.
18. Needham, Organizing Knowledge, p. 101.
19. Phyllis A. Richmond, "The Future of Generalized Systems of Classification," College and Research Libraries, 24 (Sept. 1963): p. 400.
20. Ibid.

THE LIBRARY ADMINISTRATOR AS NEGOTIATOR: EXIT THE "BOSS"*

Kenneth R. Shaffer

While few would deny that the fabric and structure of American life have changed--and continue to change--at a near-revolutionary pace, long out-dated images of our institutions and mores still remain in our popular vocabulary. One can only explain this paradox by nostalgia for "the good old days" (which, perhaps, were not so good), and by our confusion and uncertainty as to what the realities of 1975 really are. A relevant example is the refusal, in our popular vocabulary, to face the indisputable facts of change in our image of the administrator, the manager--the "boss." This is true for library management as for business corporations and other institutions.

Any administrator who expects to hold on to his job very long must be acutely conscious every moment of his working day of the ambivalent attitudes toward his authority on the part of his staff, his superiors, and outsiders. While in rare moments he may reflect with bitter amusement at the misunderstood nature and limitations of his position, all too often this misunderstanding is expressed in terms of demands and ultimata by others which he knows he cannot resolve on his own authority. Too often, the administrator's life is exhausted by threat, demands for instant and radical change, public ridicule and debasement, and recurrent confrontations. His time, energy, and patience are devoted to "putting out fires," and little may be left for him to carry on the work of a productive manager.

---

*Reprinted by permission of the author and publisher from Library Journal, September 1, 1975, pp. 1475-80.

Images of the "Boss"

To a large extent the frustrations and torment of management are directly due to the traditional and paradoxical misunderstanding of what the administrator in today's world can or cannot do. We should examine this relic which survives not only in the popular mind but also among the sophisticated from whom, by this time, one should expect a more realistic understanding.

First, is the persistent symbolization of the administrator as the "boss"--an autocrat, an authoritarian, even a despot. He is seen as sitting in his office hiring and firing staff without consultation and information--even acting by whim. Allegedly, he determines promotions, salary increments, policies and services, and above all, budget, single-handed, without full information and input, and therefore without understanding or compassion. This belief persists among those who by this time should see the realities of management more clearly. The image of the "boss" continues as a cartoonist's delight. It was epitomized by a recent cartoon picturing the "boss" sitting behind the protective barrier of a massive desk, his meticulous Brooks Brothers suit betraying a paunch reflecting years of good living, and obviously in the act of firing a thin, nervous, and intimidated employee. The caption reads: "Simpson, you have worked for the Company for 30 years. Now it's time for you to go out and work for yourself!"

The other image, frequently held concomitantly with the one I have just described, is that of the administrator, sitting in a large, posh office, drawing a fat salary--and doing nothing! He appears supine in fighting for budget for staff salaries and services, indifferent to problems, and content to let the library take its course without staff input and without taking part in the action. He enjoys his confortable salary and the prestige of his position, takes credit for staff achievements, and appears to represent an unnecessary and ineffectual appendage. After nearly 40 years in library and educational management, I cannot recall a single personal secretary (and they were, without exception, loyal and highly competent) who did not believe that I was really only <u>working</u> when I cursorily signed a stack of vouchers authorizing payment, dictated letters which were often routine, or drafted a budget or annual report which had already been carefully and thoughtfully worked out. When I was <u>really</u> working--that is, when I was thinking, which is the most difficult and vital aspect of management--their attitude was,

"Oh, he isn't too busy right now, and I'll be glad to make an appointment for you." I do not know who the author of the following definition of the administrator is, for it was given to me years ago. It is called What Is an Administrator? Administrators are a fortunate lot; for as everyone knows, an administrator has nothing to do; that is, except:

> To decide what is to be done; to tell somebody to do it; to listen to reasons why it should not be done, why it should be done by somebody else, or why it should be done in a different way; and to prepare arguments in rebuttal that shall be convincing and conclusive.
>
> To follow up to see if the thing has been done; to discover that it has not been done; to inquire why it has not been done; to listen to excuses from the person who should have done it and did not do it; and to think up arguments to overcome those excuses.
>
> To follow up a second time to see if the thing has been done; to discover that it has been done incorrectly; to point out how it shall be done; to conclude that as long as it has been done it might as well be left as it is; to wonder if it was not the time to get rid of the person who cannot do a thing correctly; to reflect that in all probability any successor would be just as bad or worse.
>
> To consider how much simpler and better the thing would have been had he done it himself in the first place; to reflect satisfactorily that if he had done it himself he would have been able to do it right in 20 minutes and that as things turned out he, himself, spent two days trying to find out why it is that it had taken somebody else three weeks to do it wrong and to realize such an idea would have a very demoralizing effect on the library because it would strike at the very foundation of the belief of all employees that an administrator has nothing to do.

Delegating

The ultimate responsibility for libraries rests in the trustees of public libraries, the trustees of colleges and universities, school boards (or equivalent agencies), and corporate management for special libraries. But these "ultimate governing bodies have historically delegated more and more of their authority and responsibility to agents or agencies of their own creation which serve them. Public library trustees--except in small communities--have tended to delegate more and more, if not most, of their responsibility to their executive officer, the library director. Trustees of academic institutions have similarly delegated responsibility to the college and university president, who, in turn, delegates it in large part to the library director whose appointment has, at least in the past, been of his own choice and judgment, rubber-stamped by the trustees. The school board delegates to its administrative officer, the superintendent of schools, who in turn will delegate it to subofficers until it reaches the librarian. The director of a special library may be responsible to the head of a department of research and development, the personnel department, or other agent whose authority ultimately derives from top company management.

All of this boils down to the fact that traditionally the library administrator has enjoyed--or has had thrust upon him--most of the responsibility for the library. He has had a responsibility to develop services and to at least propose policies and budget to his superiors. Traditionally, he has hired personnel, dismissed them, and determined what their salaries and other benefits would be. He is accountable not only for a high level of service to the constituency of his library, but also for maintaining productive relationships outside the library. He is expected to maintain a public image that not only will affect the broadest and best use of the library, but which will insure the library's receiving adequate financial support and sympathetic and informed public protection in times of crisis. For decades the library administrator has had most of the responsibility for management--with his superiors acting (wisely or unwisely) as a sounding board, generally rubber-stamping the proposals which he brought to them--but with a veto always a possibility. The administrator was in the front line and kept his job as long as his performance did not get his superiors or the library into too much trouble. Excepting small libraries, he delegated most of the nitty-gritty to his associates, freeing his own time, energy, and imagination for the larger issues of planning and management.

The library director's responsibilities in 1975 remain about the same as in the long past--<u>but with a difference!</u> The paradoxical image of him as an autocrat and/or figurehead persists, but the social and intellectual revolution of the past decade has produced radical changes in the complexities of pressure for change--all too frequently expressed by threat and violence--which may erupt not only in major areas of management, but also in the nitty-gritty. Library management, if it is realistic, can expect confrontation, newspaper headlines, legal proceedings, denunciation, withholding of funds by government agencies, disruption of library services by staff or outsiders, or worse. Alert management will sense trouble ahead, and frequently it will be able to contain it but in a library it inevitably finds itself on the edge of the abyss with no forewarning--a situation which calls for immediate assessment of the issues involved and effective diplomacy to resolve the crisis for the common good.

What follows are explicit illustrations of some of the problem areas which have greatly altered the role of management, causing it to shed the comfortable stabilities of other years and call for new techniques and attitudes in dealing with the instabilities of a changing world.

Participatory Management

This aggressive movement of both professional and nonprofessional ibrary staffs that climaxed only a short time ago, voices its claim, under the banner of "democracy," to participate at every level of library management, from policy to decision making. It embraced nearly every aspect of administration, from budget to personnel administration, from program and services to salaries, appointments, promotions, and dismissal. When library management and its superiors were not responsive, an appeal was made to local newspapers, the library press, library organizations, and to higher levels of municipal, academic, or corporate authority. This movement diverted management's proper time and attention to the maintenance of the library's image and its viable operation, the frustration of explaining and clarifying the issues, and the embarrassment of bitter confrontation with loyal colleagues for whom it had great respect and with whom it had worked productively for years. There are a few examples where library staffs took over management lock, stock, and barrel. But their administration quickly disappeared, to be replaced by new management appointed with the explicit mandate to restore the balance of administrative responsibility.

If the movement for participatory management in the terms I have described has "cooled," undoubtedly the chief contributing factor was the failure of those who espoused it to invent a structure wherein responsibility is concomitant with participatory staff management.

However brutal and uncompromising the movement for participatory management may in some instances have been, the good which has resulted from it undoubtedly outweighs the hardships which accompanied it. Library management has learned that much is to be gained by taking staff into its confidence, from seeking and evaluating staff suggestions and advice, from maintaining really meaningful two-way lines of communication. Structures of participatory management which management itself has brought into being for the simple and sole purpose of saving its and the library's skin are discussed later in this article.

Collective Bargaining and Unionization

One does not have to look back many years to remember a climate when the greatest anathema one could suggest to librarians was collective bargaining or unionization. Long after the labor movement had won general acceptance, the possibly excessive self-consciousness of librarians as dedicated professionals would have produced shock and horror at such an idea. Unionization in any form suggested a departure from professionalism and a leveling with the blue-collared worker--something (and no male chauvinism is intended) with which the librarian would not dirty her skirts.

But here we are in another depression, and things are mighty different! Librarians are different. The image of the professional is changed. The rapid rise in cost of living, the crunch in financial support for libraries, the tight job market which for decades permitted the discontented librarian to move to more satisfactory conditions in another library, have spared few of us. Perhaps it was the spectre of trash collectors, janitors, publicly employed clerks or secretaries who fared better in salary than the librarian for all his or her years of professional education and experience. In any event, attitudes toward collective bargaining and unionization on the part of library staff, professional and nonprofessional, have changed, and the movement toward collective bargaining and unionization is expanding rapidly. There can be no doubt that it is here to stay.

Attitudes of library management are undergoing a rather fascinating about-face. Management's initial reaction was usually dismay and frustrated resistance. The right of a legally recognized collective bargaining unit or union to demand higher salaries and better working conditions created a baffling impasse between a staff capable of threatening the library with sanctions and the expressed inability of the administration's superior agencies to produce funds. Many a library director grew gray and wrinkled with the task of dealing with a suddenly powerful staff and impotent or resisting trustees.

But happily, an organized staff has few fears for most administrators who have worked with it, for usually they soon discover that unionization in any form has a stronger voice and commands more weight than they can. Municipal, academic, and corporate authorities are used to dealing with organized labor and have a healthy respect for it. Management, assuming the role of negotiator, communicating productively between both groups, not only has the capacity to produce better salaries and working conditions than it could achieve by its own traditional recommendations, but even under current economic conditions, finds its job different--and usually infinitely easier. So, for management even to tacitly encourage their staff to organize is far from uncommon.

Regulation by Government

The management of any library faces a bewildering maze of government legislation and regulation at all levels. It is frequently conflicting, obscure in meaning, and far beyond the abilities or resources of the library to comply. I can recall instances in academic institutions, for example, where an employee filed a complaint of discrimination with the United States Department of Health, Education and Welfare. In one case, discrimination was alleged because others with identical qualifications and experience were promoted. Another claimed that men with the same qualifications received higher salaries for positions of the same level of the complainant. Another claimed a violation of his rights when courses he had been teaching were dropped, and he refused to teach other courses even though they were in his field of specialization. These were not members of the library staff, but they triggered full-scale investigations with hearings by HEW involving every department, anyone who applied for a position, and all personnel employed for from five to ten years. In one university, the compilation of data required by HEW was estimated to have cost more than one million dollars, and the statistical report of its library personnel for the span of time specified ran to several hundred pages. The statistics asked for were comprehensive enough to cover every possible evidence of discrimination of any kind. Not only every person employed by the library for the preceding decade, but all applicants for positions had to be statistically presented in terms of educational qualifications, age, sex, marital status, experience, salary, increments, ethnic origins, reasons for promotion, reasons for dismissal, etc. Such statistics, and there were many others, were required to be presented in terms of each individual, but also analyzed in tables by category of interest. Such a document, not to speak of its defense, measured in time, costs, or anyway you wish, is disruptive, demoralizing, and in many respects is patently irrelevant. Yet under the threat of loss of millions of dollars of HEW grants to the entire university there was no choice.

States which make grants to public and school libraries may pose a similar threat, and the regulatory criteria of their disbursing departments may be quite different from the multitude of federal agencies of which I have used HEW only as an example. Many state agencies will withhold or withdraw grants if library personnel fail to meet explicit educational and other standards or if per capita support by the municipality or school district fails to meet required levels. Library systems supported by public money may develop their own additional criteria for eligibility to participate in system benefits.

These regulations are imposed and enforced by government agencies with money to disperse--regulations, not law and the enforcement of law by judicial process. In some states it is expressly forbidden by law to ask a prospective employee his ethnic background, or to keep records of such information even after he has been hired. Yet many federal (HEW) and state regulatory agencies not only demand this information but also inquire how it was obtained--visually, by questionnaire or application, interview, or by other means. Both regulations and law enforced by federal, state, or each individual municipality make the library vulnerable to charges of discrimination of a breadth and complexity that boggle the imagination.

With this Sword of Damocles always hanging over its head, library management has changed its role. No longer does prudent library management recommend appointments, promotions, or dismissals solely upon the advice of the department head involved or a personnel officer. Instead, it acts more and more frequently upon the advice of a staff committee, sometimes appointed, but preferably staff-elected. And while management may ignore or disagree with the recommendations of such a committee even after appropriate negotiation, it does so at some peril unless it is convinced that it is acting upon safe ground. With such a device, administration frees itself from real or alleged autocratic, biased, or capricious policies, provides assurance that it has acted on broad staff input, engenders a feeling of participation and usually a high sense of responsibility by staff, and so operates from a base that will help to forestall a discontented staff and which may cause the plaintiff to think twice before he or she appeals to higher authority or calls a lawyer. The equity of staff participation through a duly constituted committee is significant and obviously productive. It also helps to take management off the hook!

Intellectual Freedom

The bitter and often tragic disputes over "the controversial book"--almost always involving the treatment of sex--that have historically plagued public and school libraries seem, for the moment at least, to have subsided. Every one of us can recall more than one instance where they reached an intensity which was violent enough to cause the resignation of trustees or the dismissal of the library director. No doubt the permissiveness which now characterizes mass media has carried over to greater permissiveness toward libraries. A more thoughtful sensitivity on the part of management in assessing the attitudes of the community they serve is also an important factor in preventing libraries from getting into hot water as often as they did in the past.

But attacks on intellectual freedom have taken new forms. Almost all literature--and now I am speaking of nonfiction and include books, periodicals, and other materials of established scholarship--has become controversial. We are a country which is deeply divided ideologically, and our division takes the form of intolerance that pervades almost every aspect of our society. Books, however scholarly, dealing with government and foreign policy, economics, minorities, religion, medicine, education, sex education, and family life--you name it--provide visible points for attack, and while this is especially a problem of metropolitan areas, it affects every library anywhere. Here confrontation usually takes the form, not of an individual objecting to a novel that he or his children may have read, but of well-organized groups dedicated to particular partisan goals. When such a group attacks the library because it does not provide material or services which conform to its particular ideologies, or when it provides books and services opposed to their beliefs, they can do so in strength. They command the immediate attention of the press, of high officials, of the public at large, and not always with a fair or impartial point of view. Because they are well organized and frequently not lacking in resources, they can employ picketing, sit-ins, and the attention of the mayor or city council or university president, his trustees and legislators. Unlike the individual who takes issue with the library, the organized group often cannot be contained by argument, explanation, or even rational discussion. Their confrontations are likely to be commanding and demanding, with no choice of negotiation, and I can recall many libraries where management exhausted itself dealing with one group after another, trying to keep the fires they create under control. All of us have witnessed administrator after administrator who, after two or three years, either resigns from sheer exhaustion and frustration--or who is dismissed. Confrontations without the possibility of negotiation is not the most gratifying way of spending our lives. This is poignantly true when management is diverted from its job of administering the library, which then must go along, for better or worse, without leadership. The ability to placate organized groups whose demands may exceed budget, good sense, or ethical commitment, and still manage library operations effectively, is beyond the capacities which most of us possess.

Performance Budgeting

This is all so obvious and so well documented that I would not have mentioned the subject--except that a new dimension has been added, a dimension which significantly obfuscates and falsifies the basis for an intelligent evaluation of the library and the justifications for its financial support, and amounts to little more than a hollow mockery. It is called "performance budgeting." Performance budgeting has been widely used for some time in business and industry and with apparent success, for it is both meaningful and easy to count (mechanically) the number of bolts an assembly line worker screws onto machines, or to count, again mechanically, the number of labels placed on cans of tomatoes. Apparently in such types of business and industrial operation, these statistics can be meaningful. They should, for instance, measure the production norm of the average worker and thus provide some estimate of the number of workers, each performing the same job, with a given volume of projected production.

But performance budgeting has become the fashionable and highly touted darling of municipalities, academic institutions, and has frequently spread from the production area to corporate administrative areas, including their libraries.

In essence, beyond the simple library statistics which have already been mentioned and lamented, performance budgeting is based on a count of every possible operational activity that occurs in a library by each classified category of worker--general administration, department heads, professional librarians, clerks, janitors, pages--the whole works! How many books are charged out and discharged is expected to determine the number of people required to perform these tasks. The number of books selected again provides a basis for the number of people needed to be budgeted for this activity. Without belaboring the point, the annual production of <u>each</u> category of employee in each <u>specific</u> operation is counted.

Performance budgeting ignores the fact that it is impossible to count the many activities and operations that occur in even our largest libraries where job specialization is to a degree defined. It also ignores the cost of such statistics even if they were possible. The mechanical counters covering each operation in the factory assembly line are not in our libraries and would not work if they were. Work, in most libraries, is highly interchangeable. If for a few minutes a circulation clerk is not charging or discharging materials, he or she may sort out overdues, send notices, or use the interval productively in a dozen other ways. The reference librarian on duty will use such intervals to examine the reference collection to determine new material that should be added, work on a bibliography or reading list, or turn to a variety of our tasks.

After many a long, tough day as an administrator, I

would try to recall what had made the day so rough, but it was seldom possible. One starts one thing, is interrupted, goes to another, the telephone rings, an appointment appears, and this goes on until it is possible to leave. A full day of exhausting work cannot be reduced to statistics.

The second limitation of performance budgeting is that it does not measure quality of service. A reference question can be handled with tact and competence and result in a satisfied client, or it can be handled superficially. Quality is paramount throughout library service. If the quality of materials and service are assured, library management can forget about quantity.

Finally, the very nature of performance budgeting begets falsity and deception. Because accurate quantification is impossible, the circulation head is likely, in preparing figures to be fed into the library budget, to gather the circulation staff together and ask, "How many overdue notices did each of you send out last year?" The total may come to 2800. That seems a little light, so the circulation head puts down 4500 in the statistics supplied to management. This may occur and is likely to occur in every operation in every department. To further compound falsity, management may feel, as it compiles the full performance report, that many of the figures are still unimpressive. The 2800 overdue notices that became 4500 now become 6200. It is not my intention to pass ethical judgments, but even honest attempts at quantification can at best be a guess or an estimate, and in competing successfully with other departments of the city, college, university, or corporation everyone knows that more than a little exaggeration is also common practice there.

Performance budgeting is usually thrust upon library management as the general policy of a municipality, educational institution, or corporation. Once management is stuck with it, it must work harder than ever, with the full participation of staff, so that the quest for and achievement of excellence throughout the library will provide a compelling mandate not only to officialdom but to its constituency for adequate support.

Each library user sees the library in terms of the kind of use he or she makes of it, and most have little knowledge of the services and materials it provides for others. The job of explaining what a library really is cannot be dismissed as merely a public relations problem. It can only be done by successful and meaningful justification of the library's public purpose with the by-product of a "soft sell" for public support. Participation in that purpose must reach far beyond management and staff to the most remote corners of the community the library has been constituted to serve.

The administrator must expect, as a normal function of managerial environment, to deal with confrontations in various degrees of strength with the complicated and frequently obscure legal restrictions enforced by the courts at all levels of government, but he must also deal with the far greater obfuscations of government regulatory agencies which hold the purse-strings. He must be prepared to face partisan and often extreme ideological groups armed with potent resources which, if exercised, could cause irreparable damage. He will increasingly arbitrate the demands and challenges of his own organized staff which also are not lacking either in legal protections or the resources of strong unions or other organizations with which they may be affiliated. He must negotiate with the agencies who ultimately control the library's financial support and program, which dicta may take the form of mandate without benefit of prior consultation or adequate information. He must be ready to survive in a human world with new expectations and values, whose needs often take the form of "instant demand without negotiation." Finally, in a sorry state of our national economy, the administrator must succeed in a highly politicized competition for funds with other departments of the municipal, academic, or corporate entity of which the library is a part.

The day of the managerial autocrat or figurehead content to delegate both his responsibility and problems to others is over, for the single-handed technique of management no longer works--or survives. The administrator who finally resorts to management by crisis is short lived. But the first to be tossed out is the administrator who throws in the towel in an attitude of "Que sera, sera."

The prime need so essential in these times is for management to attain the widest orientation to and meaningful participation in library affairs, beginning with trustees, superior agencies, and staff, but including the entire constituency of the library--the public at large, including users and nonusers, and groups and organizations with both interest in the library and "clout," the faculty, students, and alumni.

This base of orientation becomes an even greater strength as it goes beyond the geographical constituency that the library serves. The job is not an easy one or one that can be realized quickly, yet the results will not only improve the library and enhance its image, but will also arm it with broad, strong, concerned, and informed support which in time of fiscal, legal, or ideological crisis may become the crucial factor.

The human requirements for successful management in the environment I have tried to describe are rare and almost go beyond expectation. The administrator must listen as well as speak up; must arbitrate and be prepared to compromise as well as act. He or she must be calm and infinitely patient but firm in his or her convictions. The administrator must forego the spotlight of prestige to share achievements readily and widely. And last, he or she must possess an elephantine strength, energy, and patience, not only in dealing with the crises and problems of the library, but in providing the leadership day by day that will bring it to greater and greater achievement and excellence.

THE AMERICAN RESEARCH LIBRARY SYSTEM IN A PERIOD OF CONSTRAINT: SOME IMPRESSIONS*

I. R. Willison

This article is the substance of a report, submitted to the Board of the British Library in 1974, on a short visit to research libraries in the United States made in October and November 1973. The author was at that time in charge of the United States Collection and Superintendent of the North Library in the British Library Reference Division (formerly the British Museum Library); the primary purpose of his visit was to see what implications for the British Library the American situation might seem to suggest. The opinions expressed are, of course, those of the author only, and not of the Board. The original report was prefaced by a detailed acknowledgement of the great hospitality, kindness and cooperation that the author received throughout his visit, and he is glad of this opportunity to express his gratitude publicly, though necessarily less specifically.

I

As is already well known, the change from the expansionist, "post-Sputnik" phase of the late fifties and early sixties to the present phase of constraint in the development of American research libraries has been in many respects a traumatic one. An orthodox view of the change is embodied in the widely noticed article--admittedly written with some heat--by McAnally and Downs on "The Changing Role of Directors of University Libraries" in College and Research Libraries, March 1973.

*Reprinted by permission of the author and publisher from The Journal of American Studies, April 1975, pp. 21-34.

Five major factors--three, so to speak, structural and two political--have caused this change. The first is the chronic inflation of the costs of library materials--particularly serials--and services. A staggering figure quoted to me was the cost of library maintenance: $100 per square foot per annum. Second, there is the decline in the real value of institutional endowments typically based on holdings of stock rather than real property, due to the instability of the stock market. This is a factor of greater moment in North America than in Europe, since many of the great research libraries outside the Library of Congress are in private rather than state-supported institutions, whether these be private universities--Harvard, Yale, Columbia, etc.--or independent research libraries, such as the Research Libraries of the New York Public Library, the Folger, the Newberry, the Huntington. Thus in 1971 the New York Public Library was forced to reduce its opening hours from eighty-seven to forty each week, and faced the possibility of closing six of its collections to the public. I found that this was regarded as the biggest of the recent shocks in the American research library world. The third factor, affecting principally university libraries, is the decline in student enrolment, and hence in revenue from capitation fees, from the peak of the mid-sixties. This is due, it seems, to long-term demographic movements such as the passing of the peak of the post-war baby boom. The effect of this decline in enrolment and revenue has been aggravated in the case of certain state university systems, such as Indiana and Texas, by the anti-élitist policy of promoting what were originally extension sub-campuses of the main central campus of the system--Bloomington, Austin--into separate undergraduate colleges, at the expense of the central campus and its research capability.

Fourth, there has been the alienation of traditional support for universities and other research institutions, and the revival of equally traditional suspicion of the welfare state, following the shock of campus unrest during the middle and late sixties. Examples are: the withdrawal of federal support from the massive post-Sputnik expansion of graduate education and research libraries outside the old established graduate schools; the severe cost-benefit audits of the university and the university library system in California ordered by the Governor, leading to the abandonment of the "multiversity" plan of equal development of all nine campuses in the system, and with the trial version of the audit actually recommending, among other things, the sale of the rare books in the system; the similar hard-nosed attitude on the part of the regents and trustees, for example at Austin, Texas, at Ohio State, and even at the Ivy League universities on the genteel East Coast. This takes one into deep water. Though the current Watergate confusion made it difficult to get a sense of perspective, my impression, based on questioning various senior administrators involved in the crisis, was that the expansionism of the late fifties and early sixties, like the Vietnam war with which it was associated, needed a far more carefully worked-out rationale than was in fact provided by the traditional enthusiasm of the go-getting university booster. When the university students on the one hand and the federal and state governments, and the university alumni, on the other, eventually questioned the relevance of this accelerating and apparently indiscriminate expansion either to their lives (in the case of the students) or to their investment (in the case of the authorities and the alumni) the world of learning in America could give no satisfactory answer. The academic centre could not hold. Things simply fell apart.

The fifth factor is the drive towards unionization and participation in management among the middle and lower professional grades in research libraries. This concern with status and promotion prospects, and distrust of the paternalism characteristic of traditional American research library management, is clearly linked with the facts of inflation and alienation just mentioned, and it figures largely in the McAnally and Downs survey. I had the impression that the problem was most acute in the major private universities, as opposed to the state universities and the independent research libraries. The state universities presumably have a bureaucratic ethos adequate to containing the problem; the independent research libraries are sufficiently small and élitist for the director to continue to exercise traditional charismatic leadership.

Much of this experience, of course, has been paralleled in Britain and Europe: it is, after all, an aspect of the problem of high culture in an advanced industrial system common to many countries. However, I think it is characteristic of the volatility of scholarly arrangements in North America that the worst of the trauma is already felt to be over and that new arrangements are being made which are already proving successful. Morale is higher than it was two or three years ago. The main strategy employed in holding down library budgets is to minimize duplication of professional staff, in the first instance between libraries themselves, by the use of local networks or consortia designed to exploit the potentialities of computer-based on-line shared processing (especially, to begin with, machine-readable cataloguing, MARC; the other element--shared acquisitions--envisaged by the National Program for Acquisitions and Cataloging, does not seem to have got under way yet). In the second instance, it is hoped to minimize duplication of professional staff between libraries and the book trade, most noticeably by the use of specialist library catalogue publishers, such as G. K. Hall and Mansell Information, in connexion with retrospective recataloguing, and by the use of blanket approval arrangements with book-jobbers or, in the University of Toronto's more illuminating phrase, "dealer selection" order systems, as an integral part of planned library collection development.

The best-known and to date most successful computerbased shared cataloguing network is the system set up at Columbus by the Ohio College Library Center (OCLC). I was impressed by the enthusiasm of the staff of the particular cataloguing department that I visited (at Miami University, Oxford, Ohio) for participating in what was felt to be a worthwhile enterprise, despite the considerable rearrangement of procedures involved. I was impressed also by the enthusiasm of shrewd library administrators both in and outside the State of Ohio for a system which demonstrably saved money and enabled them to win back the good will of recently unsympathetic finance officers. Thus, the University of Pennsylvania has established an on-line terminal with OCLC, and the entire South East Association of Research Libraries, having completed a feasibility study, is now seriously considering a contract with OCLC. Nevertheless, I was told of three interesting limitations to the OCLC system. First, though it is a regional system it is dependent for optimum working on the speedy delivery of MARC tapes from the Library of Congress as the national cataloguing source, and at present the delay in delivery is a matter of months after the arrival of the LC catalogue proofs, with the result that an unacceptably large amount of time in the system is spent on local input of data either from the LC proofs or from original cataloguing in the participating libraries. Second, for reasons I had not the time to determine, the hardware for OCLC was provided not by the major manufacturer, IBM, but by the Xerox Corporation (Sigma 5) and is limited in capacity for extensive out-of-state use. Already the prospect of out-of-state contracts is threatening to overload the system and is causing political difficulties among the original participants; they feel that, having invested considerable staff time during the extensive and trying development period, they are now unable to enjoy the secondary benefits of the system--for example, the rapid location and provision of material not on campus--because the additional terminals cannot be provided. (Much will depend, it is felt, on the success with which the newer systems proposing to use IBM equipment--principally the New York system based at Albany--are able to "back into" OCLC. The New York system, which I was not able to visit, is still, I understand, in the planning stage, and it is not yet clear whether it will link up with OCLC). Third, the OCLC system is designed with the college and smaller university library and not the major research library in mind. From the point of view of the British Library two major research library consortia worth watching are the University of California system and, in particular, the newly-founded Research Library Group, consisting of the Research Libraries of the New York Public Library, Columbia, Harvard and Yale. Both are still in the embryonic stage. The "Academic Plan" for California, following the two audits of the university system ordered by the governor, is to replace the nine-campus research multiversity with a concentration of research resources at Berkeley and UCLA only. However, the Plan only arrived at UCLA the day I left, and the exploratory Rosenthal report commissioned by the Research Library Group is not due till the New Year.[1] Nevertheless, one operation at California that has already received political approval is the computer-based Selective Dissemination of Information (SDI) service at UCLA. Even so, because of the national pre-eminence, relative maturity and conservatism of its member libraries, it must be the Research Library Group which will be of greatest interest to the British Library. At this stage the chief thing to record is the understandable nervousness of the various administrators at the outcome of the Rosenthal report. The reorganization and change in attitude involved in implementing any forthcoming recommendations will be considerable.

The proliferation of high-cost computer-based local networks raises of course the question of their co-ordination in a national ibrary system, and while in Washington I briefly visited the two federal organizations which, so far as research libraries are concerned, are involved in this: the National Commission on Libraries and Information Science and the National Endowment for the Humanities. Both organizations were set up by the Johnson administration; and the first thing to say about the American national ibrary system is that it is still too affected by the political confusion surrounding the succeeding Nixon administration for much clear doctrine or arrangement to have emerged yet. To take the National Commission on Libraries and Information Science first. Its first working paper, a draft New National Program of Library and Information Service, only appeared in October, and is essentially a plea for "firm action by the federal government ... now" before the "disorganized aggregation" of regional networks develops "to the point of being incapable of future interconnection" (p. 5). The paper contains few specifics and I found that it was widely felt that the Commission still lacked a satisfactory identity and coherence--a point made with some feeling by the Center for Research Libraries in Chicago, which is looking to the Commission for the support necessary to enable the Center to develop a national lending service, particularly for serials, based to a considerable extent on the doctrines and techniques of the Lending Division of the British Library. The President had given the Commission an advisory function only, and not a funding function as had apparently been intended by the Johnson administration.

Further, I had the impression that the Commission was in danger of becoming involved in the political battle between the Presidency and Congress (which is not confined to the present administration) whereby the Congress is trying to regain some of the initiative it began to lose under President Kennedy, or even earlier. Thus the Commission's paper seems to me to be addressed more to the Congress than to the White House: one of the few specifics states that "building a national network of libraries to promote knowledge and progress between the among the people of the states will require the same foresight that Congress had when it invested in the Interstate Highway Act to promote travel and commerce." Again, the staff of the Commission may be required to spend a great deal of its energy in the next few years (in the view of some observers, far too much of its energy) in stage-managing public hearings in all of the fifty states, should the current, more than somewhat partisan, Joint Resolution of Congress proposing a White House Conference on Libraries for 1976 be approved by the President (the same observers expressed the private hope, and belief, that the President would in fact veto it).[2] Finally, from the point of view of research libraries, it was feared by some senior administrators, particularly in the above mentioned East Coast Research Library Group, that the inevitable involvement of a federal agency in pressure from the grass roots would result in anti-élitist policies that could require, for example, mature libraries to lend indiscriminately even from their rare book collections. Nevertheless, it was commonly agreed that, from the point of view of research libraries, the most important and encouraging feature of the Commission was the appointment of Dr. Frederick H. Burkhardt, retiring President of the American Council of Learned Societies, as its Chairman. As President of the American Council of Learned Societies, Dr. Burkhardt had been responsible for the submission of evidence on the relationship between libraries and scholarship to the Johnson Advisory Commission on Libraries (which had led to the setting up of the National Commission), and as a trustee of the New York Public Libraries and Chairman of the Board of Higher Education for the City of New York he had helped work out the arrangements with the City and the State of New York which had been largely responsible for bringing the Research Libraries of the NYPL through their recent financial crisis. As a result of my conversations with Dr. Burkhardt, with Dr. McCarthy, executive director of the Association of Research Libraries in Washington, with Dr. Fred Cole, President of the Council on Library Resources, with Dr. O. B. Hardison, Jr., of the Folger Library and secretary of the Independent Research Library Association, and with Representative John Brademas, Deputy Majority Whip, Chairman of the House Select Sub-Committee on Education, I had the impression that these five constitute a kind of research library "establishment" in Washington: coherent, effective, though at the moment, for the reasons given above, keeping to a relatively low political profile. (The Library of Congress, clearly the linch-pin of any conceivable national research library system, as is shown by the transfer of the responsibility for NPAC from the Department of Health, Education and Welfare to the Library is felt to be in partial limbo at the moment until the succession to the present librarian, Dr. Mumford, becomes clear.)

In general, when discussing the national research library system, my informants warned me against thinking of the North American system in European terms of a closely integrated, monolithic policy and executive structure. My impression was that all the effective action in the research library field at the national level--principally, financial grants from the National Endowment for the Humanities and from the private foundations with special library programmes, such as the Ford and, more recently, the Andrew W. Mellon foundations--was directed, as a matter of principle, to the support of the existing geographically separated, strong collections of research material founded between the Civil War and the New Deal by the local initiative of faculty, alumni and philanthropists on the spot. The most conspicuous example of this is the NEH/Mellon million-dollar-plus a year programme for reviving the Research Libraries of the New York Public Library: thus the Director, Mr. James Henderson, is now called the Andrew W. Mellon Director of Research Libraries. The Mellon Foundation is also conspicuous for its substantial funding of fellowship programmes in the independent research libraries, for example, the American Antiquarian Society and the Huntington Library. This can be seen, I think, as part of what may prove to be an important trend amongst university, library and foundation administrators to think of research apart from teaching, and to associate the former more positively than in the past with the mature--or relatively mature--and largely off-campus collections of rare and special material in the country. It of course raises problems for the university--but it is also evidence of what seemed to me to be the indelibly pragmatic and pluralist style of planning for advanced research in the humanities in North America, compared to what one would expect to find, if not in the British Academy, then certainly in the Centre National de la Recherche Scientifique and the Deutsche Forschungsgemeinschaft. I found no evidence of any grand design for research. On the contrary, as Dr. Gordon Ray, President of the Guggenheim Foundation, put it, North Americans are more than content with their traditional "fertile chaos," provided it continues to be fertile (and they have no reason to doubt that it will).

From all this I have the impression that in matters of high culture, certainly so far as advanced research collections of printed material are concerned, North America is still, and is likely to remain, in an ex-colonial situation, implying a dependence in the last resort on the major national and research libraries of Europe. Notwithstanding the current selective, and intensive, financial support of existing local research collections--Folger, Huntington, Newberry, Widener/Houghton, New York Public Library--eventual autonomy vis-à-vis Europe is not envisaged. Even the maturest of these collections--Harvard, say--have, like the Library of Congress itself, come into existence too late after the Renaissance to match the relevant European libraries for minor, or what one might term interstitial, printed material from, say, the sixteenth to the eighteenth centuries which can be of general, albeit not of continuing, importance for a piece of advanced research in that period. In Chicago, for example, it was put to me that a Renaissance specialist in the Mid-West would expect to conduct a piece of advanced research in three stages: a preliminary search of printed material at the Newberry; an examination of the primary texts at the more specialized Folger or Huntington; and finally an examination of the interstitial material in a major European library, most probably the British Library. We should therefore review certain aspects of our permanent obligations to our international clientèle--European and Australasian as well as North American--for example, the unacceptability to that clientèle of lending foreign material which they would expect to find immediately available in Bloomsbury on demand. Again, in collaboration with our colleagues in the other European national research libraries, we should consider the whole problem of the stock of European printed material printed, say, before 1850--its development, conservation and processing--in the light of the continuing demands that ex-colonial research systems are going to make upon it.

There remains the problem, in an age of financial restraint, of the use in depth by British scholars of those North American research libraries containing unique and crucial items acquired on a considerable scale (and therefore not available to an adequate extent through piecemeal photocopying) following the change in the balance of power between English and American research libraries early in this century: for example, collections of modern literary manuscripts. So far as the independent research libraries are concerned--Folger, Newberry, Huntington, etc.--the inauguration or expansion of visiting fellowship programmes using, for example, the grants from the Mellon Foundation mentioned above, supplemented by the British Academy scheme of travelling scholarships for British research librarians, seems to have provided a temporary solution. However, as we went on to mention above, the restriction of foundation support to the independent research libraries points up the problem of the future of the research, as opposed to teaching, capability of universities, particularly of state universities which in the Far West and South West--notably UCLA and Austin, Texas--have major holdings of modern British literary manuscripts. I was informed that the traditional device whereby visiting British scholars wishing to use these collections in depth are accommodated--a visiting professorship with a merely notional teaching load--was becoming impractical. The situation is causing the universities considerable embarrassment and the possibility of extending the scope of the British Academy travelling fellowship programmes needs to be explored.

II

Planned collection development involves the putting down on paper of one's acquisition policy or "profile" in great detail--subject by subject, level by level, language by language, even publisher by publisher--in collaboration with faculty or scholarly advisers and, more often than not, the execution of that policy, so far as books are concerned, in the first instance by blanket on-approval arrangements with library suppliers. It is, as I have already mentioned, one of the most conspicuous features of the North American library scene in the present age of financial constraint (the other being computer-based networks). Even the most conservative laissez-faire acquisition departments, I was told--Harvard, Yale, Chicago and also the independent research libraries, such as Newberry--are now, or shortly will be--requiring their selection officers to co-ordinate their activities in this way; and there is a flourishing, although still informal, Association of Collection Development Officers, of which Mr. Norman Dudley of UCLA is currently chairman. At first sight this is surprising, since planned collection development has hitherto been associated with periods of expansion: European national libraries in the mid-nineteenth century--for example, the British Museum Library in the period of Panizzi, Asher and Henry Stevens[3]--the Library of Congress at the end of the Second World War and, most recently, American university libraries following the lead of Cornell and UCLA in the late fifties. It was used as a means of preventing a library's identity from being seriously distorted as a result of the traditional system of single title-by-title selection by faculty member of staff subject specialist, and single title-by-title ordering by the purchasing department, being overwhelmed by the vastly increased intake of material. It might be said to have represented the final stage in the transition from personal to institutional collecting of scholarly material. I was told that the reasons for the survival, and indeed promotion, of planned collection development and the use of the blanket order in an age of constraint were, first, that an explicit, reasoned and exhaustive statement of acquisitions policy helps retain the confidence of finance officers in a library's competence in a major area of expenditure and preserves the acquisitions fund from its traditional fate of being the soft option when economies are necessary. Second, collection development, since it requires the library to become intimately involved with scholars in a manner which preserves the initiative in the hands of the library, gives management the chance not only to meet the demands of staff associations for a career structure implying parity with academic faculty but also to persuade finance officers that the parity is a real one and therefore requires suitable budgeting. Third, library profiles show a substantial degree of homogeneity between themselves, and the use of the expertise of an established jobber by a number of libraries to select as well as process titles in the first instance minimizes unnecessary duplication of expensive professional effort in a notoriously labour-intensive occupation.

The problem of blanket approval systems does not lie, as is sometimes thought in North America as well as this country, in the fact that a research library may lose to a book jobber the responsibility, and the satisfaction, for developing its own collections. It is true that in the period of rapid expansion in the late fifties certain of the smaller North American research libraries, when faced with the demand on the basis of presumed national security that they expand into new fields, chose to give jobbers virtually complete responsibility in the interests of speed; but normally the system of blanket approval both requires continuous monitoring by the library's selection officers of the books offered in the first instance by the jobber so that the acquisition guide lines and directives to the jobber can be progressively refined, and also allows the selection officers to conduct retrospective surveys of their collections and develop arrangements for out of print, reprint and antiquarian purchasing. In one sense, the whole point of the blanket approval system is to exploit the jobber's special relation with the book trade so as to allow the library actually to see far more material on approval, and to see it far more speedily and with far less paper work, than would be possible when dealing direct with publishers. Like the exercise of progressively refining acquisition policy, the consequence of blanket approval systems is in fact to sustain the morale of the professional staff in the library.

The problem of blanket approval systems is rather the extent to which the jobber is "established," that is to say bibliographically and commercially experienced, and I noticed the contrast between the respect all the North American research libraries I visited have for European jobbers as professional equals and collaborators and the doubts they have regarding the North American jobbers. On visiting the jobbers themselves, however, I was impressed by the bibliographical expertise of their selectors: their difficulties are primarily financial. The problem of cash flow, now becoming acute in all sections of the world's book trade depending as it must on extended terms of credit, is in their case compounded by the necessity of basing the entire operation on a capital-intensive computer system in order to exploit the homogeneity of library profiles. Moreover, American jobbers tend to be less mature and diversified than their European counterparts; their capital base, relatively speaking, tends to be much smaller. They are involved in the classic American dilemma of a one-man business having to aim at Pike's Peak or bust, in a highly volatile economic situation; and the classic solution of seeking the long-term protection of a financial conglomerate presents hazards, in the form of conflicts of personality as well as policy, not yet mastered.

III

The most conspicuous feature of the current situation of rare book collections in North America that I noticed was, not surprisingly, their apartness from most of the problems mentioned above. The positive aspect of this is that, on the whole, unlike general research libraries, rare book libraries do not feel that their purchases have been seriously affected by the recession of the last few years. The reason given for this was that the rare book library budget is almost always a relatively small item in the general library budget where staff costs, for instance, bulk extremely large, and is less vulnerable to the restraint called for by the central administration. As it was put to me, Houghton does not _have_ to buy a certain number of books within each financial year, whereas Widener does; and for any extraordinary item a private donor or alumnus or other philanthropist can often be found. So far as the independent research libraries are concerned, where rare or special materials are the centre of operations, a new generation of enterprising directors has arisen--Hardison at the Folger, McCorison at the American Antiquarian Society, Towner at the Newberry, _et al._ They have been remarkably successful in raising money from private sources and have occasionally caused raised eyebrows amongst the older generation of scholar librarians, it appears.

All this means that practically no thought has been given, so far as I could tell, to the desirability of the kind of sustained collaboration in acquisitions which is felt, though not yet acted upon, by general research librarians. None of the rare book librarians I spoke to thought that concern about the relations between their collection and the national rare book stock would be particularly meaningful, nor did they think a national directory of rare book and special collections either useful or practical. The three main intelligence networks in North American rare book librarianship--the Independent Research Library Association, the Conference of Rare Book Librarians, the American Library Association's annual Pre-Conference on Rare Books--are highly informal and do not communicate officially either with each other (though they may have individual members in common) or with the Bibliographical Society of America. The local societies of bibliophiles--in particular, of course, the Grolier Club of New York--are far more effective at getting things done than the BSA, and the Conference of Rare Book Librarians, though it represents the cream of the cream of the institutional rare book libraries when compared with the ALA Pre-Conference, and though in the course of its brief history it has addressed itself, or is proposing shortly to address itself, to serious matters such as editorial standards in facsimile reprinting, conservation and security, has not developed any substantial agreed body of doctrine and practice. (It must be admitted that this is in part because it is felt that there is in fact no solution to certain problems, for example the problem of security in a rare book collection, and that even rare book librarians are as liable to fetishism in their thinking as are general librarians: for example, it was put to me that book conservation laboratories are in danger of becoming the fashion of the seventies as "computers in libraries" were of the sixties.) There is a noticeable contrast between this looseness and the relatively compact establishment in Britain represented by the Council of the Bibliographical Society, the British Academy, the Rare Books Group of the Library Association, the Oxford and Cambridge Bibliographical Societies and the various major national and research libraries. Nor is this contrast primarily due to the far greater size of the American continent and the pluralist tradition of arranging things mentioned above. Rather is it a case of Dr. Ray's fertile chaos, which in the world of rare books reigns supreme--to everyone's satisfaction.

The negative aspect of this apartness of the rare book world, I found, was the common feeling among administrators of rare book collections--even including directors of the independent research libraries with their Mellon-supported fellowship programmes, and the Library of Congress rare book collection--that their collections have been under-used by scholars or by suitably inquisitive laymen and, in the case of the university rare book libraries, the feeling that faculty and qualified students not only have not used the rare book collection much, but have been positively resentful of its privileged position. Moreover, the cry of "sell the rare books" was not confined to the auditors of the University of California system, and although repeated largely as a joke by faculty and administrators on one or two campuses, I detected some "needle" beneath the remark. The reasons for this apartness are, I suspect, first that most special collections are twentieth-century creations; and the presence of the original private philanthropist-founder of the special collection--for example, Mr. Lilly, Mr. Scheide, Mr. Barrett--or, if he is dead, the presence of his family or associates, is still strong, and there simply has not been time yet for the original core collection of high spots to be generalized into a structured research collection. The independent research libraries, just because of their independence--and their size--are of course more advanced in this respect. Second, in the case of university rare book collections, limitations of space and staff have inhibited that conspicuous progress in withdrawing rare books from the general library which would integrate the collection more firmly in the general life of the university (however, half of the new Pusey building at Harvard is intended to enable Houghton to do just this). Third, notwithstanding impressions on this side of the Atlantic concerning the North American passion and expertise for bibliography and textual criticism, the temper of American scholarship in the humanities, taken by and large, is still new-critical rather than historico-philological. It was the directors of the historical, rather than literary, special collections, such as those at the Library Company of Philadelphia and the John Carter Brown Library, who were somewhat surprisingly most concerned about this. The problems of apartness, in other words, are not new, and I had the impression that the solutions being adopted are an intensification of the traditional methods of promotion. On the one hand there are the high-gloss exhibitions and conferences: for instance, the Beinecke and the Folger are contemplating ambitious extra-mural programmes for the citizens of New Haven and Washington, perhaps involving educational television. On the other hand, academic courses in historical and other types of bibliography are being contemplated to train not only rare book librarians, felt to be in short supply, but a new generation of bibliographically-minded faculty; for example, the Humanities Research Center at Austin, Texas, is thinking of an Institute of Bibliography on the lines of the Institute at Leeds. This points up another fundamental American dilemma: the geographical remoteness of the typical rare book collection (particularly those not on the East Coast) from a really mature general collection of printed books. The easy symbiosis of the British Library and the School of Librarianship at University College London, or the Bibliothèque Nationale and the Ecole des Chartes, is noted with some envy.

IV

In summary, there seem to be three general implications for the British Library. First, I have suggested that the disarray of American research libraries and scholars in the face of financial and political constraint was due in part to their lack of an informed understanding of their raison d'être. I suggest that, similar national pressures being imminent in this country, the British Library should now take steps to review its own understanding of its raison d'être and indispensability, not so much in the short-term view of its relations with the national library system, but in the longer term view of its relations with the world of scholarship at large. This rationale should be stated publicly and repeatedly in considerable detail. That this would in turn raise the larger question of the rationale of scholarship itself in a mass industrial democracy makes the task more exacting, but not impossible.

Second, looked at from abroad, the indispensability of the British Library so far as printed materials are concerned lies, I have said, in the richness of its holdings of pre-1850 materials, particularly when considered in conjunction with the other major national libraries in Europe. We should now consider the feasibility of a more substantial survey of our holdings than is to be found in Esdaile's or Edward Miller's histories of the British Museum Library, or F. C. Francis's summary description of the published catalogues of the Department of Printed Books; and this should be done, preferably in connexion with similar surveys made or to be made by our European colleagues, in order to estimate the amount of material still not found in the libraries, any identifiable categories into which this material may fall, and the feasibility of acquiring any desirable section of it in a systematic way. One of the categories that would lie outside as well as inside the local responsibility of each national library for its own printed archive, and would therefore be a matter of common concern, may prove to be scholarly works written in Latin before, say, 1750, when major scholarship began to be assimilated into the local vernacular.

Third, as an attitude and discipline of mind appropriate to this task as well as an executive technique, we should consider reviving, no doubt with modifications, our own nineteenth-century practice of planned collection development, not only for current but also for retrospective acquisitions. It would give us the invaluable sense of bringing the forward movement of the library under our own control as, one hopes, the introduction of computer-based processing will likewise do for our housekeeping.

Notes

1. It was subsequently presented in the spring of 1974.
2. With the change of President, the Joint Resolution has in fact now been approved.
3. See I. R. Willison, "The Development of the United States Collection, Department of Printed Books, British Museum," Journal of American Studies, I (1967), 79-86.

PART II

TECHNICAL SERVICES/ READERS' SERVICES

REGULATION OF PHOTOCOPYING: A WORLD-WIDE QUANDARY*

Curtis G. Benjamin

As Shakespeare sagaciously observed, one's wish often can be father to one's thought. Possibly this is why so many librarians and educators think that the regulations of certain foreign countries should serve as guides to how photocopying for educational purposes should be regulated in the United States. One often hears this rationalization argued in favor of a liberal exemption from copyright protection of photocopying for educational uses in our country. How often has a librarian or educator said in effect, "They have worked this thing out in a sensible and equitable way in Sweden and other countries, so why can't it be done here?"

Sweden is nearly always mentioned. This is because so many people have been led to believe, or do believe of their own volition (the wish being father to their thought), that the Swedish government has found an easy and simple solution to a dilemma that has for several years troubled educators, librarians, authors, publishers, and lawmakers of the United States. When this belief is questioned, one finds more often than not that the person who so wishfully cites the Swedish solution actually has little knowledge of it, much less any concrete notion of how well or ill it might be applied to the problem of a country such as the United States. Obviously, some homework needs to be done before the Swedish system is conveniently seized upon as a promising guide for action by this country.

So what can be said about and for the Swedish system? First, two general observations can be made: 1)

---

*Reprinted by permission of the author and publisher from Library Journal, September 1, 1975, pp. 1481-3.

it is the first of its kind to be nationally adopted, and for this reason alone it has been widely touted as an enlightened model for other countries to follow; 2) it was established by a Special Agreement, not by copyright law. The Agreement was negotiated in 1973 between the Swedish Government and 17 private organizations, which include national associations of authors, book publishers, newspaper editors, journalists, photographers, artists, composers, and music publishers. It was entered into voluntarily by all parties concerned following proposals by the Chancellor of the Swedish Universities and the National Board of Education.

The Swedish Agreement

Although the Agreement is quite complicated in its safeguarding qualifications and limitations, a few of its basically important features can be described quite simply:[1]

It concerns copying for school use only, and it applies only to compulsory comprehensive schools. It does not apply to colleges and universities or to private educational activities at any level.

It applies only to works of Swedish authors or other authors domiciled in Sweden, and to works of foreign authors first published in Sweden. It does not apply to works published and copyrighted in other countries.

It applies to works of only those authors who are members of one or another of the private associations that are parties to the Agreement and who have formally given power of-attorney to one of the contracting organizations.

It applies only to the kind and amount of copying that is needed for classroom teaching. It does not apply to any other kind of copying that may be useful in a school system, such as information for the staff.

It permits the making of up to three copies of a work or part thereof without restrictions. If more than three copies are made, there are several restrictions concerning the use and disposition of the copied materials. For example, copied materials cannot be substituted for other suitable materials that are available to the teacher.

The State pays for photocopying rights at specified

rates which vary for 12 described categories of copyrighted works. Periodic payments are made to a consortium of the 17 contracting associations, called BONUS. BONUS in turn decides how the total income is divided among the member associations, each of which is free to determine how its share is used. The Agreement itself contains no specification of the end use, but in the negotiations preceding the Agreement it was stated that in the main the money would be used for collective purposes, not for direct recompense to authors and publishers.

School authorities are responsible for keeping exact records of all copying of more than three pages for specified six-month periods. However, only ten per cent of the schools have this task for any period. The total volume of copying of each of the 12 categories of works is determined from the reports of this sampling, and an accounting must be rendered to the State every third year.

The term of the Agreement is three years from July 1, 1973. Each contracting association is required to maintain for this period a specified rate of accession of "title-holders" for its kind of works. For authors and journalists and for book publishers and newspaper editors the rate is 95 per cent. The State can cancel its contract with any association that fails to maintain this almost full enrollment of all copyrighted works in its area of interest.

It is, of course, too early for a prediction of how well this national system of voluntary regulation will work in Sweden. The architects of the Agreement look upon it as a system that probably will require substantial revision by trial and error as time goes on. Indeed, the method of reporting on a sampling basis has already proved to be unsatisfactory. Teachers and school administrators object to the effort required on their side, and authors and publishers claim that no more than one-tenth of the actual volume of copying is being reported. Accordingly, it is widely predicted that the system will not be continued in its present form for another term.

How well such a system would work in the U.S. is, to be sure, quite another question. Most knowledgeable assessments suggest that several of its basic features are unacceptable to either public or private interests of this country. To begin with, it would be all but impossible to get our many trade associations and professional organizations to agree on a plan for collective representation of all interests. Moreover, most organizations of copyright proprietors would not buy a scheme under which remuneration would be spent only for collective purposes, such as unemployment and pension benefits. The private-enterprise thinking of the U.S. still is quite far removed from the quasi-socialistic "middle way" political economy of Sweden. Besides, many U.S. authors and publishers certainly would want and need direct recompense to support their lives or their enterprise.

Further, it would be folly to think that our federal government could be persuaded to organize and finance a system that would operate in local public schools. As everybody knows, there is a strong trend away from this sort of thing at both federal and local levels of government.

Finally, one can safely assume that public schools would not readily accept the burden of detailed record keeping and reporting, even if only ten per cent of them were involved at any one time. In fact, I think one can be sure that our local school administrators and librarians would solidly resist the imposition of such a burden.

Any one of the foregoing objections could be enough to disqualify the Swedish system as a likely model for the U.S. to follow. It seems, then, that we should look elsewhere for guidance--if indeed we must look abroad for a model on which to fashion a solution to our own national problem. Nevertheless, we should closely observe how Sweden handles the more complex problems of dealing fairly with photocopying privileges at the college and professional levels where the literature is far less homogeneous and where international copyright agreements must be observed. The authorities are reported to have found it much more difficult to devise an acceptable system for regulation at the higher levels.

The Nordic Council

Further it will be interesting, but not very pertinent, to observe what comes of the deliberations of the recently organized Nordic Copyright Council. This is an ad hoc committee appointed by the governments of Sweden, Norway, Denmark, and Finland to study better conformity of their copyright laws in order to allow the other three countries to follow Sweden's lead in the regulation of photocopying in a way that would permit an interchange of copying privileges among the four countries. It is reported that the Danish and Finnish members of the council have objected to the Swedish practice of collective payments of compensation to be spent only for a common purpose. Moreover, they have raised a serious question of whether such payments made internationally would not require their countries to forfeit membership in the Berne Union. The method of international compensation will be especially critical for the Nordic countries because all of them extensively use foreign language publications in college and professional education. It may well prove to be an insuperable barrier to a snug agreement among the four countries.

In other continental European countries the trend appears to be toward stricter policing of photocopying under the law, and the principle of fair compensation is being established more firmly.

West Germany

In West Germany, a change in Articles 53 and 54 of their Copyright Act, which pertain to copying rights, has been proposed. Further, the national book trade organization Börsenverein des Deutschen Buchhandels has an agency (V. G. Wissenschaft) that collects payments for copying rights under a recent agreement between that organization and the Federal Association of German Industry. (The Börsenverein agency also collects royalties for the lending of scientific books by public libraries.) However, it is still legal to make one copy of a journal article or a "small part" of a book for private use. But an unauthorized photocopy may legally be made for private use only--it must not be distributed to a "third party." And everyone who wants to copy for a commercial use must deal directly with the copyright owner. Unfortunately, the West German system has not yet set up a mechanism for dealing with other-country copyright owners.

The French Committee

In France librarians, publishers, and the Ministry of Cultural Affairs are trying to rationalize photocopying without resorting to a revision of the national copyright law. This effort has followed a court decision won by the publishers association against the government-financed Centre National de la Recherche Scientifique (CNRS). In this pivotal decision, the court found that CNRS had infringed copyrights by all but unrestricted copying of protected works. The case had strong similarity to Williams & Wilkins v. the United States Government but unlike the U.S. case, the decision of a lower court was upheld on appeal. Thereafter, the Minister of Cultural Affairs appointed a Committee on Intellectual Property and charged it with responsibility for recommending how photocopying permission might be handled on a negotiated basis. Meanwhile, the French National Library refuses to supply photocopies of parts of protected works without written certification in each case that the copy is intended only for personal use of a qualified researcher. And the Conseil National du Patronat Francais (the French counterpart of our National Association of Manufacturers) has reversed an earlier stance and conceded that its members should negotiate with copyright owners to work out formulas of compensation for any kind of reproduction of protected works.

In Austria, where the law allows photocopying of only a "small part" of a work, a Vienna court confirmed last year that photocopying of whole journal articles by a copying service was an infringement. It is reported that other kinds of possible infringement will soon be tested in the same court.

In Switzerland, a second draft of a new copyright law has been published. This draft corrects an imbalance of the first draft, which proposed general and free copying privileges for educational institutions, public authorities, and commerce and industry. Moreover, the second draft entitles copyright owners to compensation, and the national publishers association is setting up an agency called "Pro Litteris" for the collection and disbursement of fees.

Revision in the U.K.

In the United Kingdom the Whitford Committee has responsibility for recommending revisions of the Law on Copyright and Design of 1956. Last year both the Publishers Association and the British Copyright Council submitted to the committee statements which expressed grave concern over the impact of institutional photocopying on authors' rights and on the welfare of book and journal publishing. Early this year the Inner London Education Authority submitted an opposite statement, arguing that education is a "special case" in relation to copyright law and hence the revised statute should somehow provide liberal copying privileges for educational uses. After its study of the matter, the Authority concluded that there is "no practicable method of satisfying the interests of all three parties at interest," namely, teachers, authors, and publishers. Nevertheless, it did propose three possible methods: 1) direct control (permission) and payment; 2) blanket agreements between the parties at interest; and 3) indirect subsidies. The Authority opted for the third method, but failed to specify what kind of indirect subsidies would be fair and workable--leaving the question open with no more than a suggestion that some sort of tax relief for authors might be an acceptable solution. (The question of compensation for foreign copyright owners was completely ignored.) It appears, then, that the opposing sides are squared off in a confrontation that will not be easily reconciled.

The Netherlands Solution

To date the Netherlands, more than any other country, has dealt decisively with the total problem of regulating photocopying. Its Copyright Act states four main rules with respect to reproduction, which came into force on July 1, 1974:

1) It is not an infringement to reproduce small parts of books, pamphlets, or musical scores. Journal or newspaper articles may be reproduced entirely. The reproduction, however, must be made only for private use of the user.

2) Public services and public-service institutions are subject to special treatment regulated by a Royal Ordinance which entered into force in August 1974. They all enjoy various copying privileges, but each has to pay a fee per copied page: 0.10 guilders (about U.S. $0.04) for all uses except educational, for which the rate is 0.025 guilders (about U.S. $0.01). A system for the collection and disbursement of fees is being organized by a foundation jointly established by organizations representing copyright owners.

3) A commercial enterprise does not infringe the law

if it makes photocopies of small parts of scientific books or of entire scientific journal articles for persons employed by the enterprise. The number of copies allowable must not exceed "the reasonable requirements of the enterprise." An equitable remuneration must be paid by the enterprise to the copyright owner, and the rates, not being fixed under the Royal Ordinance, have to be negotiated.

4) Lawfully made reproductions may not in any instance be transmitted to third parties without the copyright owner's consent.

Two points of the Dutch system are worthy of special note. First, the works of foreigners who are nationals of a member country of the Berne or Universal Copyright Convention are given the same protection as those of Dutch authors. Second, libraries are allowed to make reproductions under certain conditions, one of which is that they may do so for loans to other libraries, provided that the recipient libraries are in the same interlibrary loan network. End users of interlibrary loans may not give or sell the copies to third parties; the law says "loan," not "transferral." The source library must account for all copies made and pay copyright owners at the rate of 0.10 guilders per page.[2]

Litigation Down Under

On the other side of the world, everyone in Australia who is interested in copyright is anxiously awaiting a decision of the High Court on an appeal of the Moorhouse and Angus & Robertson v. University of New South Wales case. In May of last year, the Supreme Court of New South Wales found the University guilty of copyright infringement because it failed to oversee the use of photocopying machines at the library and thus contributed to breaches of copyright by users of the machines. In its verdict the court reprimanded both the vice chancellor and the librarian of the university for their indifference to abuses of the law and for the refusal to allow a representative of the Australian Copyright Council to monitor sampled use of the machines. The court directed the university to mend its way and pay the cost of the lawsuit, which amounted to about U.S. $15,000. The appeal was heard by the High Court in November, but the decision has been reversed for an indefinite date.[3]

Meanwhile, a committee appointed by the Australian

government (known as the Franki Committee) has been charged with responsibility for recommending desired changes in the copyright law. And the Australian Copyright Council, a private organization representing the interests of copyright owners, has formed a limited company for the collection and disbursement of fees for copying and performing rights as negotiated with the university libraries and other large users of protected works.

In other parts of the world, several countries have recently enacted copyright laws or issued decrees that deal with copying rights in general terms. For example, Brazil has a revised statute which has not yet been tested in the courts. And Iran now has its first taste of copyright protection by an Imperial decree that is not likely to be challenged in any way. Under this law photocopying is allowed only for nonprofit teaching and scientific research, and authorization must first be obtained from the Ministry of Culture and Arts.

From the worldwide welter of legislation and regulation, several realities can be distilled for our own guidance. Every country has its own distinctive set of problems prescribed by such considerations as size, complexity of political organization, plurality of educational and informational systems, socio-economic philosophy, tradition, or private versus government control, homogeneity of language and ethnic culturation, etc. The problems are intensified in countries that are technologically advanced, which is to say those countries that are liberally supplied with copying machines which are habitually used. Solutions would be much less difficult if the importance of international copyright conventions were not a fundamental consideration. All these realities, and many others besides, must be kept in mind as we move ahead in a national effort to devise fitting and fair solutions to the photocopying dilemma in the United States. By looking abroad we can perceive how different and how difficult our own task is--and how urgently we need to get on with it.

References

1. Those who want a more detailed description of the Agreement are referred to a report of the Swedish Ministry of Education and Cultural Affairs: Joran Mueller, Copying for Educational Purposes in Sweden. Stockholm, 1973.

2. For further details of The Netherlands system see: Copyright: A Monthly Review of the World Intellectual Property Organization. No. 2, Geneva, February 1975.
3. For a complete report on the Moorhouse case see: Australian Law Reports, 24 June 1974, Part 1, p. 1. Butterworths, Chatswood, NSW.

LIBRARIES AND LENDING RIGHTS*

Rudolph C. Ellsworth

In most countries libraries are part of a literary tradition and a way of life that are essential to authors and publishers. In the English-speaking world, however, the long-standing discussion on the establishment of a public lending right for authors represents one area where the book trade, authors, and librarians have not yet come to any substantial agreement. But times change and popular moods change with them. A breakthrough in the idea of paying authors for the use of their books in libraries may now be at hand. In 1973, New Zealand began a system of payments to native authors for use of their books in libraries; significantly such payments are made by the national government from a special fund appropriated for this purpose. A year later Australia began a comparable scheme.

The idea of such payments to authors has been generating heat as well as light in Great Britain, North America, and Australia for at least the past generation. A wide variety of opinions pro and con--with some subtle variations in between--have emerged from authors' groups, publishers' offices, and library associations. In brief, just as a composer or a dramatist receives payment under performing rights legislation whenever his work is performed in public, so authors have sought to establish their right to an analogous "public lending right" (PLR), by which they would receive a payment (sometimes called a lending or library royalty) when books are borrowed by public library readers. There is no exact precedent which might help to distinguish between public performance and private enjoyment of library materials by an individual reader, nor is there any precise parallel with other legal rights to prove a moral claim. This debate

*Reprinted by permission of the author and publisher from Canadian Library Journal, Vol. 31, No. 6, December 1974, pp. 502-508.

has waxed and waned most vigorously in Great Britain, where some advocates claim that PLR is a right due to all copyright proprietors to receive remuneration for the use of their works in libraries, namely "payment for use under copyright," while others define PLR as "the right of authors (or their estates) to payment for the public's use of in-copyright books in public and non-public libraries."

A more pragmatic approach, such as that now being worked out by New Zealand and Australia, avoids the issue of copyright by establishing criteria concerned with the use of native literature as indicated by the provision of this through the libraries of the country as a whole. Such an approach embodies two principles that characterize the schemes of payments (called "library compensation") to authors for use of their books in libraries that have been operating in the Nordic countries for several years. (Denmark 1946, Finland 1961 authorized, 1964 started, Iceland 1968, Norway 1947, and Sweden 1954.) First, the money is provided through a state grant (that is, monies appropriated for this purpose by the central government). Second, no charges or fees are levied on users of the libraries. The latter principle is in keeping with the UNESCO Public Library Manifesto of 1949 (issued in revised form during International Book Year 1973) which states in part that the public library "should be maintained wholly from public funds, and no direct charge should be made to anyone for its services" and "To fulfill its purposes, the public library must be readily accessible, and its doors open for free and equal use by all members of the community regardless of race, colour, nationality, age, sex, religion, language, status or educational attainments."

New Zealand Authors' Fund

New Zealand's third Labour Government, it has been said, resulted in new style and new substance in the country's politics. Among these must be included the creation of the New Zealand Authors' fund. The biggest single contribution to establishing this fund as the vehicle to compensate authors for use of their books in libraries was the willingness of the Labour Party to provide central government finance. This was a proposal cited in the party policy statements emphasizing the need for "sound advancement of the people." It was put into effect with some dispatch by the late Prime Minister, Norman E. Kirk, after the party's electoral victory on 25 November 1972. The fund became a reality some seven months later. The New Zealand Centre of International PEN (the world association of poets, playwrights, editors, essayists, and novelists) had been campaigning for such a scheme for about seven years. The New Zealand Authors' Fund is administered by the Department of Internal Affairs through an interdepartmental Review Committee which consists of an independent chairman and members nominated by the New Zealand PEN Centre, the Literary Fund Advisory Committee, the New Zealand Library Association, the Secretary for Internal Affairs or his deputy, and the National Librarian or his deputy.

How It Works

In brief, the scheme works as follows. Authors are required to apply each year for payment in respect of their eligible works. Only books which total 50 copies of each title held by the libraries qualify for payment. Such books must be listed in the *New Zealand National Bibliography* (that is, be published in New Zealand, or published overseas dealing wholly or in part with New Zealand, and written by authors normally resident in New Zealand) and consist of at least 100 pages of photographs or art reproductions, 50 pages of prose, or 25 pages of verse. Eligible titles are determined through a census of books held by a sample of libraries according to details worked out by a technical sub-committee representing the organizations and officials on the Review Committee plus the Treasury Department. The libraries directly affected are mainly public, university, and teachers' college libraries. The royalty is a flat rate of payment per book which is calculated by dividing the total number of eligible books into the annual appropriation, less administrative costs of the census and committee activities. It is expected that a census will be required every third year and that this will be kept current in the interim by supplementary yearly reports from the libraries concerned.

For the first year (1973), 354 of the 385 authors who applied were found eligible. A preliminary estimate had indicated that this figure would be around 600. The initial appropriation was $140, 000 and the royalty worked out to $1. 30 per volume. The minimum payment was $65, the average around $300, but some authors received more than $1, 000. The top earner was the 98-year old Dunedin author, Alfred Hamish Reed, whose book *The Story of New*

Zealand was most widely held in the libraries. The runner-up was his nephew Alexander Wyclif Reed. Other top earners included: Ngaio Marsh, Janet Frame, Maurice Shadbolt, Barry Crump, Mary Scott, John A. Lee, Errol Braithwaite, Frank Sargeson, and Sylvia Ashton-Warner.

The regulations pertaining to the New Zealand Authors' Fund make no mention of any PLR nor is any aspect of copyright involved in administering the fund.

"There's no doubt in my mind that Whitlam is going to be right with Kirk," said Wellington author Ian Cross shortly after the New Zealand Authors' Fund caught the attention of Gough Whitlam. In the policy statement of the Australian Labour Party made on 13 November prior to the general election held 2 December 1972, the present Prime Minister Edward Gough Whitlam advocated the principle of payment to authors for library use of their works. Such a scheme became a fact of literary life in Australia as of 1 July 1974, retrospective to the preceding three months. The Australian scheme of library compensation to authors is similar to that functioning in New Zealand, but there are differences--most notably, eligibility for this royalty may extend beyond the lifetime of the author, and Australian publishers receive a royalty per volume of one-fourth the amount awarded to the author. The Federal Government appropriated $106, 000 to cover the initial payment, for the final quarter of the financial year 1973-74 (1 April-30 June), to be made after 1 July 1974. (The total cost for this period and the first full year of operation will be just over half a million dollars.)

All Australian authors listed in the Australian National Bibliography, whether published in Australia or abroad, whose works are stocked by at least 50 public libraries in the country are entitled to 50 cents a year for every library copy of their books. Here, as in New Zealand, the number of borrowings or loans do not count. Thus, the minimum library royalty is $25 per year. This scheme considers the "life" of each title to extend from its date of publication through the life of the author, or, on the death of the author, 50 years from the publication date.

The funds are provided by the Australian Council for the Arts and are administered by the federal coordinating and entrepreneurial organization, the Arts Council of Australia through the Literature Board. A reorganization in January

1973 made the Literature Board, which includes representatives of the Australian Society of Authors and the Australian Library Association, directly responsible to the Arts Council. Australian publishers receive a royalty of 12-1/2 cents a copy per year for each of their books stocked in the public libraries.

Authors' Returns

A statistical survey and sampling made at the beginning of 1974 indicates that, for Australia's leading novelist Iod Idriess, the scheme could amount to an annual income of $5, 000, for travel and children's writer Colin Simpson, between $2, 000 and $3, 000, and for Nobel Laureate Patrick White, up to $2, 000.

This scheme of library royalties should be viewed in the context of two other recent developments on the Australian literary scene. First, the Literature Board has established an extensive program of grants and guaranteed incomes for writers. Second, the principle of paying royalties for photocopying was recently affirmed in a case decided in the Equity Division of the Supreme Court of New South Wales. In some way not yet worked out, writers will gain a small amount of money when their works, or part of their works, are photocopied by people unable or unwilling to buy them from a bookstore. As a start, the Australian Copyright Council has formed the Copyright Agency Limited to negotiate with universities and education departments to establish a royalty payment system and to collect these fees and distribute them among the authors. Comparable royalty payment systems are also being worked out in the Scandinavian countries, the United Kingdom and Canada.

Discussion about lending royalties has gone on in Great Britain for almost 25 years. Three phrases which limn some of the high points of this debate are "Brophy's Penny," "Books are Different," and "Public Lending Right." The first refers to the proposal made in 1951 by the novelist John Brophy to charge for each loan of a book from a public library--the proceeds to go to a fund for the benefit of the writers of the books. The single penny in time became two, to accommodate the administrative costs to the libraries for collecting the money. However no such pennies ever materialized. The second epitomizes the rationale behind the court decision in 1962 that upheld the Net Book

Agreement of the British publishers, but applied here first negatively, later positively in another context, that of the author's right to a form of compensation for use of his books in public libraries. The third is the term invented in 1959 to describe this right by Sir Alan Herbert who has long been one of its most zealous protagonists.

This debate has been lively and literate, displaying polemic, even pyrotechnics at times, as well as indifference. Despite two reports by government-appointed working parties one cabinet was characterized as showing inverted Micawberism and "an open mind but a closed purse" to PLR. However, both main political parties now support the principle of payment to authors (and publishers) for library use of their books, but differences within what has coalesced, more or less, into the PLR Lobby (the Society of Authors, the Publishers' Association, and the Writers' Action Group) about means of funding and determining the fees have led the movement toward PLR legislation to be described as moving crabwise but slightly forward. During 1973, an "early day motion" in the House of Commons to amend the Copyright Act 1956 to include the PLR, evolved into an all-party Private Members Bill for the same purpose. Such an approach premises extending the "natural right" of copyright to include use without ownership of literary activity analogous to the protection accorded to the products of creative and artistic activity. This route contrasts sharply with the lending royalty schemes now functioning. But as yet Great Britain has no PLR.

PLR and Imported Books

However, in anticipation of some form of lending royalty, one issue already in the talking stage is the application of PLR to imported books on a reciprocal basis with countries which have their own version of library lending royalties. This is an issue that has not been dealt with in any country yet. Nor has much enthusiasm been shown by any of the authorities now involved with library royalties to explore this area.

At the request of the Authors' League of America, a bill (U.S. House of Congress: A Bill to Establish a Commission to Study and Make Recommendations on Methods for Compensating Authors for the Use of Their Books by Libraries, 93rd Congress, 1st Session, 1973, H.R. 4850) was introduced by Representative Ogden R. Reid (D., N.Y.). The approach proposed here is flexible and open-ended. Funds for such lending royalties would be provided by the Federal Government and any system recommended by the Commission would not affect the Copyright Act. This bill has been referred to the Committee on House Administration.

In Canada, during that watershed decade of the sixties, debate and discussion began on library lending royalties along with so many other issues. In due course, library associations heard glad (or sad?) tidings from Denmark, England, and Sweden, and authors wrote wistfully about how nice it would be to have PLR. But with the recent emergence of the Writers' Union of Canada on the literary scene, this debate has changed. Insight as well as outlook are now apparent in this scenario which is certainly leading towards action which remains to be outlined and then clearly defined.

The final report of the Ontario Royal Commission on Book Publishing issued in 1973 is "not opposed to the Public Lending Right principle as such" but recommends only that the Federal Government be "earnestly requested" to keep an eye on what is happening about library royalties in Great Britain and the United States. In *Saturday Night* for March 1974, the case for the PLR was presented with eloquence and logic in the article "When You Read a Library Book Should the Author Be Paid?" by George Woodcock, author and editor of *Canadian Literature*, and Basil Stuart-Stubbs, University Librarian, University of British Columbia. A brief and impassioned statement for making readers pay for their library book loans entitled "Our Authors Are Being Ripped Off" by Toronto novelist Marian Engel appeared in *Maclean's* for June 1974. Mrs. Engel is chairman of the Public Lending Rights Committee of the Writers' Union of Canada which recently submitted a brief on the Public Lending Right to the Bureau of Intellectual Property of the Department of Consumer and Corporate Affairs. The Ontario Library Association has formed its Canadian Authors' Public Lending Rights Action Group. The group prepared a 16-page report, "Public Lending Right A Survey of Practices, Options and Opinions," that was discussed at the OLA annual conference in Ottawa in May 1974. This report led to a motion in favour of the PLR that was passed at the OLA Annual General Meeting, 12 May 1974. The OLA action group is now studying ways and means of providing a "practical and simple method of compensating creative artists for the use of their works by libraries." The Canadian Library

Association Committee on Authors' Lending Rights is in the process of being established.

Relationship of Library and Writer

Before PLR becomes established as a comfortable, if not entirely accurate, cliché in North America, it may be well to pause, look above and beyond the clutter, confusion, and loose ends of the present debate, and wonder a bit more widely about the world of books, authors, and libraries in this connection. Inequities to authors have a long history. But to fault the libraries today for making available more native literature, among many other things, to their readers than has ever been done before in most parts of the world, is to overlook completely the ferment of cultural development during the previous century that produced, roughly about the same time, national and international copyright legislation of literary property, and the Public Library Movement, both to further the growing demand for reading matter and education. The complementary thrust of both of these actions was then, and is now, to bring books and people together. Over the years the challenges of how to do this have become more rather than less demanding, to the point where the world of books, authors, and libraries now needs all the cooperation and understanding within its environs that it can muster. One of the searching questions that is being asked throughout the Learning Society of today is: What is the place of literature and how can its appreciation be encouraged inside as well as outside the institutions of this society? "In the twentieth century the symbiotic relationship of library and writer has become one of the basic facts of literary life." Moreover, integrating the Welfare State with the Learning Society is generating an array of measures to encourage individuals, as well as institutions, in the development of national cultural policy. Most of the concern in this sector so far has concentrated on the performing and creative arts at the expense of literary arts. It has been less fashionable to recognize among this array of measures the pragmatic approach of lending royalties to provide authors with some financial means of fulfilling the cultural mission to which their talents call them. Likewise, that such an approach, which really originated in the Scandinavian States during the twenties, has a cross-cultural dimension capable of refinement and readjustment to a variety of cultural milieus. But this may now be changing. Early in the present century New Zealand had a reputation for pioneering social reforms which later came to be accepted as commonplace in other parts of the world. Viewed in such a tradition the New Zealand Authors' Fund seems to fall naturally within the short term "social objective" for individuals as well as institutions announced, and now being implemented, by the present government of that country.

The only satisfying reward for effort is achievement, which generally is a product of compromise. Establishing library lending royalties (a public lending right) in Canada offers a formidable area for compromise, but it would also be a very real contribution to national cultural policy through the agency of the public library.

IMPACT OF NATIONAL DEVELOPMENTS ON LIBRARY TECHNICAL SERVICES AND PUBLIC SERVICES*

Paul J. Fasana

Documents describing current efforts in the area of serials automation are difficult to get hold of. Even when one is successful in tracking down a document, there is the annoyance, the frustration in discovering that it has been superseded or replaced. In addition to ferreting out written documentation, I spent considerable time talking with colleagues at NYPL and other institutions. Though interesting, this was not always very informative because my colleagues were having exactly the same problem that I had had--inability to gether any authoritative information. Rumors, half-truths, and misconceptions are rampant, it seems, in libraries throughout the nation.

Initially this paper was to take the form of a "technology assessment"--that is, describing the current state of affairs and then projecting what this might mean for the next decade in terms of libraries. Because of the rapidly changing context in which current serials efforts are taking place, this approach proved impossible. There are too few facts available to allow anyone to attempt anything as practical or systematic as an assessment.

Depending on one's training, the current state of affairs can be described (or characterized) as being "dynamic" or chaotic. To the system analyst and the computer technician, the current scene is dynamic; the forces that have been unleashed by the International Standard Bibliographic Description (ISBD), International Serials Data System (ISDS), and CONSER (i.e., CONversion of SERials, or CONsolidation

---

*Reprinted by permission of the author and publisher from The Journal of Library Automation, Vol. 7, No. 4, December 1974, pp. 249-262.

of SERials) are fertile and challenging. The librarian's view, in my estimation, is less positive: a dynamic situation implies that there is control being exerted directing the various forces at play, and further, that this direction is exerted to insure that the result will be progress or advancement and not simply change.

A large number of librarians that I spoke with conveyed the impression that they looked at current efforts as verging on the chaotic. This attitude on the part of librarians may or may not prove true. It may or may not be paranoid. What is important, however, is that the attitude exists to some degree in the minds of a goodly number of technical and public service librarians, the very same groups which will have to implement many of the projects being planned and then live with the results. The success or failure of any effort is a direct function of the attitudes of all participants.

The most positive contribution that could be made by this paper would be to analyze the reactions of librarians and to attempt to convey their attitudes. Being a cataloger by training (and disposition), I had to try to find some unifying theme or organization. Therefore, for the purpose of this paper this mass of data has been synthesized into three broad categories: The Apprehensions of Librarians; Their Frustrations; Their Concerns.

APPREHENSIONS

Focus of Authority

For decades, the Library of Congress has gathered unto itself the trappings of cataloging authority. It has taken on, with the kind permission of the ALA Descriptive Cataloging Committee, the responsibility of drafting cataloging codes and standards, and of developing classification schedules and subject heading lists. It has made itself even more indispensable by becoming in effect the sole interpreter and implementer of these codes and standards. There is hardly a cataloger in the nation today who does not begin his or her day without dipping in and freshening his memory or art with the wisdom of the LC Cataloging Services Bulletin, the LC Subject Heading List (and many supplements), or the invaluable AACR.[1] These trappings are more than comforts and supports for overworked catalogers. They are the tools by which consistency, excellence, and continuity of library catalogs have been achieved. The United States today is blessed with card catalogs that provide a degree of effectiveness and overall control not found in any other nation in the world. This has been achieved, to a large extent, by the fact that there has been a national cataloging service (rather than a national bibliographic service) which has been in a position to provide millions of catalog cards to assist thousands of libraries. LC has done this not as so many national bibliographic services have done, by describing bibliographic units and printing them into noncumulating lists and bibliographies, but by acquiring the materials themselves irrespective of subject or country, cataloging them according to widely accepted and promulgated rules, and integrating them into its own catalogs and collections.

The various centers, programs, and consortia currently working pose a palpable threat to this subtle concept, and, in so doing, potentially will undermine the integrity and quality of catalogs throughout the nation. In this context CONSER perhaps poses the most alarming threat. By admission, CONSER would undertake in the area of serials to create a data base (perhaps "file" would be a more exact description) of serials according to standards which may or may not be acceptable or consistent with previous records or emerging standards. It would attempt to do this by setting up a legally complex entity, making use of bits and pieces of technology and files, and involving a number of libraries having widely differing objectives and standards. It might work, but then again it might not. A project as important as the building of a national serials data base must have a firmer base if it is to be effective and win the confidence of librarians. It must begin with more guarantees than the proposal that the national libraries of Canada and the United States will participate by postediting records and being verification centers and eventually, probably, take over the maintenance of the project. Catalogers are conservative. They are not against change *per se*, though they are insistent that proposed changes be adequately evaluated and developed in advance. This caution or conservatism has proved in the past to be beneficial.

Programs such as CONSER and ISDS have begun to disturb and unnerve catalogers because they are a threat in their minds to the stability and orderly progress that has existed for many decades. The significance of this reaction will become more obvious as we examine the situation.

Affection for Standards and Standardization

The basis of cataloging done in the United States up until 1960 was codified and made an international standard (or at least an "international agreement") in the Paris Principles of 1961.[2] These same principles were used as the basis of the Anglo-American Cataloging Rules of 1967.[3] Many people recently have gone back to the Paris Principles to prove or disprove a particular point or argument. Many of these same people have intentionally (or unintentionally interpreted one or another principle to their own purpose. Or they have said that one or another of the principles is no longer valid or worthwhile. It is very disturbing to me as an ex-cataloger to see this happen to what is, in effect, one of the milestones of cataloging theory. It is even more disturbing, it appears, to reference librarians.

What are the Paris Principles? Are they, as some have insisted, a restrictive, outmoded set of rules for determining headings for a work? I would suggest that a full and unbiased reading of the principles (together with the working papers that were prepared for the IFLA International Congress in 1961) would reveal that they constitute a statement of theory which is encompassing, pragmatic, and still quite viable. The Paris Principles implicitly comment upon:

1. Authorship--they assume that it is important, at least for research purposes, to relate and/or collocate all works by an author (corporate or personal). This includes editions, translations, etc. That this often is translated into a battle over which of several forms of name, or which of several names listed on a title page, should be chosen for main entry is beside the point. The basic intent is to establish authorship responsibility in order to relate, logically and helpfully, materials in a collection for users.
2. Form of material--printed information, regardless of its form, can and should be described, organized, and displayed consistently in a catalog. An author responsible for a monograph should get equal and consistent treatment if he authors a serial. He should not be treated in one way when he prepares one kind of material and in another when he prepares a different form.
3. The catalog--the catalog itself has certain functions and objectives. Among the more important functions

> in this context is the ability to integrate and relate records. On one level this is the ability to integrate the records themselves because of consistency in entry (or responsibility for intellectual content) and format of entry. On a more important level, it allows the integration of the materials themselves in terms of their record surrogates (i.e., catalog cards) used to control materials on the shelf.

The importance of these three concepts is enormous for current collection building and reference. Increasingly we see information being packaged in a variety of forms. Increasingly we have library users and researchers requiring an approach to all the material on a subject. The catalog, and indirectly the rules used to construct a catalog, must be able to provide this integrated but "multimedia" approach. In the various standards being promoted for use with serial materials there is an underlying feeling that serials are different--so different that a separate standard is needed to catalog them. In effect, these standards assume that they should in all instances be entered under title.

The ISDS is the only standard which states this principle explicitly, but it is implied in the ISBD(S) and also the CONSER Project (at least early in CONSER's development). Philosophically I can't help but be concerned that if this attitude holds sway over future cataloging practice and theory, the disservice to library users will far outweigh the technical advantages that may be realized in the immediate future.

The *AACR* is an implementation and elaboration of the Paris Principles. The *AACR* and the Paris Principles are in terms of cataloging theory not only satisfying but usable. In their use they have proved practical because they allow, wherever the principle of the authorship becomes too diffused or opaque, the alternative of entering under title. This flexibility is important and should be preserved by future standards.

Continuity and Integrity of Records and Collections

A library is a concept that embraces the past, the present, and the future. Many similes have been used to characterize this idea. A library instructor once grandly described cataloging and collection building in terms of building a great medieval edifice, like Chartres. Catalogers as they integrate a catalog card and/or piece of material into the collection are satisfying some vast design but doing it in an anonymous fashion. Someone recently described the same concept in a far more vivid manner. To him, the collection of books and catalogs in his library were like a vast placenta, the umbilical cord of which was attached to him. Every book cataloged or acquired becomes a painful gestative process. He continued his metaphor by saying that when LC announced its proposal to close its catalog and start fresh, he suddenly felt some hope that he might be delivered of this retrospective nightmare.

Both metaphors reveal different but important attitudes relative to the cataloging process. The library today is continually having to struggle and contend with the past, to rationalize this struggle in terms of current developments and current additions, and anticipate the future. Let us look at several current developments to see how they affect these issues and what impact they can have on existing collections, catalogs, and technical service librarians.

There are probably three impending events that should be considered:

1. LC's announced intention to "de-superimpose,"
2. Machinations on the international level in terms of ISBD--both for monographs and serials, and
3. The ALA Catalog Code Revision Committee.

LC in all of its wisdom decided in the mid-sixties not to conform fully with AACR because of the expense that would be involved in changing records. To a large degree, LC's decision was not of its own accord but rather the result of substantial pressure brought to bear by research libraries throughout the nation.

In any event, LC's alternative, that of "superimposition," has proved to be costly and vexing, not only to LC itself but to all libraries attempting to use LC cards. LC's recent announcement that it would in some way as yet to be decided upon give up superimposition in the near future caused a shudder in every large cataloging department. Though catalogers have complained bitterly about the problems of attempting to deal with superimposition in local cataloging and catalogs, the prospect of having to redo thousands of records in the near future is even more frightening. Unless one can envision doing de-superimposition in conjunction with closing of the catalogs, cataloging departments will either have to "patch" catalogs with confusing and unsatisfying reverse references (of the type that read "For work cataloged before a certain date see this form," and "For works cataloged since a certain date see a second form") or do a lot of recataloging, thereby reducing "productivity." This prospect is made even more odious when applied to the literally thousands of corporate serials that will be involved. Consider, for example, the thousands of university publications issued in serial form that will be affected by de-superimposition.

At the same time, cataloging librarians are confronted with proposed ISBD conventions. Contrary to what some have said, the implementation of ISBD for monographs is requiring considerable retraining of cataloging personnel. The impact that these supposedly minor changes in descriptive cataloging will have on cataloging productivity, though still impossible to quantify with any precision, will be negative. The new collation requirements of ISBD(M), for example, if followed, will add appreciably to the cataloging time for a title.

ISBD for serials is another problem and seemingly more divisive and troublesome. In spite of the ALA Descriptive Cataloging Committee's hasty endorsement "in principle" of the proposed IFLA standard, which to some might have suggested that the committee had studied the standard and established that there was consistency between ISBD for monographs and serials, significant differences are emerging. For example, in monographs the "/" is used to introduce, in all cases (except the series statement), author information. With serials, however, for generic titles the author statement is added onto the generic term with a "space hyphen space"--a different symbol convention which violates one of the prime objectives of ISBD, that of coding data consistently.

Another, and perhaps more important, example is the ambiguous footnote on page 19 of the ISBD(S), where we are told that the "organization of this area [the series area] is not the same as in the ISBD(M) ... due to the differing functions of the two standards."[4] Nowhere is there an elaboration as to what this "differing function" is. If one reads the preface carefully, however, one begins to develop certain fears. The first paragraph states that ISBD(S) is intended to find a "common basis for the cataloguing of serials." In monographs the authors carefully specified "descriptive cataloguing" only. Therefore, one might assume that "cataloguing" here means only descriptive cataloging of serials. However, further on one reads that this was an "appropriate moment to look afresh at the cataloguing and description of serials because ... of ISDS ... and ISSN." Note that "cataloguing" and "description" are distinguished.

Though not explicitly stated, the evidence seems to point to the fact that serials are to be treated differently from other types of materials and probably will have to be cataloged in all cases under title. If this is in fact what will happen in the next several years, what will the local library be forced to do? Again consider recataloging thousands of serials? What effect will this have on productivity and the concept of an integrated catalog?

At this point, this is only conjecture. However, it does indicate the mood of influential and well-organized groups on the international and national levels. The ALA Catalog Code Revision Committee is beginning its work on what we thought would be a revision of the Anglo-American Cataloging Code _in its entirety_. The word "entirety" is important because it implies that the revised code, if developed as a whole, would have a greater chance of being consistently developed. However, at a recent public meeting, a speaker stated that in fact LC was considering its current charge from the Descriptive Cataloging Committee to "_rewrite_" Chapter 7, "Serials," to conform with ISBD(S) to mean "_revise_" Chapter 7 as the first part of the revised _AACR_. If this is true, it is disturbing. Because of the pressures alluded to above to go to title entry for serials, together with the unexplained "urgency" to implement CONSER, ISDS, and the like, Chapter 7 may turn out to be inconsistent and at variance with other parts of the revised _AACR_ and past practices if it is developed in isolation.

I have attempted to highlight above the context within which technical service librarians are having to try to function at present. Each of these possibilities in itself will require study, revision, retraining, and patching of existing catalogs. When overlayed, the situation becomes nightmarish. What decision should they make with respect to local cataloging practice today? Will it be valid tomorrow? And then, of course, there is the nagging realization that regardless of what is done, the cataloging department will have to try to accommodate the increased workload without additional staff and then be called to task for decreasing productivity.

Carrying this one step further, the cataloger can look forward to the complaints of reference librarians about the complexity and cumbersomeness of the public catalog.

FRUSTRATIONS

Technical service librarians, in addition to their apprehensions, are beset by a number of frustrations. Those which seem most important at present are:

1. Attempting to know what is in fact going on and who, if anyone, is in charge;
2. The volatility and rapid change which are characteristic of all current serial efforts; and
3. How to influence and have input to these various projects and efforts.

In the past two years librarians have been confronted with an array of acronyms and projects. Let us sort out the sequence of events and personalities of the past two years in the area of serials only. In 1972, the Association of Research Libraries issued the final report of the National Serials Pilot Project.[5] The conclusions and recommendations of that report are modest, straightforward, and reasonable. The more important are:

That a national data base be built
That the MARC record format be used with minor modification
That an authority file be an integral part of the NSDP system design to insure consistency and authentication
That some thought be given to the peculiar and unique capabilities of the computer relative to cataloging theory
And finally, that the project itself be established as a separate entity but within the public control and trust.

How these recommendations were interpreted and implemented by the National Serials Data Program during the past two years is rather murky. The project started with the appropriate amount of fanfare and initially sparked interest and cooperative feeling.

Very soon, however, efforts and objectives became rather ambiguous and confused with politics. NSDP began to take on more of an international rather than national flavor. The cordiality that seemed to exist initially between it and the national libraries seemed to evaporate overnight and be replaced with a sharp sense of competition, especially with the MARC serials effort of LC. Eventually it became apparent that the NSDP considered itself not an effort to create a national serials bibliographic control system and data base, but rather a link with the International Serials Data System, a progression that might have been logical and defensible if the library community had been aware of what was being done and felt that it had participated.

In the meantime, another force emerged and began to exert influence. At first it was called the Toronto Group, or the Anable Group, and reflected the interest of a number of librarians whose only affinity seems to have been the need to create a data base for union list activities. By January of 1974, the Council on Library Resources emerged as the agency "selected" by the library community to carry the ball in this area of serials automation. Since January, activity has been fast, furious, confusing, and occasionally contradictory. At present we have the existence of CONSER, a project which has espoused the original objectives of the original Toronto Group (i.e., a union list project) and has grafted on several more goals, i.e., to become the source of data for both a national serials bibliographic control system and an international serials control system.

These developments should not be perceived as negative. As a technical services librarian I am more than a little confused as to what has happened, who is causing it to happen, and what in fact is the real objective of all this activity. I and a number of my colleagues would like to be able to direct queries and questions to someone to find out the whats, whys, and wherefores. But there seems to be no one person or agency to whom questions can be directed. There is no body of literature to which one can go to study or evaluate--unless, of course, one is a member of the inner circle and is involved in the planning and direction of the project. But even those few are often unable to say what the project is doing or to lay their hands on the document which would purport to be official or reflect the latest stage of planning or development at any point in time.

To a large degree, perhaps, the sense of urgency that has fired recent serials developments is a reaction to the long years of study, deliberation, and inactivity that went into the original National Series Data Program. This is perhaps understandable, but I don't think that it should be used as an excuse to get something done, where getting something done becomes an end in itself. Technical services librarians have for the past decade watched the development of library automation and have resigned themselves to the reality that serials automation is an area that could not and should not be attacked locally. The cost of converting serial records is high. The need for compatibility with other libraries is critical. The requirement that any system or data base created be consistent with (or at least cognizant of) records and collections already extant is paramount.

Therefore, librarians have a vested and vital interest in any project that takes on the characteristics of being national in scope. Since they have spent years waiting and have modified local plans and projects to dovetail with the national development, they have a keen (perhaps exaggerated) sense of interest and responsibility. It is inevitable that any national serials project will have great impact on what they are doing locally. Therefore, they have an overwhelming obsession to contribute and participate. CONSER is rapidly emerging as a serials project with national implications. It is in fact doing everything to espouse and incorporate the perquisites of a national system. By so doing, it must also take on the responsibility of a public trust. The question must now be posed, Is CONSER willing to take on these responsibilities?

Again, my comments are not intended to be critical of CONSER. Rather I am trying to convey the sources of frustration that I sense among my colleagues. Perhaps this sense of frustration or moral indignation can be focused more precisely by actually posing some of the questions that librarians have asked:

Who is in charge? What are the credentials of those in charge?
How can I keep informed of technical developments within CONSER so that I can evaluate and make valid decisions on a local level?
What is the status of the CONSER format? Is it/will it be compatible with the MARC serials format?
What is the time schedule for implementation?
What are the objectives of the OCLC/CONSER Pilot Project that is being set up? Are they valid? Technically feasible? Will the records created be freely available to the library community? When and how?

What are the technical and quality requirements of CONSER participants? Has CONSER in fact rejected the idea of authority control for entries? If they have, should they be allowed to?

What will be the nature of the file created by CONSER? Will it be a file of disparate records usable for union list activities only? Or will it be truly a data base exhibiting the essential characteristics of quality, consistency, and accuracy?

What kind of evaluative and review mechanism is there (if any) to insure that what is being done will meet the stated objectives of the project and the acknowledged needs of the library community?

What mechanism is there (again if any) to allow feedback and input from the library community?

What validity is there in the urgency and pressure to create a file of 200,000 to 300,000 records within two years? Is this reasonable, especially considering the highly volatile state of affairs in the area of standards development?

Perhaps the frustration of both technical service and reference librarians can best be summed up or stated in terms of physical laws. An impetus is being created by the interest, need, and activity of a relatively small group. The momentum that may be created if this impetus is successful will be persuasive and pervasive. It will eventually affect all libraries. The force of momentum is _amoral_. It can destroy everything in its path or it can carry everything forward with it. We are at that point, it seems, in the development of an automated serials program where it is still possible to influence and affect the direction and velocity of this gathering force.

CONCERNS

The comments so far have been rather general, attempting to convey feelings, attitudes, and reactions. We should now examine several rather specific matters which reflect the kinds of concern that technical service and reference librarians have.

These fall into three distinguishable areas:

1. Analysis of the problem--has there been adequate analysis of what impact proposed standards will have

on cataloging and reference activities?

2. Technical evaluation--has there been adequate evaluation of the objectives and proposed products of these efforts in terms of practical and/or conventional library needs and objectives?
3. User evaluation--has anyone given any thought to the impact that these efforts will have on the library user?

As for quantitative analysis of the problem, little or no attention seems to have been given to any aspect of the impact that ISBD and CONSER will have on the workloads or productivity within libraries. It seems that the prime movers in this area are all convinced that the anticipated benefits of being able to manipulate serials data within the computer in an on-line mode will more than offset any disadvantage, temporary or otherwise.

This may in fact prove true in the long run, but there are legitimate questions or reservations that can be raised and should be answered now. What in fact will be the result in the immediate and medium-range future? Let us look at one narrowly focused aspect of this issue, that of encoding serials into the CONSER format (or what it seems that the CONSER format will be).

According to a planning document prepared by CONSER (dated 9 April 1974), the CONSER format is designed to reconcile or accommodate AACR, ISDS, and the ISBD(S). This is an interesting challenge, since each of these standards has unique requirements. Whether it can be accomplished technically is at this point irrelevant. Let us assume that it is possible to accommodate these three standards and that a library begins to encode its records in this hybrid format. A major problem exists in the recording of author information for works having generic or nondistinctive titles. ISBD(S) in rules 1112 and 1113 gives instructions for creating what it calls "distinctive titles" for works with generic titles. The result will be an element that corresponds closely to (if not identical to) the "key title" of the ISSN. This seemingly trivial matter may in fact have significant consequences. At a meeting recently at which the CONSER project was being described, the question was posed as to whether this had been considered; the speaker answered yes. A further question asked how many titles might this affect, to which the speaker answered that he *had been informed* that it would affect less than 1 per cent of all serial titles.

Based on my experience at NYPL, this seemed unrealistically low. Therefore I sampled the NYPL Central Serial Record to see what the magnitude of effort might in fact be. I drew a random sample of approximately 1,260 titles from a file of approximately 90,000 current or active titles, the size of NYPL CSR. This is admittedly not a statistically valid sample, but sufficient to indicate whether or not "less than 1 per cent" would be affected by the ISBD generic title conventions. The results of the sample are as follows: 54 per cent of the titles reviewed were entered under author; 46 per cent were entered under title.

Of the 54 per cent entered under author, more than 96 per cent were entered under corporate author. Of the 96 per cent entered under corporate author, 45 per cent had titles which probably could be considered distinctive, and 55 per cent of the titles were nondistinctive or generic. A simple arithmetical calculation reveals that, based on the small sample, more than 25,000 titles would be affected by the generic title rules of ISBD. This is a significant number of titles, and potentially a major problem area, if one keeps in mind the fact that ISSN requires that when key title changes, a new ISSN must be assigned. Anyone who has worked at cataloging corporate serials knows how frequently corporate names change. If the two standards (ISBD and ISSN) are followed strictly, therefore, there will be potentially a great deal of recataloging required.

My purpose in describing this small exercise is not to give you hard facts, ratios, or comparisons. It is, rather, to emphasize that this kind of quantitative analysis is highly essential in developing plans and procedures. To my knowledge, little or no analysis of this sort has been done and it is critical that it be done, ideally <u>before</u> decisions are made committing a program to a course of action.

Let us now focus upon technical evaluation. By technical evaluation I mean "library" technical rather than "computer" technical. I circulated copies of the proposed ISBD(S) standard to a number of catalogers and asked for their reactions. There were numerous comments about the complexity and seemingly overly detailed and overly structured nature of the rules as a whole, as would be expected. Each cataloger noted and commented on different aspects of the format; all, however, noted that:

1. The designers of the format had obviously never had

to catalog serials in a library and integrate serial records in a live catalog.

2. The resulting product of cataloging with ISBD(S) was a description eminently suited for a bibliography but perhaps not so well suited for a library catalog.

The arguments used to support these comments are that if rule 1. 2, Parallel Titles, Sub-titles, and Other Titles and 1. 3, Statement of Authorship, were to be strictly followed, the title paragraph would be long and would include information which is highly volatile and traditionally more suitable as notes. They also noted that LC's current policy, that of cataloging new serial titles from the first piece acquired (rather than from the first bound volume), would probably result in a great many problems.

It would be difficult if not impossible to quantify all aspects of these problems in advance. However, it does seem rather obvious that the impressions and evaluations of line serial catalogers need to be taken into consideration. I would hope that at some point some group will attempt to evaluate the theoretical niceties of ISBD(S) in a practical serials cataloging context--hopefully before it is adopted and used as a standard in any major library project.

IMPACT UPON USERS

Finally, it is necessary to comment on user or end-product evaluation. This perhaps is the most important aspect of any activity in our service-oriented society. Libraries are in the business of providing service. How well are we serving the library user? How efficient and effective are the catalogs that we prepare for public use?

There are those who have claimed that the library user does not understand the library catalog or the cards that are filed in it anyway, and therefore as librarians we don't really have to be too concerned about them and their problems. This comment was made by a cataloger at a public meeting about a year ago when trying to defend the symbol convention required by ISBD. The implications of that comment are repellent. Have we taken the time to evaluate the impact that ISBD, ISSN, ISDS, CONSER, and all of the other projects, standards, and efforts currently whirling about will have on the user? I would submit that we have been too busy, all of us, with our own concerns and problems to give much thought to the user interface.

What impact will title-entry cataloging for serials have on the library user's ability to find what he is looking for in a library?

What effect will de-superimposition and ISBD symbols and cataloging conventions have on the quality, consistency, authoritativeness, and integrity of our library catalogs?

What impact will title-entry cataloging for serials have on the integrity of collections? Of retrospective catalogs?

These are the questions that must be addressed. It seems, however, that these are exactly the questions that are being ignored in the current welter of serials work.

Technical planners are too involved with the politics, it seems, of what is going on in the national and international arenas. The desires, objectives, and opinions of too small and too capriciously chosen a group are being allowed to hold sway. The decisions that this group is making are not being properly communicated to the library community. They are complex but they should be communicated and explained so that relevant feedback from the library community can be generated.

The technical planners are not alone in being at fault. Librarians themselves are shirking their responsibilities. It is not sufficient to say that since matters are complex, technical, and/or political, there is no simple way of participating or contributing. A way must be found. Librarians have a professional responsibility to be sure that what is being done in their name reflects the objectives of their profession and satisfies their sense of professionalism.

CONCLUSION

Libraries in the United States have always attempted to provide a level of service to users which is rarely equalled and almost never excelled. This has been achieved by adhering to standards, such as the AACR, which are sensitive to the needs of researchers and users first and foremost. We have created collections and catalogs which attempt to bring together all forms of materials, to analyze them in a way which reveals meaningful interrelationships, and to make them available via tools such as the card catalog which attempt to do something more than simply describe an artifact in all of its uniqueness.

There is a real danger that current efforts in the field of serials will undermine these major achievements because they fail to understand or take into consideration the overall context of the library and especially user service. It is irresponsible for anyone to argue, as has been done, that because of the problems of checking in or cataloging serials, we should arbitrarily enter all serials under title. This in effect destroys the important concept of bibliographic control and integration, the cornerstone of cataloging in the United States. It is equally irresponsible to argue that because of the new computer technology and its ability to store and manipulate large quantities of data rapidly, established conventions, traditions, and procedures should be discarded before that potential has actually been demonstrated. The ability to store and manipulate data rapidly is not the same as, nor does it replace, the important characteristics of library catalogs, those of consistency, accuracy, and authoritativeness. And finally, it is not only irresponsible but folly to insist that getting something done (translate that to mean converting 200, 000 to 300, 000 titles in two years) is reason enough to forge ahead regardless of the consequences.

The momentum of automated serials control develop ment work is beginning to be felt. I would hope that we will be able to control and direct it rather than be controlled and directed by it.

References

1. Anglo-American Cataloging Rules; North American ed., ed. by C. Sumner Spaulding (Chicago: American Library Assn., 1967).
2. International Conference on Cataloguing Principles, Paris, 1961, Statement of Principles Adopted by the International Conference; annotated ed. with commentary and examples by Eva Verona (London: IFLA, 1971).
3. Anglo-American Cataloging Rules.
4. ISBD(S): International Standard Bibliographic Description for Serials; Recommended by the Joint Working Group on the International Standard Bibliographic Description for Serials set up by the IFLA Committee on Cataloguing and the IFLA Committee on Serial Publications (London: IFLA Committee on Cataloguing, 1974).
5. National Serials Pilot Project, Toward a National Serials Data Program (Washington, D.C.: Association of Research Libraries, 1972).

OSBORN REVISITED; OR THE CATALOG IN CRISIS; OR, FOUR CATALOGERS, ONLY ONE OF WHOM SHALL SAVE US*

Michael Gorman

Andrew Osborn's celebrated polemic, "The Crisis in Cataloging," appeared some thirty-four years ago in the October 1941 Library Quarterly. Though in certain respects it was a forlorn trumpet blast against walls that stand to this day, it is overall one of the most influential documents in the history of cataloging. Osborn's statement is both short and pungent, and therefore superior to almost all other works on the subject if we hold with P. G. Wodehouse, who once observed that his books are better than Tolstoy's because they were shorter and had more jokes in them.

In "Crisis," Osborn discerned four types of catalogers: the misguided "legalistic," "perfectionistic," and "bibliographic," and the sensible "pragmatic." These types seen today have the dated charm of mother's wedding photographs, for we have moved from a mere crisis in cataloging to a crisis in catalogs and catalogers. Never has there been such unanimity on the theory of cataloging and such disarray in its practice. In many libraries the catalog has taken over, becoming an end rather than a means, and catalogers have become willing or unwitting accomplices of its waste and muddle. Theirs is not to reason why, but to catalog.

I now offer four revised categories of cataloger: the Decadent (in the nineteenth-century literary sense of the term); the Stern Mechanic; the Pious; and the Functionalist. Each in a different way is contributing to the resolution or the aggravation of our central problem: How can we stop the catalog from being the monster that is devouring our libraries? How ought we Frankensteins to regard the Thing that we have made? Some watch with worry; some with

---

*Reprinted by permission of the author and publisher from American Libraries, November 1975.

horror; and some, amazingly enough, with smug satisfaction.

The Decadent

The Decadent is easy to spot. Many unlikely people can be seen as bibliographic Baudelaires or Brummels, concerned only with the exact placement of a comma, the precise square bracketing of pages in a collation, and the nice distinctions between such categorical inventions as "periodical" and "continuation." This dandyish elevation of form over content is pernicious not only because it is thoughtless, but because it preserves outdated and irrelevant practices in the catalog. All good catalogers recognize the importance of detail, but also its proper place in life.

Still less should the catalog exist merely to display the virtuosity of the Decadents, who, in some libraries, reach their apotheosis by accepting centralized cataloging data and then altering it to suit their own sense of the fitness of things. Thus they subtly demonstrate their credo that form comes before all else. The savings of money and human resources that accrue from the use of centrally produced cataloging data are as nothing to the Decadents' desire to show that they, and they alone, understand the exact fit of a hanging indentation or the correct cut of a pair of square brackets. I have even witnessed a senior Decadent ruling out (in immaculately straight red ink lines, of course) information given on a Library of Congress card that somehow offended his sense of propriety. Only tapdancing comes to mind as an equally preposterous and futile expenditure of human energy.

Library school education is probably as much to blame as any other cause for the spread of Decadence. The endless mazy intricacies of Cutter-Sanborn numbers are treated as a proper subject for professional consideration in some cataloging courses, while the crucial purpose of the catalog is ignored. Lost in contemplation of the niceties, the fine print, and the minute details, such educators produce either Decadents or cynics. The former are turned on by the means and know nothing of the ends; the latter are left with the lifelong conviction that cataloging is an avocation suitable only for loonies and little gray people.

The truth is that cataloging is a serious business, too

serious to be left to the mercies of catalogers. The crying need of the profession is not for more catalogers, but for more people with an informed and sensitive understanding of the nature of catalogs and their importance to the library. The Decadents not only waste money and time; they pervert the general professional understanding of cataloging until the catalog becomes undervalued at best, and, at worst, a despised object of ridicule. The inevitable consequence of Decadence is the Goth at the gates. The movement ineluctably produces the counter-movement. The Decadent is threatened not with sanity and moderation, but by the new barbarians of bibliography--the Stern Mechanics.

The Stern Mechanic

This sleek and solid-state invader bears a no-nonsense approach to the whole problem of cataloging and a touching, almost childlike belief that machines will solve everything. Reminiscent of a WWI general, the Stern Mechanic believes that too much damned talk goes on, mostly by long-haired types, and that what we need is a spot of action. Install a machine here, do something (anything) decisive there, and the whole shooting match will soon be over.

The only trouble is that the simple solution tends also to be the simpleminded solution. The country is littered with punched-card machines that were going to solve the problems of five decades in a week, but turned out to add two more staff to the cataloging department and two more months to the cataloging backlog.

The xerographic copier usually figures in the more outré fantasies of the Stern Mechanic, who extols its speed, cleanliness, and ability to be used by even the lowest intelligence. One library decided at the urging of its head of technical services to obtain a vastly expensive copying machine to produce its catalog cards. These were to be copied from single Library of Congress cards or any other centrally produced cards, and to be disseminated among all the libraries that made up the system. By the time this particular application of Stern Mechanics had run its course, the library had acquired an enormous amount of card stock, an expensive guillotine for cutting the stock into 5 x 3 cards, and a machine for making rod holes. This last machine, a death-dealing and fearsome object to behold, stood in magnificent idleness for all but thirty-five minutes each week. A timely operations and management study finished off this particular piece of foolishness, but the lesson is there to be absorbed.

The lesson is simply this: no machine will ever solve the central problems of cataloging. Even the most progressive and efficient of machine systems will fail if they are merely mechanical cosmetics. For instance, the Ohio College Library Center (OCLC) system, considered by many to be the most significant development in Western civilization since the invention of printing, can be indicted on a charge of cosmetology. OCLC was intended to be a genuine advance in shared cataloging and in the progression to forms of catalogs suited to the last part of the twentieth century; in fact, it is being used as a means to perpetuate a form that was ideally suited to the last part of the nineteenth century--the card catalog. One hopes that the more imaginative persons connected with OCLC see the use of a computerized system to produce cards only as an interim measure, and that it may indeed prove to be so.

To use the computer in such a perversion of technology is a product of the "horseless buggy" syndrome. Advances in technology should be used in the creation of new systems and new things and not just a new whizz-bang version of what we are doing already. The spectacle of many libraries getting together and using all the resources of modern technology to produce--WHAM, POW--the 5 x 3 card is one not likely to be treated with much kindness by future library historians.

The card catalog reached the end of its useful life in large libraries about twenty years ago, and is the chief reason for the near breakdown in technical services in many large libraries today. The problems that the card catalog poses are too wearily familiar to the staff and users of libraries of all kinds; it is more instructive to think of the state of the large library when the card catalog is finally done away with. No filing backlogs, no vast halls full of gloomy cabinets and even gloomier would-be catalog users, no waste of money and human resources on the unending and mind-messing task of card filing. Instead, lovely books and other materials will occupy the prime space that the catalog now usurps, and library users will use terminals or microform readers strategically placed throughout the library and the library community. Cataloging will have become what it was always meant to be; a vital task in the library that enables library users to gain access to the documents and information which the library can supply.

In many ways the unthinking use of machines to achieve the illusion of progress is more harmful than unabashed stagnation. Left to themselves, outmoded systems will rot and collapse. The Stern Mechanics are not only keeping some of them alive too long, but carrying over the worst traits of the old era into the new. Why, for example, do bibliographic machine formats (MARC chief among them) preserve the concept of the main entry? It has been obvious since the invention of the unit card that, except in some specialized applications, the idea of the main entry in an irrelevance in modern cataloging. We still, however, agonize over the choice of the main entry. Why? Because the code tells us to do so, and the creation of MARC records requires us to do so. Thus are the time-consuming and increasingly irrelevant concepts of the past preserved.

The Pious

The Stern Mechanic has some belief in the power of reason, or at least a neo-Victorian belief in progress based on reason. The next category, the Pious, have no such belief. Theirs is the blind faith of the true believer. There is convincing evidence that cataloging is a form of religion for some people. It has its sacred texts, sacred objects, central body of doctrine, and high priests.

Everyone is familiar with the room which in many large libraries houses the most sacred object of all, the cataloger's holy tabernacle--the card catalog. Sumptuously fashioned of wood and polished brass, the card catalog often occupies a room with vaulting and church-like arches. There is a busy but hushed atmosphere; filers file like so many oblates telling their beads. Should filers laugh or speak in a voice above a low murmur, they will soon be visited with shocked and reproving glances from the rest of the congregation. Stray library users are seen as well-meaning but irritating intruders into mysteries of which they can know nothing.

In rooms adjacent to the main house of worship, the Pious pore over the sacred texts like so many theological students. What is the precise significance of the introductory note to Rule 17 of the Anglo-American cataloging rules? What awful punishment awaits one who maketh not the reference, "Art. See also Dentists in art," as called for by the LC subject heading list?

Probably the most depressing feature of meetings to do with cataloging is the contribution of the Pious. Questions which are not questions but demonstrations of piety are voiced; rules are invoked to the letter, and not in spirit; and the devils of common sense and efficiency are exorcised. The late Paul Dunkin in his book Cataloging U.S.A. entitles one section "The Prophet and the Law." The Prophet is Cutter and the Law is the body of rules that have been created after Cutter--usually a long way after. And herein is the weakness of Piety. The Prophet gives us the word and lesser people codify the word until its clarity of thought is lost. All prophets need deliverance from their followers, far more so than from unbelievers. The pattern is easily seen in the wake of Panizzi, Cutter, Dewey, and Ranganathan. In cataloging at this very time, the clearheadedness of Lubetzky and the great breakthrough that came about because of his work are threatened, not least by the Pious--to whom even the wooly phrases of the Paris Principles are Holy Writ.

The Functionalist

Faced with the threat of Decadence, Stern Mechanics, and Piety, what are we to do? The answer lies with the fourth type: the Functionalist. Believing with William Morris and the Bauhaus that beauty and utility are indivisible, the Functionalist can perceive the elegance of a useful catalog record without thinking (as the Decadents do) that elegance is an end in itself. A Functionalist is prepared to use all modern mechanical aids that will make the catalog a more efficient tool, but does not see mechanization as an end in itself. The Functionalist believes in the importance of standardization in cataloging and that it can best be achieved by agreement on cataloging rules and other standards; but Pious adherence to the letter of the law rather than the spirit has no place in Functionalist doctrine, which is simply this: Catalogs are instruments of communication between the library user (and library staff) and the documents the library can make available. Anything increasing this communication is good, and anything detracting from it is bad. When one is converted to these concepts, the crises of catalogers and their catalogs seem infinitely more manageable. Converted Decadents delight in the elegance of usefulness; converted Stern Mechanics are able to use their mechanical expertise in a fruitful rather than a sterile manner; and as for the Pious--at last they see the light on the road to a bibliographic Damascus.

Cutter wrote in 1904 that the Golden Age of cataloging was over. It seems to me that another Golden Age is developing at this time. Never have there been more complexities to grapple with and so many exciting developments in the field. Will catalogers be obstacles in the way of progress, or its most important agents? It will depend upon their understanding of the purpose of the catalog, and their vision of the best techniques for achieving that purpose.

COLONIAL CATALOGING*

Cavan McCarthy

Where does a library keep its books? Silly question--books are kept on shelves, people take them off the shelves to use them. That happens everywhere, in Western, Socialist and Third World countries.

Well, almost: it doesn't quite happen like that in Third World countries. Some libraries there get no regular supply of books: we won't talk about them today, they are too depressing. Many do accession regularly, but they don't put their books on the shelves. They go into cataloguing where they lie around in piles or even unopened parcels; they don't get to the public for a very long time.

I have even seen a library where two-thirds of the collection was in the back; that is exceptional, but 20% is not rare and the average might be as high as 10%; most Third World cataloguing departments are piled high with books. The professional librarians are in the back too, puzzling over tortuous cataloguing rules. The readers are out front trying to unravel monstrous catalogues without professional guidance. They are playing a lottery in which there are only second prizes: should they find something, it will by definition be an old book: the new ones haven't been processed yet. Backlogs caused by complex cataloguing rules keep materials off the shelves at the time they are most useful: when they are new and up-to-date.

Innumerable examples could be given: at one time the backlog in Brazil's National Library was so large that if it had been organised as a separate collection it would probably have been the third largest library in the country. One Nigerian state library has a 15,000-volume backlog: the en-

*Reprinted by permission of the author and publisher from New Library World, March 1975, pp. 55-56.

tire collection in another state is not much larger than that. I showed a draft of this article to a man who had previously taught in a Caribbean university; he promptly told me that when he took up his appointment there he discovered that the cataloguers had a fine basic collection on his special subject. He had extreme difficulty in wresting books away from them, even overnight; there were only a couple of hundred volumes, but he claims that when he left a year later 90% had still not been catalogued.

The whole system is a monstrous waste of human and material resources, and it is western librarians who are responsible, not the librarians of the Third World. We are responsible by default, if not by action, for allowing AACR/ISBD to be dumped upon world cataloguing as internationally applicable world standards.

Which they are not.

But cataloguers all over the world still follow them, because they purport to be the best Western practice, because there are no decent alternatives and because adoption leads towards world bibliographical unity (on our terms).

The US version of the AACR was translated in Brazil shortly after it came out, although that code contains distortions of the Paris Principles which were inserted to please huge US libraries with jumbo-sized established catalogues. That is not a problem in Brazil: a more typical situation there would be the production of a university's first union catalogue, and they would have been better advised to adopt the UK version of the AACR. This particular story has a happy ending because the Brazilians quickly realised their mistake and put out their own simplified code, which begins with a translation of the Paris Principles.[1] They had also learnt a lesson about foreign codes of practice, and when the local translation of ISBD(M) appeared, one of the most eminent librarians in the country published a fierce attack on it.[2]

Third World countries are notorious for two things, a literal belief in the printed word and a rampant bureaucracy. It is, for instance, almost inconceivable for a Nigerian not to follow full Western cataloguing practice down to the final full stop. His entire schooling has beaten one fact into him above all others: it is essential that he read and answer examination questions about the white man's books if he is to have any kind of a decent future in modern Nigeria. (NB: he does not have to understand the books, just answer questions about them). After such an upbringing it is extremely difficult for him to reject a part of the rules, especially if he is a qualified librarian who has been trained on these codes and has heard lectures on standards, international bibliographical control and so on. He must be taught AACR at some stage, and this makes it difficult for him to learn simplified cataloguing. If he learns simplified first he resents the "waste of time" when he gets on to the "real stuff"; vice versa, and he does not see why he should simplify when he knows how to do it "properly."

So he adopts complex rules which even we find difficult to understand, and which produce lengthy entries which can only be transcribed by a skilled typist. These are difficult to find in Nigeria: a typist with anything resembling an education will devote his time to getting either promotion to senior clerk or entry to a higher education course. One Nigerian State Librarian recently wanted his divisional librarians in the "bush" to adopt simplified cataloguing, but they flatly refused: an amazing action in a country as authoritarian as Nigeria. But they are acting in tune with their environment, which is very bureaucratic and where delays and complex minutiae are normal, so it would not seem strange to them to have the same in the cataloguing room. Especially if the most advanced Western books demand it.

A further, more philosophical but perhaps more basic objection is that the whole AACR/ISBD axis is firmly based on "correct" western publishing style, and that in turn is based on individualism. That is, the majority of books are expected to have a standard title page upon which an individual is named as the person chiefly responsible for the book. As long as the library materials conform to these purely traditional principles, they are easy to catalogue by AACR/ISBD, but why should they conform?

In the Soviet Union a book is frequently the combined effort of an editorial committee, e.g., a collection of articles compiled by half a dozen people. They are listed in alphabetical order on the back of the title page and one is distinguished by "chief editor" after his name. The title page will have an issuing body as well as a title, but no personal name. A similar Western compilation would be considered the work of an individual who will be given on the title page as editor. Now the Soviet system is perfectly valid, perhaps even preferable, yet it is difficult to handle by AACR/ISBD, whereas the individualistic Western book is straightforward.

Why should that be? Take another example: government publications are notoriously difficult to catalogue. Tough if most of your national book production consists of government publications, as is the case in many less-developed countries. It is equally awkward if you are a Tiv or an Icelander and your name does not conform to the WASPish 'Brown, John' pattern. A lot of publishing outside Europe and North America is difficult to handle with AACR/ISBD, and a Third World librarian trained in them must come to accept the traditional Western view that the individual monograph is the normal, correct form for a book to take. He has been through an extremely subtle indoctrination into Western individualism. It supplements the blatant indoctrination he got at competitive school.

We need a package based on the twin principles of service to the public and internationalism, which will produce brief sensible entries for all types of library material. The package should be short, easily comprehensible and preferably published by something like Unesco to give it authority; it could be layered, so that different levels could be adopted by libraries of various sizes. It should cover filing as well as headings and description. If you learnt to write your native language in Arabic letters, then discovered that the only newspaper in your language uses Roman letters, and after that you attend an English-language library school where they talk about the difference between letter-by-letter and word-by-word filing, you are apt to be a little confused about filing order. Some of my Hausa students are in precisely this position. I haven't been discussing classification here, but it is obvious that the same problems and solutions apply and that the package would be infinitely stronger if an international classification were to be included. There is no reason why this should not be done, as long as we do not accept AACR/ISBD as the eternal solution.

Such a system would give a product similar to the catalogues we have now, but there is no reason to stop there. A Soviet CIP entry contains a short entry followed by four or five sentences of blurb which are obviously intended to be transcribed onto the catalogue card. Perfectly feasible in a cheap-labour country using classified catalogues; essential because closed access is normal there. But equally valid where readers select books from a distance, as between libraries within the large co-ordinated systems which are now standard in developed librarianship. And equally feasible using centralised production methods.

Western cataloguers are obsessed with headings, and scarcely mention annotations, which are considered impossible on a large scale. But a group of youthful amateurs, who hadn't been told that annotated bibliography is impracticable, produced the Whole Earth Catalog, which was successful beyond their wildest dreams and founded a whole new area of publishing. But these publications are basically nothing more than annotated bibliographies which deliberately break away from the cold whiteness of conventional bibliography and attempt to be interesting reading in their own right.

It is doubtful whether this will ever be absorbed even into fringe librarianship. From the service point of view it would be wonderful if we were to develop interesting informative catalogues which readers enjoyed consulting; the practical and technical problems are large, but could be solved with less effort than it took to produce MARC, COM and all the other acronyms. For instance: descriptive leaflets or "flyers" are already produced for many books; printed cards often arrive with the books or are ordered from a central agency; looseleaf folders are readily available. So in addition to its traditional catalogue, a library could have a descriptive catalogue of a part of the stock, A5 punched sheets with CIP entry plus description, held in looseleaf binders. The whole thing could even be a free service to libraries from publishers: don't forget they will want their books to be borrowed if loan-based PLR comes in. The system doesn't have to operate like that; I'm just outlining one possibility.

Imagine that a Nigerian comes into my office and says that he is setting up a library service for the numerous literacy posts round about and that he needs advice on the type of catalogue to produce. I could show him a Whole Earth Catalog and point out that a publication along those lines would be something that new literates would enjoy consulting and which would make them want to read the books they saw described. Those are two vitally important things which cannot be said about any library catalogue in the world today.

He might accept this and with luck, enthusiasm and

hard work produce such a catalogue: it could be extremely effective, revolutionary even. The point is that he would only try if he was an amateur, and had a certain amount of courage: if the scheme flopped he would be risking his job. On the other hand a professional librarian would immediately realise that I was ignoring everything he had been taught in long arduous hours of cataloguing class. He would not begin to understand my "unprofessionalism," and in the end I would have to tell him the address of the best supplier of metal card cabinets.

So it goes.

References

1. Cordélia Robalinho Cavalcanti. Código simplificado de catalogaçao. Brasília, Universidade de Brasília, 1971.
2. Edson Nery da Fonseca. "Posfácio," Revista de biblioteconomia de Brasília 1(2), 1973, 166-8.

THE GREAT COMPUTER HOAX*

Jeanne V. Schramm

One very slow evening in 1973 I was sitting at the reference desk reading an article on computerized card catalogs. It seemed that we were somewhat behind the times here at West Liberty State College [W. Va.], in that we weren't in a position to utilize these fantastic technological advances in library service. To be truthful, I didn't really understand the article, and I didn't really understand computers, but then I was sure that not many other people did either. But it occurred to me that one might take advantage of the public's fascination with and acceptance of computer technology without actually possessing a computer.

I immediately set to work designing a nonexistent computer system. First I put up a sign saying that the library had acquired a computer and that any student needing help should submit a blank punch card indicating his or her topic or problem. We would then punch the card and feed it into the computer; out would come a list of all subject headings pertinent to the student's needs. Blank punch cards were attached to the sign, which was placed in front of the catalog.

Business was slow at first, but soon the idea caught on. Students submitted cards and were told to return in 24 hours for the results. The reference staff then researched the topic and had the appropriate subject headings typed in computer print-out style on computer print-out paper. Soon the typing of the subject headings got to be so time-consuming that we left them in longhand, explaining that to speed things up the computer center phoned in the subject headings and the librarians simply wrote them down for the patron.

---

*Reprinted by permission of the author and publisher from Wilson Library Bulletin, April 1975, pp. 577-579.

(There was an actual computer in the administration building, and our computer was mysteriously tied into that one.)

The name selected for this magnificent bit of hardware had to sound authentic (like computers' names that sound as though a computer thought them up), and at the same time had to be somewhat truthful about what the device actually was. Since the computer was in reality the library reference staff, I selected the acronym HOLAD (for Heads Of Librarians At Desk). And of course, since there were seven of us, it became the HOLAD 412.

We discovered that students who were too shy to ask a librarian for help had no qualms whatever about asking the computer. And those students who normally were rather impatient with us if we didn't provide answers immediately were only too happy to wait 24 hours for the HOLAD 412 to do its work.

If, after a quick glance at the student's card, we felt that we could provide help immediately, we regretfully announced that the computer was broken and that we would be glad to help. On several occasions the students informed us that they would really rather wait for the computer!

The students weren't the only ones taking advantage of HOLAD. Faculty members also submitted cards, and during library tours, several freshman English instructors were heard reminding students to utilize the computer in their research.

The hoax was exposed after several months of operation, when we divulged our story to a reporter for the campus newspaper. During the time that the computer was in use not one person realized that it was fake. (Would a librarian purposely mislead?) Even the dean of administration, who served as chairman of the campus computer committee, commended us on our computer utilization project.

In doing her story for the newspaper, the reporter interviewed several students who had used the HOLAD 412. One student informed her that his term paper had been "saved" by the computer. He had looked for days for something on the Teapot Dome scandal with very little success. He hadn't wanted to "bother" the librarians and finally decided to submit his topic to the computer. Twenty-four hours later he had received a list of six subject headings which he had not used, and they really saved the day. He informed the reporter that he was really lucky to be able to attend a college with such advanced technology available to assist students in their research!

Unfortunately, the HOLAD 412 has been retired and is now in storage. Perhaps one day we really will have a computerized catalog. I only hope it works as well as our HOLAD. I'm sure it won't be as much fun.

PART III

COMMUNICATION AND EDUCATION

THE CONTINUING EDUCATION BANDWAGON*

Walter Brahm

"You all comin' to the meetin' to get some of this here continuin' education? Haven't seen you at any of these workshops. You too busy to come and grind an ax?"

Americans are notorious faddists, and librarians are no exception. Their current craze? Continuing education. In the past they climbed aboard the bandwagons of intellectual freedom and social responsibility doped with a full shot of mob psychology. But the continuing education bandwagon looks so inviting that it's joined by all without hesitation. You can find nothing in library literature but exhortation for more such education. It stands beside Motherhood and the Bible.

The cloak of continuing education covers every area of library work. It has become an end in itself rather than a means to an end, thereby threatening to reduce the quality of service provided the library user, dulling the individual initiative of staffers, directing the competent away from the primary duties of service, and raising the cost of staffing libraries out of reason.

Librarians, in the guise of continuing education, go to what used to be called meetings--now workshops. To vary the monotony of the name, we sometimes label one an institute, or a seminar, or a clinic, or to be more erudite, a colloquium. The most recent is a hybrid, "semshop." Workshops can be scheduled for any area of library work; there are even workshops on how to conduct workshops. If a workshop on "Nothing" were scheduled, I believe a full complement of librarians could be induced to attend.

---

*Reprinted by permission of the author and publisher from American Libraries, May 1975, pp. 288-289.

Sacrilege

Admittedly, these comments are negative and will be unpopular. It may be sacrilege to question continuing education, as well as intellectual freedom or social responsibility. Librarians have assumed the value of such education to be axiomatic: no proof needed. If one pill is good, two are better. Let it be stated emphatically: We believe in and encourage continuing education, but we question group meetings as an effective approach to the problem. There must be some way to limit them or provide them in a less chaotic fashion than the present free-for-all.

As I write this, the mail contains an announcement of a two-day conference on automation. For the past fifteen years the library profession has been deluged with automation and state-of-the-art conferences. Are so many, so frequently, necessary to keep us up to date? Except for improvement in hardware, automation theory and areas of library application--repetitive tasks--have not changed significantly. A few examples of meetings which demonstrate the plentitude of CE opportunities: "Alternatives in bibliographic net-working, or how to use automation without doing it yourself" (two-day conference); ...eleventh annual clinic on "The application of minicomputers to library and related problems'" (four days); "Minicomputers in libraries" (two days); "Evolving standards in library automation" (two days in Maryland; repeat two days).

Jangled Jargon

The jargon of continuing education also has passed understanding. We may anticipate shortly a workshop or institute on workshop language! Some examples that leave you wondering: a) "December Continuing Education Section's meeting was an introduction to Values Clarification. It ... got everyone thinking about the things that influence our value judgments. To quote: 'Our differences are things that we each really have to give to each other'"; b) A workshop on the Humanism Explosion and its role for public libraries; c) A workshop to create or train Change Agents; d) Prototype Intellectual Freedom workshop;* e) "The program's dynamic will be the interplay among participants and faculty."

---

*Workshops beget workshops! "The money, time, and planning invested in the ALA Prototype Intellectual Freedom (Continued on next page)

I have yet to see any evidence that there is a need for group-style continuing education; a true demand for it; or that such CE has produced noticeable improvement in library service, at least sufficient to justify the enormous cost of current involvement.

CE supporters may foam at the mouth at such a sweeping statement, but experiences in my own bailiwick have compelled me to say it.

The Cost of Continuing Education

The Connecticut State Library's budget in 1973 projected 60 "library science training seminars." We didn't produce 60 programs, but managed to execute about 35. Attendance estimates approached 2,500. Public library employees in the state number about 2,400 (including parttime). These one-day workshops at eight hours per day took 20,000 man-hours, or 500 weeks. That's the cost or loss of service just from attendees.

Perhaps Connecticut isn't typical. Perhaps its state library staff, its librarian and trustee associations and its library schools are doing much more in the field of continuing education. I doubt it. The California Library Association some time ago announced plans for a series of short courses and institutes. An Arizona State Library Association newsletter reports that a recent study recommends the association assume responsibility for developing a meaningful and viable continuing education program for the region. Multiply Connecticut's activities in this field by 50 states, and imagine the man-hours spent on preparing the programs, and on the travel and participation. Estimate the staff time consumed in organizing and conducting the programs and the supporting services: publicity, correspondence, registration, food and hotel arrangements, and often the publication of the papers presented. And gasoline for travel? Enormous.

What does the library or the library user receive in

Workshop ... are beginning to bear fruit. The purpose ... was to prepare key-people on the State-level to plan and carry out similar programs in their home states. In the first six months since the Prototype, twelve ... have sponsored workshops; and fourteen other State Committees have workshops scheduled...."

return? This question never fails to raise the hackles of workshop devotees. We are promptly deluged with testimonials from participants: "I was so stimulated"; "I returned home refreshed"; "I got a different viewpoint on things"; "The leader of the workshop sure knew her stuff." But no one has yet told us how such reaction translates into better service for the user, or why the same or even better effect could not have been accomplished by individual reading in the professional literature. There is a member of the Connecticut State Library staff about whom we receive almost daily compliments on the service he provides. The praise comes from members of the legislature, attorneys, and the public throughout the state. Far more than any of us at the top administrative level in the State Library, he is responsible for the library's current reputation for service. He seldom goes to meetings; he's too busy. But he knows his territory, and everyone knows he knows it.

A Model for a Model

The institute has become more important than its purpose: improving service. It is promoted and evaluated as a model for other institutes. The conduct of a workshop seems to be the measure of its success. Putting on a good show swells the pride of the promoter, and obscures the search for the elusive answer: whether the workshop helped the public. Indeed, the search for the answer is seldom initiated, so eager is the workshop devotee to get on with another institute.

Is such education promoted to satisfy a real demand or because there is a surplus of manpower in library advisory and education areas? The preparation and conduct of workshops and institutes may be the easiest, most interesting way to consume the time and energy of such manpower. Is it the most effective way? How valid is the demand? "We have to limit the enrollment because of the demand. We planned for 60 but 90 came." What staff member wouldn't want to go to a workshop if the employer paid the cost and gave him time off to do it? It's fun to go to a meeting and get away from the job. The employee doesn't have to put his physical and mental energy to the task on his time or put his money into it. Perhaps continuing education without individual sacrifice has lost its glamour, its sense of accomplishment. We find it difficult to reconcile the demand with requests from the promoters for wide distribution of of program announcements and a pitch to the employer to pay expenses for staff attendance.

Do We Really Need Mr. CLENE?

How much opportunity for group learning must be provided?

Who determines the extent and subject of these opportunities?

Are the many group programs provided currently and in previous years--many are repeats--inadequate for the task?

The answer is always a resounding "yes" from within and without the profession. This is pure assumption. There is no proof that more is needed, or that what exists is inadequate. Librarians have an inferiority complex in this area, a psychology that the working staff, administrators included, are inexperienced, not knowledgeable about personnel development; that library school faculty are too traditional and theoretical to be effective in staff development; that state agencies and associations are not staffed or free to do a systematic job. Consequently solutions proposed urge everyone to do more, and more. There is now a proposal and design for a super Continuing Library Education Network and Exchange (CLENE) before the National Commission on Libraries and Information Science. CLENE is not intended to disturb or replace existing local, state or regional programs but to "reinforce, augment, and provide more effective utilization" of them. Our citation of this center is not to pass judgment on it but to document the additional time and effort spent on the group education ethic. What we have is good, but more is better! We may spend so much time learning to do the job, we won't have time to do it!

Read ... or Retire?

Are current practices which encourage continuing education the best in the long run for motivating staff? If an individual were required to attend programs on his own time and at his own expense, every continuing education program would be evaluated immediately in a new and meaningful way. Promoters would have to assure themselves and others of their value to guarantee attendance. Stimulation and encouragement for individual development could be more effective. Academics have their mandate to "publish or perish." Ought ours to be, "Read or retire"?

If we believe that the library provides informal education for all who individually use its collections, then should we, as librarians, forsake our own individualized education for the social group approach? If the public were to do this, there would be little need for libraries except to provide assigned reading for education programs. The library is a continuing education instrument for its users, but its working staff is being seduced to disdain this approach to their own education.

Educational pundits say: Although the ultimate responsibility for learning rests with the individual, learning is a social process greatly sparked by group reaction. This heretofore universal assumption of the success of group learning is now being questioned. The establishment of independent study and external degree programs, a trend toward individual learning, is currently gaining some favor. The library itself exists for the user solely on an individual basis. Ralph Besse, speaking at the 1974 Ohio Library Association Conference, left no doubt about libraries and self-education!

> I confidently assert that the book is the greatest tool of continuing education for a learning society. I believe that reading is the core of continuing education. It is essential to all other methods. It is the only comprehensive method most adults have time for, it is the only comprehensive method that is available all our lives, it is the only comprehensive method that is available wherever we are. It is the most complete, it is the quickest, it is the most current.

A bit corny perhaps, but it does raise a question: Do librarians have faith in their own product?

WORD OR IMAGE?

David Gerard

> Every created thing has ways of pronouncing its ownhood. (Auden)

It was good to see Fiction and the Reading Public (Q. D. Leavis) mentioned in New Library World (F. T. Bell: "Conversation in a train," October 1974), an indication of this journal's panoptic qualities. It is a book which ought to be the vade mecum of every practising librarian, within easy reach on his desk, yet it enjoys almost total neglect by the profession and--more surprisingly--it is missing from these essential reading lists so beloved of library schools. Yet perhaps not so surprising; as a profession we have been traditionally uncouth.

Why is the book so important? One or two observations need to be made before answering.

Firstly, imaginative recreation in our contemporary culture should be of paramount concern to all of us in the book trade, especially public and academic librarians. Yet it is a singularly tepid obsession to judge from the evidence of our professional press. Now the art of fiction has been and still is a most sensitive register of the condition of society at any time, and a test of our personal response to an imaginative statement made by the novelist. Fiction, whether we like it or not, is still the chief source of nourishment for most public library clients, yet our concern for it has always been superficial, perhaps because we are unsure about our own individual response to it.

If we grant that librarians should be concerned about imaginative recreation (for are they not now Directors of Leisure and Recreation under the post-1974 dispensation?), then the tangible object on which that interest should focus is quite simply the novel, a major part of their stock-in-trade. But to understand fully the nature of this thing we need to know more about the commerce of the novel, the interaction of the reader, writer and the intermediary publisher who are composite and indivisible: the librarian must see them as such or not at all.

Which brings us back to Fiction and the Reading Public. That particular enquiry into the relationship between the novelist and his readers reveals profound evidence for librarians about the true state of recreation as enjoyed by the vast novel-reading public. The author penetrates the self-delusions of novelists and readers in her analysis of the motives and mechanism which produce novels at every fictional level, from the simple novelette to the few examples of supreme creative expression, as in Hardy or Lawrence. You recognise yourself in her picture of the common reader because it is more uncomfortably real, more familiar than the equivalent in, say, Richard Altick's English Common Reader, where it is a statistical abstraction. And the distinction is bluntly made between the unserious and serious novelist, between the best-seller and the rare creative artist. Though written in the early thirties, the book is as valid today.

Test of 'Ownhood'

But why should a knowledge of such distinctions be important for librarians? Simply as a test of their "ownhood." Very few of us need expose our ignorance any more after the demands of school are over; there is an unwritten rule in adult society that we do not embarrass by pressing people to prove the bland assertions that are the constituent parts of most conversations. But as professionals we ought to be tested. And it would be an impressive demonstration of our fitness to administer our fiction stocks if we ran a series of critical articles by librarians, each taking a novel for its theme. That would be concrete evidence of our understanding of the medium we talk so much about in the wrong way.

Proof of such understanding is nowhere to be seen in the professional press; when a critical verdict is explicitly avowed it turns out to be someone else's, or is a safe received judgment, or the work of an outsider, not a librarian. Quantities of speculation about the provision of fiction, but the nature of this huge communications industry is never investigated; it is all quantitative (like the extension of responsibility under recent reorganisation) but, alas, not necessarily qualitative. None of the claims about fiction provision are ever tested by explicit demonstration, any more than conversational small change is ever scrutinised, and there is rarely a reference to what actually makes a novel what it is.

Of course I am not saying that such demonstration of our powers of understanding a novel would be the only way to understand what recreation in our culture means, but it would be a start. We need a concrete point of reference on which to locate ourselves if we are to avoid yet another round of those vapid generalities. To repeat: fiction is the prime example of the functioning imagination in our sphere and therefore the point at which the librarian comes into his own. It is the symbol of leisure for librarians, the clue with which to judge the quality of leisure, and it is present in abundance upon our shelves. Ergo, librarians can best come to <u>their</u> definition of the best use of leisure by way of the novel which it is part of their responsibility to administer. In short, it is the symbol of our ownhood.

Context of the Printed Word

The habit of method, of starting from fixed points and making the ground sure as we go, distinguishing what we know from what we do not know, is surely the soundest basis for training? If this principle is agreed then this argument which began with the simple, concrete example of fiction can lead into a whole universe of discourse about the context of the printed word.

"Imagination I hold to be the living power and prime agent of all human perception," said Coleridge, an influential witness, and we in libraries know him to be right--we are probably in libraries because we have felt this, though less articulately. Obviously it is not the possession of ample leisure that creates a flourishing culture (see any working class housing estate, or the purlieus of W1), but rather the latent possibilities in any given society for constructive work. For librarians the interest in any discussion of leisure must be the life of the imagination, because that is the dimension which librarians exist to support. Therefore the investigation into what constitutes the most constructive basis for a leisured society must, for librarians, relate directly to those agencies which provide for the imaginative release of those energies common to all humanity. It must not, for example, deviate into narrowly political, or sociological, or anthropological discussion of abstract principles allegedly responsible for this or that kind of community. Such theories inevitably return to repetition of those tired clichés of the Left about man making himself and the need for cooperative endeavour, or the even more dishonest reassertions of the Right about the freedom of the individual. Imaginative recreation is as important as food or physical recreation; if only the profession could prove that!

Because the librarian is naturally associated with the printed word or its equivalents, then language and its transmission is his prerogative, surely? When it is loudly claimed that the era of the book, that most easily handled parcel of transmitted imagination, is at an end, we ought to be able to define what it is that makes us defend the book, because it is important that our defence is not mere academic self-indulgence. At a time when new electronic media may appear to offer new modes of recreation, it may be worth rehearsing (whether or not the old medium is about to pass away) the consequences of printing, very briefly. We have been so long at the Book Fair, we ought to know what it has done to us.

New Features

We don't have to be virgin pure marxists to accept that the appearance of a materially new commodity may radically change the way in which men see things. Hence the printed book once in being was soon found to need certain new features, like a title page, a contents list, an index, illustrations, clean-cut chapters, headings and subheadings: all the adjuncts of elementary information retrieval. And, above all, a new industry to produce it. What was a unique and laborious process by hand, when processed into an exactly repeatable product in theoretically illimitable quantities demands new skills, new trades, a new mixing of men. The earlier product, created singly for the glory of God is today created by wholly commercial means. More importantly, many more decisions bear upon the product and open the way for other minds than the author's to obtrude on the reader; the entrepreneur is indispensable and the way that publisher-entrepreneurs and editors select and shape the subjects and contents of their commodity alters readers' ways of seeing the world. More subjects, more books at lower cost, wider, more diffuse reading, is possible; a multiplicity of new kinds of book, making all sorts of comparisons take place in the reader's mind. Mental contrasts with other works, reliance on the private inner eye, the sense of up-to-dateness, the pictorialising element, that is, space rendered pictorially, and ideas expressed by diagram.

All these inherent factors made man new in his own image as a reader and thinker, yet tended towards uniformity of reference, the growth of printed conventions, universal, recognised systems of notation, all for economy and convenience. Print, like everything else, was a mixed blessing, yet no revolution in European history has been as fundamental as the one that made the word-in-print the focus of life, personal and public. So the reader, internally noisy, externally silent as he reads, has virtually complete freedom to drown in seas of reading matter, to choke on visual excess, whether reading for pleasure, gossip, to indulge erotic fantasies or primly acquire more information. An invisible public was created and today groups, parties, new ideologies are continually being created through the circum-tradition of printed ephemera.

What has happened to reading? This essay began by suggesting the novel as a criterion by which to judge and take evidence about the inner state of the reading public, or rather, the two reading publics into which our society is now divided, the minority and the majority, the serious and the profane, or the clerks and the laity. There are undoubtedly two such sectors, and we recognise them: for the lay reading public, reading has never been more than a pastime as easily satisfied by other means; for the clerks whose numbers rise with every extension of higher education, reading is becoming a specialised occupation, in fact almost a total occupation.

Critically Important

We are at a stage now critically important for the future of our common language, tradition and for our profession, and it isn't a moment for solemn reappraisal but for excitement. The librarian is the servant of the reading public(s) and he is located socially like everyone else and acutely affected by the changes in reading habits. One such change is in book ownership, and in the context in which reading is done today. Just as the new mechanised processes produced new kinds of books and new kinds of men in time past, so those very books as a concomitant of personal life have always depended on certain economic, material and educational preconditions--the factors which made for that division into two reading publics. As book ownership has been made more possible through intensive industrialisation of the book trade, so the act of reading has itself changed and changes us. The aura of the sacred must have been strong about the book as an object for many years after the first printed book revolution, when the very look and sound, when read aloud, and the whole meaning of the physical object must have transformed the book virtually into an icon.

Today that imagination which was for Coleridge the prime agent of perception, the reading experience, takes place in a specialised framework. The old order produced an upper class readership in country houses, in proprietary libraries, then by extension into the world of cities and of mundane living though the public library movement: each could be described as a stage in the growth of imaginative recreation. The book has emerged from its private world (part of that moral and social order which Mrs. Leavis approves in her Fiction and the Reading Public), but its concomitant authority, once the preserve of the small and influential reading class, has now disintegrated as the class has become diluted by whole generations of intellectual parvenus. Its "authority" is pervasive now, not through the cohesion of one social class, but through institutions and national collections.

Full Circle

In a way we have come full circle, for in the day of the pre-printed book, collections were communally owned. We have evolved from the privileged, private (both words from the same root) library to the days of mass libraries. But--and here is the paradox--the day of the mass library is the day of the specialist. Serious reading today takes place in a specialised environment, either the study or the university library. And our example of the novel finds itself in a curious state either as pastime consumer product or the object of heavy attention by academic specialists. It seems that we must read with heavy seriousness, a kind of drab utility, or be merely diverted. Books are now professional tools; silence and communion with the printed word is now institutionalised.

Where it is still vestigially private, the book has become a paperback, a temporary thing for casual use, disposable. It is a great leveller: Mickey Spillane and Plato are not far apart in the bookshop. Among the young, reading is done to music, like lovemaking; a transistor is at least as likely in the back pocket of jeans as a paperback, and the two are not mutually exclusive since the paperback so readily allows reading anywhere, even in company. In the modern bedsitter or semi the slim row of paperbacks shares a modest corner of the wall with the hi-fi installation.

The new, strictly divisible modes of reading, serious professional and casual amateur, are potent hints about the change in beliefs about the book. The primacy of the book was unquestioned while it gave off a strong whiff of learning, privilege and orthodoxy, but now that it is dispersed into transient amusement or corralled (one might say carrelled) into the campuses of our educational establishments, it has curiously lost its position of authority.

Now there are new competitors about; new shapes and shadows creating new sight lines. The tradition is passing and with it language is turning into something else. The world of language through the printed book is the world modern librarians have inhabited since 1850, and it has been the main agency for transmission of imaginative life, cultural diffusion. We have been its protectors with a total vested interest in it. But from now on that form of cultural diffusion looks like being for mandarins only; in fact for some mandarins the crisis is already imminent, (for example, Ian Robinson's The Survival of English, CUP 1973). If this is a fact and the Word is changing, or turning into Image, then that will affect us in libraries. If we are too anxious to accept the change, to "make it new" (one of the current shibboleths), then will we be accessories to the act of destruction of the traditional Word?

Decline of Confidence

This is not the place to account for the decline of confidence in language. Perhaps we have been too much hypnotised by the tyranny of words in the past in any case, and the demolition work done by the linguistic philosophers and by science--which is quite able to evaluate, describe and prescribe without words--has been salutary. Our experience of the dehumanised language of the caption, the politician and the adman might even make us sigh for an alternative.

What is the significance for librarians? Increasingly the programming of knowledge goes on silently in libraries. The remodelling of libraries which this will entail needs no effort of the imagination to foresee, not only in the physical structures but in the thought structures too. Data banks, as somebody said, are not for browsing. New environment means new men, new modifications in habits of mind and in seeing which will be as radical as at the invention of printing; changes possibly in sensibility. There is some suggestion that reading may have to be taught as a specialist art. What we cannot count on any longer is the supremacy and power of print coming down to us from a controlling tradition which dictated reading and at its most serious level a whole civilisation of inherited meaning and coherence. The leisured, cultured minority no longer holds power; other, broader, coarser even, elements are now in charge--but we are not to lose the point by getting lost in judgments of value at present. The process is what needs bringing to notice. We may as well accept that old idea(l)s about literacy may soon be as dated as the wandering rhapsodists of Homer's day became when writing was invented. The paradox is that in becoming an easy, perhaps facile acquisition, the act of reading is passing into illiteracy at one end of the scale in our leisure society and into an esoteric practice at the other.

What do we do about it? We can see in our own libraries that our techniques are already ahead of our obsolescent philosophy conditioned in a print culture. We need not fear decline--it is not a question of decline--but of rediscovery, finding out the potential of the new instruments of the image-makers. Ponder the word with which we began: imagination, still the clue, and the root word even when it is truncated and used to describe something that the traditionalists fear will impoverish us, namely "image," a vogue word that is already tainted. At least let us try to understand how the new symbols work, the graphic illustrations which do so much to illuminate (!) our days and nights indoors and out. The new stimuli are all a form of display, working by direct arousal of the feelings; they frankly assault us, as do light shows and rock music, a massive form of self-abuse (to take the extreme example).

Feelings are so easily transferred under this form of stimulation, and the distinction is not easy to make between the experience of looking at a travel film and turning the pages of a glossy magazine, yet we can ask why a film which makes such a heavy initial impact does not bear repetition, while print so often does? How much is left in the mind of the viewer the morning after the latest episode of The Mighty Century or Bronowski's Descent of Man, both enormously expensive, consuming quantities of energy, brain and material in their production? Why is listening harder than reading (was it always?)?

There is no space to continue into this territory, exploration of the new means of what almost seems like ecstatic communion, but the need is patent, the obligation professional, to read the signs, the literal signs of the graphic revolution in progress, and make sure of our ground. Is our ownhood due for a change of pronunciation?

That is the question, and it is far from academic.

The above article is reprinted by permission of the author and publisher from New Library World, April 1975, pp. 78-80.

DETENTE ON THE REFERENCE SHELVES?*

Patricia Kennedy Grimsted

The translation and publication by Macmillan of the 30-volume third edition of the Bol'shaia Sovetskaia Entsiklopediia, in association and coordination with the Soviet editors in Moscow, will undoubtedly be cited as one of the most striking manifestations in publishing circles of the expansion of East-West cooperation and trade in the 1970s. Yet, despite the publisher's commendable dedication to the promotion of cross-cultural understanding and to the production of a major new reference tool in English, the multimillion dollar project unfortunately suffers from many of the ills and uncertainties of the policy of dêtente that fostered it.

A general encyclopedia is necessarily a mirror of the culture and civilization of the country that has produced it, and it is rare that the images in such a mirror can be faithfully reproduced abroad in another language without their losing a considerable amount of their reflective power. If the first five English-language volumes and their newly published cumulative index can be judged as a representative sample of the ongoing project, the official Soviet encyclopedia is no exception.

A Foreign Ancestry...

Ironically, publishing circles in the Russian Empire discovered the difficulty of encyclopedia transfer between languages and cultures less than a century ago, when they started preparing a comprehensive general encyclopedia more extensive than any then existing locally.

---

*Reprinted by permission of the author and publisher from Wilson Library Bulletin, June 1975, pp. 728-740.

Initially the St. Petersburg firm of Efron turned to the well experienced Leipzig firm of Brockhaus, which had been producing encyclopedias for over 100 years, and launched a team effort to translate the highly respected 13th edition of the Brockhaus Konversations-Lexikon, which had appeared in 16 volumes between 1882 and 1887. The Russian publishers soon abandoned such simplistic cultural transplantation as would be involved in the direct translation of a general encyclopedia from a foreign language and opted for a completely revised, augmented reference tool more suitable to Russian needs.

Skilled translators rendered many of the German entries into Russian, with statistics and other data carefully updated; leading scholars prepared entries about the Russian Empire. Some articles were translated from other national encyclopedias. The German maps were recast with Russian place names; most of the illustrations were reproduced with translated captions. All entries were realphabetized, and ample cross-references were added.

The end result of these monumental efforts was a comprehensive and efficiently arranged Russian-language reference work of the first magnitude and highest scholarly standards, which ranks beside any in the world of that period. [1] This Brockhaus/Efron production still necessarily remains on the reference shelves of every major Soviet library and research institute and of every research library abroad supporting scholarly studies in the Russian field.

...For a Presumptive Heir

As a comprehensive reference tool the third edition of the Bol'shaia Sovetskaia Entsiklopediia hardly measures up to the standards or quality of its prerevolutionary predecessor. The present article is not the place for a detailed discussion of the relative values of the Brockhaus/Efron encyclopedia or the limitations of the BSE. But what a strange twist of fate that this current heir of a strong Russian encyclopedia tradition was the one chosen for complete translation into English. And the irony becomes more striking when one considers that it is being published in a country that has already seen 15 editions of the Encyclopaedia Britannica (which even commissions Soviet authors for parts of its Soviet coverage), to say nothing of several other distinctive general and specialized encyclopedias, dictionaries, and statistical handbooks indicative of American capacity to produce high-quality reference books.

In contrast to the prerevolutionary Russian effort, the present translation project would almost seem to be a product of a society of abundance, to be sold to the library that already has three or four first-rate encyclopedias, but that must be sold something extra. Those librarians who have received the first five volumes and cumulative index now available should expect many questions and complaints from their readers; they may even begin to wonder whether they have purchased a high-quality, comprehensive modern reference work suitable for an English-language readership.

Alphabet Soup

The American tourist who has difficulty comprehending that the sign PECTOPAH in his Moscow hotel should really be read as RESTORAN (the Russian phonetic adaptation of the French _restaurant_), until he becomes hungry enough to give the long line waiting for tables a try, will readily recognize the problems of dealing with a different alphabet.

Nevertheless, a library reader looking through the first volume of the English edition will undoubtedly be taken aback when after 500 pages of _A_ entries--from _Aalen Stage_ to _Azurite_, including the long entry "Azerbaijdanian SSR"--a remaining hundred pages is found covering the rest of the alphabet from _Babylonian Captivity_ to _Zulu War_. Turning to the second volume, the user will wonder again at 516 pages of _A_ entries from _Aachen Coal Basin_ to _Azuela_, including the long entry "Armenian SSR," 150 pages with entries from _Baader_ to _Byron_, and 37 pages covering _Cabin Atmosphere_ to _Wire Glass_. And then in the fifth volume a reader will be even more perplexed by 408 pages with entries from _Absorption_ to _Upsetting_, 238 pages from _Vagina_ to _Vzmor'ev_, 108 pages from _Wallachian Sheep_ to _Wyspianski_, and a final page with a single _Y_ and two _Z_ entries.

In despair the English-language user looks for an explanation and finds in the small print above the initial list of articles for each volume except the first (and not mentioned there in the foreword, either) the note that the articles in each successive volume of the Russian-language original are translated and realphabetized in English _only within each volume_. Thus the first five volumes now available in English translation essentially cover entries starting with the first three letters of the Cyrillic alphabet.

With such a volume-by-volume translation and exact page and column references to the corresponding original, the reader will have an easy time locating and comparing the original Russian text. And area specialists with a minimum of Russian-language training will be glad to have easy access to an authoritative translation of this basic Soviet reference work.

But whatever the set's merits, the lack of alphabetical order in a 30-volume work consisting predominantly of relatively short specific items is certainly not going to assist any non-Russian-language specialist in finding information about the USSR. It is going to perturb even the most patient student interested in determining "the Soviet point of view" on a given subject. And even the reader who has mastered the Russian language will be lucky to locate a single article by pulling a given volume off the shelf.

No Way Out

Reasons for the choice of format are not difficult to find. There was no easy solution for a publisher wanting to start the project before the Soviet third edition was completed. When the translation project began in April 1972, only eight volumes of the Russian third edition had appeared (the first volume was published in 1970), and the entire 30-volume original Soviet edition is not scheduled for completion before 1978. To await completion of the Russian-language version and then to realphabetize over 100, 000 entries before printing and binding would have involved an eight- to ten-year delay. Macmillan obviously was not prepared to make the kind of investment required by the project without being able to market any portion of it.

The Soviet editors could not have been expected to furnish advance copy from later volumes, since even if the articles were completed, the editors might be required to make updatings or remove some entries in the ensuing five years. And had the American editors delayed publication they would have been faced with the requirement of updating articles from earlier volumes if they wanted to avoid a ten-year spread in the date of preparation of items within any given English-alphabetized volume. Hence the decision for a volume-by-volume translation, with English alphabetical order provided only within individual volumes, and separate cumulative indexes after each five volumes.

From the standpoint of libraries and reference users, the solution is hardly a satisfactory one. Not only is the result a less-than-efficient reference tool, but it is one whose full utilization must await completion. The Russian-language reader using the BSE in May 1975 knew not to expect any entries after the letter O. But not knowing the Russian language or the classification system used by the Soviet editors, the English-language user will have no idea whether a given subject will be covered until the final cumulated index can be consulted--not promised by Macmillan until approximately 1980 (barring any publication delays).

Nowhere in the preface to the first volume or in any of the promotional literature is this problem mentioned or explained. Nowhere in any of the five English-language volumes is the reader advised that the index volume must be consulted before proceeding. Reference librarians would be well advised to post the sign "Consult Index First" or affix one to the cover of each volume.

For Specialists and Generalists

One of the major selling points of the American publisher for this English-language translation is that it provides a "wealth of information about the USSR and its peoples that has been previously unavailable in English." Comprehensive reference works on the USSR are at the most scant and at their best outdated for present-day purposes.

Compared with the general 626-page *Concise Encyclopaedia of Russia*, edited by S. V. Utechin (N. Y., Dutton, 1961) and the 624-page *McGraw-Hill Encyclopedia of Russia and the Soviet Union*, edited by Michael T. Florinsky (N. Y., 1961), certainly more "information," *qua* information, will be available in the Macmillan translation of the BSE. With due accounting for publication lags, these reference works are now 15 years out of date and in their size and compass leave much to be desired. Products of the cold war era, they reflect a distinctly Western, often anti-Soviet point of view; because of this, however, they include coverage of a number of leading Soviet personalities and events that are excluded from the BSE.

It will indeed be helpful for many libraries to have available in English many BSE articles for both their factual content and their presentation of the Soviet point of view. The lengthy coverage of many of the lesser-known areas or peoples of the USSR would certainly not be duplicated in any general or even specialized Western encyclopedia. Many of the BSE articles are signed by the most distinguished Soviet scholars, and their availability in smooth English translation to many non-Russian readers is a tremendous advantage for specialists and non-specialists alike.

Some Missing Persons

Non-Russian-speaking librarians and readers should understand, however, that because this official Soviet encyclopedia is being translated exactly as it appears in the Russian edition, without any editorial comment or modifications, there will be certain limitations they might not expect. One only has to recall the now-famous publisher's instruction to subscribers of the BSE second edition to replace carefully pages 20-24 of the fifth volume (the sheets that included a large biography and portrait of L. P. Beriia) with a new set of pages that included a whole page of pictures of icebergs, etc., in the Bering Sea, to realize that from a Western point of view, coverage of all personalities and events may not be as comprehensive as Western reference users might wish.

To be sure, Beriia's name has not been restored to the third edition; hence it does not appear in the English translation. Nor does one find the name of V. S. Abakumov, the Minister of State Security from 1946 to 1952, or L. L. Averbach, the literary critic and infamous leader of the staunch Communist literary organization RAPP, who was purged in the 1930s.

Other more prominent disgraced Soviet leaders such as Trotskii, Bukharin, Kamenev, Zinoviev--as well as Beriia himself--will all be treated amply in general Western encyclopedias such as the Britannica, so their omission from the BSE (and English translation) will not prove to be so much of an inconvenience.

However, the value of the BSE biographies for lesser-known Soviet personalities is underscored by the fact that even before Macmillan started its mammoth translation enterprise, the U.S. government's Joint Publications Research

Service had been issuing the series Contemporary Biographies from the Large Soviet Encyclopedia, which by 1973 included English-language translations of the biographical data from the first nine volumes of the BSE. Regrettably, however, these publications were discontinued after Macmillan acquired exclusive rights to publication in English. [2]

All the Facts that Fit

Aside from the problems of omission of biographies of disgraced personalities, there are many other drawbacks in the factual content and presentation that will leave reference users unsatisfied. A comprehensive English-language gazetteer covering the Soviet Union would be a welcome addition to reference collections, particularly if it were to identify precise alternate spelling, foreign language renditions, and official changes of geographical nomenclature. [3] The BSE provides a wealth of gazetteer-type entries; but these never cite latitude and longitude, fail to provide precise local-language variants, and are often vague about previous names and dates. And in the coverage of the western areas incorporated into the USSR during World War II, the BSE rarely provides their previous foreign-language designation, official status, and territorial divisions.

Equally frustrating, these users will be disappointed to find only vague references to Soviet production statistics in the articles on many industrial and agricultural products. There are no exact figures for Soviet production of such metals as aluminum, for example, although published statistics for foreign production--readily available in other sources--are furnished. Furthermore, Western economists often find they cannot rely on the Soviet statistical data that are given.

Many of the historical articles will obviously be of more interest to English-language readers for their interpretive rather than factual content; but factual limitations often make them a poor source for reference use. For example, in the article on Alaska the reader will find almost nothing about the problems or extent of activities of Russian traders in Alaska (which one might hope to find in a Russian source). The user will, however, be treated to an appraisal (that may warm the hearts of American conservationists, but has limited factual content) of developments after the United States purchased Alaska--to the effect that "American capitalists embarked on rapacious exploitation of its national wealth. The native population ... was subjected to cruel oppression and doomed to gradual extinction" (Vol. I, p. 195).

Granted there is considerable factual historical data in the Soviet encyclopedia that is not readily accessible in Western encyclopedia sources (proportionately less, however, than in the prerevolutionary Brockhaus/Efron). Nevertheless, the frequent substitution of propagandistic overtones for precise statistics and comprehensive factual background raises questions about the suitability of the GSE as a fundamental reference source for study and research on the USSR.

Good Intentions...

One can only applaud the aim of the American publisher, who wants to provide "a richer knowledge and understanding of the contemporary Soviet Union," and indeed the reopening of trading possibilities heightens the need for information on the part of American economic and business specialists involved in manufacturing and commerical ventures in the USSR.

Capsule treatment of key Soviet economic terms, often found in an encyclopedia, could be helpful, for example, for an American banking official to have on hand. But what banker, with little time for research, is going to think of looking under such varied articles as "Advance Payment," "Absolute Rent," "Anarchy of Production," "Assets Volume in Bookkeeping," or "Detailed Cost Register?" Given the arrangement of entries in the BSE, and the difficulty of locating them through the index in the English translation, it would be much more appropriate to furnish the banker with a translation of an elementary Soviet economics textbook and a specialized, well indexed, cross-referenced glossary of Soviet economic terminology.

The American publisher has good reason to claim that in addition to its factual content the Soviet encyclopedia has as one of its prime values "its consistent statement of the Soviet point of view." But did the publisher and advisors stop to ask themselves seriously if, by presenting the materials in the Anglicized format they devised, with all the organizational problems inherent in the Soviet encyclopedia itself, they were going to succeed in adequately conveying this point of view with clarity, consistency, and comprehensibility to English-language reference users?

Thus if readers would like to find out the Soviet point of view on the Vietnam war, they will have to know that in addition to the long article on the country under "Vietnam" in Volume V, they will have to turn to a first-volume article on the war entitled "American Aggression in Vietnam." Even if they succeed in locating it in the first place (without the guidance of cross-references), they will be disappointed to find that the article has not been updated beyond 1969.

Although the fifth-volume "Vietnam" article was obviously prepared in 1971 on the basis of predominantly earlier publications, the editors indicate the subsection South Vietnam has been updated. But a comparison with the Russian original reveals that the only updating beyond 1971 events is the addition of a final sentence: "An agreement to end the war and restore peace in Vietnam was signed in Paris on Jan. 27, 1973."

Such inconsequential updatings will hardly satisfy librarians, who will invariably query the provisions for keeping information current.

A Coming Data Gap?

The American publisher mentions in the introduction that its Soviet colleagues have updated some articles for the English translation. A comparison of texts reveals, however, that such indications are few and far between (for example, in the fourth volume only a single entry--the historical survey of Bhutan--is marked updated by the editors) and relatively inconsequential, bearing in mind the time lag involved until the whole set will be completed.

For their Russian readers the editors of the BSE produce a separate Supplement on the USSR and an annual yearbook.[4] So far Macmillan has not announced any plans to translate and publish the ongoing yearbooks or supplements in English, although obviously the data contained would be more current. The gaps will become more noticeable because even before the publication of the final cumulative index--which will ensure the full utilization of the early volumes of the encyclopedia--the early volumes will already be a decade out of date.

Puzzling Omissions

The English-language editors state that only one per

cent of the Soviet text is omitted in the translated version, but if they are translating 99 per cent, why cause possible confusion at all by omitting a handful of articles? How does one justify the omission of the article on the French West India Company versus the inclusion of the entry "Dutch West India Company." And why should the city of "Worcester" in South Africa be included while the slightly longer coverage of the cities of Worcester in Great Britain and Massachusetts were dropped? In the fields of natural science, mathematics, and engineering, the editors have seen fit to cut a considerable number of short technical articles from the translated edition. Understandably the general reader or high school student would have little cause to turn to the encyclopedia in these fields.

But if a stated aim of the editors is to picture the development and achievements of Soviet science, then why omit any articles at all? And even more important, if the extensive scientific content of the BSE is to be included as part of the "complete" translated version, the editors should have clarified their exclusion policy.

Even more frustrating in scientific fields, the awkward arrangement of overlapping entries and lack of cross-referencing between short articles will only serve to deter science teachers from sending students to this source.

For example, although almost all of the group of ammonium entries have been dropped in translation, the very short article "Ammonium Nitrate" is retained. It explains that two types of this compound are used in explosives and one is widely used as a fertilizer in the USSR. But since the cross-references of the Russian edition are omitted, the reader does not know to go back to the preceding entry, "Ammonites," covering the explosives, or to the other cited article, "Nitrogenous Fertilizers," an entry of over a page of text with bibliography, which appears much later in the same volume.

No Way In

Quite understandably the editors have decided to drop many short articles that provide mainly dictionary-type definitions. However, this policy, coupled with the deleting of cross-referencing (which will be discussed further below), leads to other difficulties. Some small entries, while not vitally important in and of themselves in the original Russian edition, provide a "way in" to other entries for the readers and a key to help them locate related articles or fuller explanations of the subject.

A case in point is the entry for Abacus, which, according to a list of entries at the beginning of Volume I, was not translated. However, a reader familiar with computation techniques in Soviet shops, whereby a cashier will rely on the abacus despite the existence of total and subtotal buttons on the cash register, may wonder why this entry would be dropped in English. This omission becomes understandable with reference to the Russian edition because, in fact, the original entry provides only a dictionary-type definition of the word abacus as used in Latin and Greek, etc., and refers the reader to the entry Schety (the Russian word for abacus) for coverage of the use of the abacus in the USSR.

One can only wonder how the English-language editors will deal with the title for the article about schety when they come to the S volume. (A page and a half, with illustrations, was devoted to it in the second edition of the BSE.) Certainly there is no other word for it in English but abacus. But the English reader consulting the article list for the first volume has already found that the entry has been dropped.

No Maps, No Photographs

From the standpoint of reference use and visual understanding, much more serious than the exclusion of a few minor articles is the omission from the translated volumes of virtually all the maps and illustrative materials in the Russian edition, except for a few black-and-white line drawings.

Pictures accompany a large percentage of the biographical entries in the original (especially of Soviet personalities). Furthermore, there are abundant illustrations for other kinds of articles, which would be especially useful in helping the English-language reader have a better visual sense of the USSR, its land, peoples, and cultural development, and hence to perceive the official Soviet point of view. The maps that accompany the original articles on many local regions in the Soviet Union, and especially the elaborate maps that accompany the major articles on the Soviet republics, are a significant reference contribution. They are badly needed to elucidate many articles, even if the expense of recasting them with transliterated place names would have added to Macmillan's cost.

Translation Quality--First-Rate

The actual translation of the material is on the whole to be commended from a linguistic standpoint. Macmillan has brought together a high-level group of well qualified translators, and the result of their efforts is usually a smooth idiomatic English. A spot check reveals a high standard of translation and a consistent devotion to preserving the exact tone and meaning of the original. Problems arise, however, because often the literal translation does not prove meaningful to a non-Russian reader. This is most serious in article titles, where occasionally the attempt to preserve the literal rendering of the Russian results in severe confusion.

For what reader, anxious to find the most extensive treatment in the encyclopedia on labor problems in the capitalist world, could be expected to consult a two-page article entitled "Absolute and Relative Deterioration of the Proletariat's Situation?" Understandably this awkward article title (the English translation is faithful to the Russian) proves too much for the index. The article's general importance is not indicated either under the index entries of LABOR or LABOR MOVEMENTS, neither of which even carries *see also* references to the shorter index entry PROLETARIAT, where the article in question is cited as a subentry with the understandably altered heading of ECONOMIC DETERIORATION.

Another entry example, "American Trotter," is a literal translation from the Russian, but without so much as a reference in the article to the common American name Standardbred for that breed of horse. (It is listed as such in the *Encyclopedia Americana*, although the *Encyclopaedia Britannica* uses the designation American Standardbred.) In the case of the entry "American Monitor Lizard," the translator helpfully adds a parenthetical note that it is the Russian name for the Teiidae family of lizards. (Indeed the *Britannica* explains under its Monitor Lizard entry that such creatures have not been known in America since the Eocene epoch, 35-65 million years ago!) But in the first cumulative index the reader looking under Teiidae (lizard fam.) finds no page citation, but merely is told *see* AMERICAN MONITOR LIZARD.

The real fault in such relatively minor cases lies not so much with the American editors or even with their Soviet counterparts, who were merely perpetuating established Russian usage. Rather, such instances are illustrative of the basic difficulty of attempting to translate directly a general encyclopedia from one language to another.

Encyclopedia or Conglomerate?

The discussion above has already suggested some of the content limitations that are to be found in the *Great Soviet Encyclopedia* and a few of the shortcomings that might lead librarians to question some of the claims in the publisher's foreword and in the sales promotion materials. But the commendable purposes of the publishers and the factual and cultural contribution of a translated version of the *BSE* are further impaired by other technical and organizational problems that face the user of the English version.

The organizing principle by which the Soviet editors have broken down major subjects into a diverse and overlapping proliferation of short entries renders these parts of the coverage difficult to use even for the Russian-language reader consulting the original. For example, English-language readers might be interested in the Soviet treatment of airplanes or the general subject of aviation, but the proliferation and awkward arrangement of articles proves to be a labyrinth through which the index hardly begins to guide the reader.

The Indispensable Index...

Encyclopedia users in general may expect to have to use an index more often when they are searching for complicated entries or obscure subjects; indeed the new organizing principle for the 15th edition of the *Encyclopaedia Britannica* is forcing further reliance on indexing and cross-referencing. But with the Soviet encyclopedia, even when the whole set is completed, the reader is going to have to consult the index before looking up the most simple and straightforward item. And this is even more perturbing because much of the potential reference use of this encyclopedia will undoubtedly involve the identification of relatively short Soviet biographical, institutional, and geographical entries that would not be covered in other reference sources.

Aeronautics
aerodynamic control surfaces, 5-2c
aerostation, 5-2d
aircraft modeling, 1-175b
aviation medicine, 1-531b
design advances of 1930's, 1-527c
first flight attempts by man, 1-525b
jet propulsion design, 1-528d
pressure suit, 5-324c
United States
American Rocket Society, 1-399a
USSR
Antonov, O. K., 2-182b
aviation insts., 1-531a
Beriev, G. M., 3-192b
Biushgens, G. S., 4-31c
Bondariuk, M. M., 3-452b
wind tunnel, 2-700d

Aerospace industry
capitalist monopolies, 1-125c
capitalist monopolies *(table)*, 1-126a
noble metals, 3-729c
--by country:, 1-1a
France, 1-125c
German FR, 1-125c
Great Britain, 1-125c
Italy, 1-125d
Japan, 1-125c
United States, 1-125c
American Telephone and Telegraph Co., 1-340a
see also Aviation industry
Aerospace monopolies in the capitalist world, 1-125c
(table), 1-126a

Air transport, 5-21b
airports, 2-69a
airway, 1-176b
Atlantic Ocean routes, 2-470b
automated facilities, 1-503a
passenger traffic, 5-151b
--by country:, 1-111a
Afghanistan, 2-35d
Algeria, 1-260d
Argentina, 2-285c
Armenian SSR, 2-335c
Australia, 1-433d
Austria, 1-457d
Azerbaijan SSR, 1-564a
Belgium, 3-124c
Bulgaria, 3-565a
Burma, 3-598a
Great Britain, 4-291b
USSR
Aeroflot, 1-529b
airways, 1-176c
arctic regions, 2-271a
military, 5-287a
terminals, 2-69d
Vietnam DR, 5-445d

Airfield, 2-68a
pavement, 2-68c
Airfield pavement, 2-68c
Airmobile troops (Amer. mil. units), 2-69a
Airplanes
amphibious, 1-358b
automatic pilot, 1-485b
carrier-based aircraft, 1-594a
engines, 1-174a
historical development, 1-525b, 525c
jet propulsion, 1-528b
USSR, 1-530c
military, 1-646b
passenger aircraft *(table)*, 1-529b
training aircraft, 1-529c
see also Jet airplanes; Piston-engined airplanes; Seaplanes
Airports, 2-69a
air terminal, 2-69c
France
Le Bourget (Paris), 4-401d
hangar, 1-622b
see also Airfields
Aviation, 1-525b
aircraft modeling, 1-175b
airfield facilities, 2-68a
artificial air, 5-10b
aviation insts., 1-531a
aviation medicine, 1-531b
USSR
Aviatsiia i kosmonavtika (jour.), 1-532b
famous aviators and flights, 1-527a
see also Aeronautics; Aircraft; Civil aviation; Military aviation; Supersonic aviation
Aviation industry, 1-530a
capitalist countries
production 1963 *(table)*, 1-530d
--by country:, 1-111a
Brazil, 3-535b
Great Britain, 4-289b
monopolies, 4-287d
Russia and Russian SFSR
Bolkhovitinov, V. F., 3-424c
USSR, 1-526d
All-Union Inst. of Aviation Materials, 1-283b
Aviation medicine, 1-531b
aviation psychology, 1-532a
Bárány chair, 2-638d

Be your own index analyst. *A selection of entries from the index relating to aviation. Should there be, for example, some* see also *references under* Air Transport? *Should a choice have been made between* Aeronautics *and* Aviation, *with all subentries under one or the other?*

Can the busy reference librarian ask a telephone inquirer to wait for a search of the interim cumulative index and then the volumes indicated in the hope of finding the information requested in the volumes now available? Obviously, the librarian will first consult another source. Librarians are expert in using indexes; but are contemporary American students going to take the time for this type of search, when they can turn to other encyclopedias that list their material in alphabetical order? And will teachers insist on the Great Soviet Encyclopedia when they come to recognize the difficulties involved?

The index that Macmillan has created is the result of a monumental effort, and its computer program should doubtless provide much interest for similar large-scale reference works necessitating the printing of a series of cumulative indexes. The four-column 203-page fine-print name and subject index is obviously the essential key to finding one's way through the first five volumes. All articles are included as separate index items, and the breakdown into two levels of subentries avoids long strings of citations under a given entry. The addition of parenthetical explanatory phrases following most main entries is a helpful key where so many of the names and terms will be unfamiliar to the English-speaking user. Citations are printed clearly and include references to the quadrant of the page in addition to the volume and page number.

So far so good. Unfortunately, however, the deficiencies of the initial cumulative index are so many that the editors should seriously consider redesigning it. Only a few of the most salient problems can be mentioned here.

Indispensable, But Flawed

One inconvenience that strikes the user at once is that there is rarely the possibility of determining whether an index citation refers to a separate article or merely to a reference within an article. The preface explains that in cases where there is more than one citation under a given entry, the separate article is always indicated first. Given the index format, however, there are few such cases, and with this system no indications are possible in the case of subentries, which make up the essential bulk of the index. Furthermore, since only the start of an entry is cited, there is no indication of the extent of coverage of the subject or length of the article if a separate one. Hence the reader has no way of determining which of a series of subentries might prove the most fruitful starting point.

Particularly frustrating, given the proliferation of short entries and general difficulties of the organizational structure of the encyclopedia, is the index's falling short of optimal cross-referencing and multiple citing of article titles under subject headings or entries recognizable to the English-language reader.

Under WORLD WAR II, for example, there is no sub-entry for USSR or clue that one must consult the many

Revolution of 1848
Bakunin, M. A., **2**-560b
--*by country*:, **1**-111a
Austria, **1**-451d
Academic Legion, **1**-44c
France
Barbès, A., **2**-642b
Blanc, L., **3**-357b
Marx examines, **5**-109d
Germany
Baden-Pfalz Uprising, **2-536a**
Hungary, **4**-373c
Batthyány, L., **3**-69b
Revolution of 1905-07, 4-321b
All-Russian Railroad Union, **5-27c**
anarchism, **1**-389c
Armenia, **2**-327c
Baltic Fleet, **2**-603d
Bolshevik agrarian program, **1-145d**
Bolshevik military and combat **orgs.**, **5**-253a
Bolshevik press legalized, **3-432b**
Buriatia rebels, **4**-193b
fighting *druzhinas*, **3-674c**
Lenin evaluates, **5-330d**
Milestones criticism, **4-408a**
military press established, **5-275b**
Vladivostok uprisings, **5-540d**
Revolutionary Art of the Ukraine, Assoc. of (1925-32), **2-414b**

citations under GREAT PATRIOTIC WAR (as the Russian phase of the war is called in Soviet usage); there is a see also reference to this latter main entry following all the separate subentries by country. Under the GREAT PATRIOTIC WAR entry, however, there is no cross-reference to WORLD WAR II and hence no indication that the user should also see the completely different citations given there.

A subentry GERMANY is to be found under both WORLD WAR II and GREAT PATRIOTIC WAR, but the 13 citations under the former repeat only two of the eight citations under the latter, with no apparent rationale for the inclusions or exclusions.

Another series of perplexing problems confront the reader who might want to locate information on the Russian Revolution. There are entries for the REVOLUTION OF 1848 and REVOLUTION OF 1905-07, but no further reference in the Revolution section to 1917. Since there are no cross-references under either REVOLUTION or OCTOBER REVOLUTION, what English reader will know that one must look under G for GREAT OCTOBER SOCIALIST REVOLUTION to find citations for 23 subentries? Then if one happens to check under RUSSIAN HISTORY, one will find a subentry titled OCTOBER REVOLUTION AND CIVIL WAR PERIOD with 28 sub-subentries, including a separate one, OCTOBER REVOLUTION, which actually gives the pages of the main article, GREAT OCTOBER SOCIALIST REVOLUTION. But only three of the 23 subentries that are listed under the main entry are repated under the subentry OCTOBER REVOLUTION AND CIVIL WAR PERIOD, again with no seeming rationale.

Great October Socialist Revolution (1917), **4**-319c
All Power to the Soviets!, **5-24c**
anarchism, **1-389d**
Archives of the Russian Revolution (jour.) (1921-37), **2-266c**
armed forces, **5**-37b
Aurora (cruiser), **1-427c**
Baltic Fleet, **2-604a**
Bolshevik press role, **3**-432a
bourgeoisie liquidated, **4-44b**

This lack of meaningful structure--too often found in computer-based indexes--leaves one wondering if sufficient editorial attention was given to the creation of an adequate subject authority file. Such an underlying flaw unfortunately would be an exceedingly difficult and expensive one to remedy.

For Lack of a Cross-Reference...

A transliteration table (using a modified Library of Congress system) is provided at the beginning of each volume and the index. But when divergent spellings are used or alternate English-language versions are common, it would be helpful to have more cross-references. Thus the encyclopedia has adopted the spelling _Byelorussia_ (following U.N. usage) instead of _Belorussia_, as appropriate to the LC system, without any cross-reference from the latter form. In this instance it also might have been appropriate to include a cross-reference from the alternate English-language variant, _White Russia_. Although this latter form is usually disapproved by specialists, it is the official subject and corporate entry still used by LC (following the U.S. Board on Geographic Names).

An index citation is given under TCHAIKOVSKY, P. I. (Russ. comp.), but since the reader is instructed that the LC transliteration system is used predominantly, should not there at least be a cross-reference under _Chaikovskii_? To cite an opposite example, the entry ARKHANGEL'SK faithfully follows the LC transliteration system; but there is no cross-reference from Archangel, the more common English spelling of the city. Some of these index deficiencies, one hopes, can be corrected by the time the final cumulated index is prepared.

...The Subject Is Lost

But whatever the other faults in the organization and conception of the English-language index, one of the most grievous is that it is being given a task that it cannot possibly perform, namely, to serve the function of cross-references within the texts of articles.

The Russian-language _BSE_ has an elaborate system of cross-references within the text or at the end of articles, but in the volumes published so far all of these are omitted in the English translation and are not consistently picked up in the index. Of course the cross-references would be hard to use in the English edition because they would still have to be located by means of an index, due to the lack of re-alphabetization throughout the set. And the American editors might not be sure of the appropriate title of an article in a future volume not yet translated. But if anything, when translated into English many of the articles need more, not fewer, cross-references to make them accessible.

Less Than the Sum of Its Parts

Given the Macmillan decision to proceed with a volume-by-volume translation, the English-language index is obviously the key to using the translated version of the BSE. The extent to which the American editors are able to improve the index format and increase access to the multiplicity of awkwardly organized and entitled articles will be the most important determining factor in the potential utility of the whole project. Such refinements as the expansion of the index to include more cross-references, restructuring of the basic subject authority file, and inclusion of the more common English equivalents for many of the awkward article titles would indeed be welcome improvements. Yet would these really compensate for the basic organizational problems and reference limitations of the Soviet encyclopedia itself?

There is no question but that some of the interpretive contributions and factual content--particularly the biographical, geographical, and institutional entries covering the USSR--are worth presenting in English and are a valuable addition to the meager sources available. But when one starts to reflect on the problems and limitations, one keeps wondering if the costly translation of the entire encyclopedia is really the most satisfactory answer to the still lingering reference needs in the field.

The problems of using the Russian edition will prove minor in comparison with the problems of using the translation for the non-Russian reader. So much so in fact, that it would be hard to justify its purchase by those libraries that do not already possess or consider purchasing the original third edition in Russian (available at less than one quarter the cost of the Macmillan translation). Obviously

Macmillan is not providing a general encyclopedia suitable for most school and public libraries. And the cause of cross-cultural understanding is hardly well served by a translated encyclopedia in which so much of the content is so difficult to locate.

One is left with a certain sense of tragedy and despair at the apparent waste involved in the massive project undertaken by Macmillan to make the official Soviet encyclopedia available to English-speaking readers. The United States has recently seen such severe cutbacks in funds available for support of research, libraries, and other facilities in the field of Russian, East European, and Soviet studies that it is a shame to see such a large-scale, well intentioned project beset with so many glaring problems at the outset.

The era of détente may see a 30-volume English-language version of the BSE added to many library reference collections. But will the Macmillan version last as long or prove as valuable to researchers in the long run as the Brockhaus/Efron effort undertaken before the Russian Revolution and before the computer revolution brought so many new possibilities for information storage, printing, and indexing techniques?

Worthy as may be Macmillan's aim to present English-language readers with "The World of Today (and Tomorrow) Through Soviet Eyes," the result of their multimillion-dollar, decade-long effort may unfortunately prove difficult for many librarians to justify in terms of the expense and space required on their reference shelves.

Notes

1. The first volume of Entsiklopedicheskii slovar appeared in 1890; the 41-volume production (in 82 parts) was completed by 1904, with supplements in 1906 and 1907.

   For publication details about Russian general encyclopedias, see the pamphlet by I. M. Kaufman, Russkie entsiklopedii--Vol. 1: Obshchie entsiklopedii. Bibliografiia i kratkie ocherki. Moscow, 1960, 103p. Summary details in French are in M. Seydoux, "Les encyclopédies générales russes: Essai bibliographique," Cahiers du monde russe et soviétique, 6:245-63, 1965.

2. All nine of the volumes are available from the National Technical Information Service, Springfield, VA 22151; \$4.25 each, except for Vols. 3, 4, and 9, which are \$4.75. Also, NTIS can supply biographies from the BSE yearbooks--1971 (\$12) and 1972 (\$6.25).
3. The official gazetteer of the U.S. Board on Geographic Names is limited to current usage and simply lists place names with technical latitudinal and longitudinal locations; the 1952 Columbia Lippincott Gazetteer is dated and incomplete for the Soviet Union and fails in most cases to indicate precise or alternate local names.
4. The two previous editions of the USSR Supplement (Vol. 50) of the BSE second edition were also published in official German translations. An unacknowledged abridged translation of this volume is available in English under the title Information USSR, edited by Robert Maxwell: New York/Oxford, Pergamon, 1962, 982p.

TOWARD A NATIONAL PLAN TO NOURISH RESEARCH IN CHILDREN'S LITERATURE*

Frances Henne

The widespread interest in, and manifold activities relating to, study and research in children's literature, make even more apparent the need for systematic planning in research libraries for the acquisition and use of resources in this area. Too long and too often left to chance, to haphazard or spasmodic acquisition procedures, to dependence on gifts of donors or sample copies from publishers, or to miserable amounts in the allotment of funds, the development of children's collections in research libraries is now beginning to assume its rightful place. It is finally receiving the serious consideration and respect that heretofore has usually been accorded only to materials in the traditional branches of knowledge.

A brief enumeration of the many types of collections of children's literature now in research libraries provides a background for the discussion that follows on recommended planning among and within these libraries. Children's literature is defined in its broadest sense, covering books, films, magazines, tapes, and resources in other formats that have been published or produced for children of all ages, including young adults.

What Do Research Libraries Collect?

Collections of children's literature in special research libraries tend to be historical, although those with certain defined interests, such as a geographical area, a religion,

---

*Reprinted by permission of the author and publisher from Wilson Library Bulletin, October 1975, pp. 131-137. Copyright © 1975 by The H. W. Wilson Company.

an ethnic culture, or an art form, have both historical and recent items related to their specializations.

The collections in public research libraries vary in scope, nature, and location. Many of these libraries have historical collections (generally housed in rare book departments or their equivalent in the central children's room); others have materials which may also include modern items. These libraries, of course, also have the extensive resources of their children's departments, for use not only by children but also by adults working with children or doing research in children's literature.

In university research libraries, a like diversity prevails. In these institutions the requirements and needs of the users are in some ways more precisely defined than in either the special or public research library. Materials must be provided for courses in library science, education, and other disciplines.

Since many students taking introductory courses in children's literature do not have even a rudimentary knowledge of books and other materials in this field, the university library must provide a basic collection designed for children and young adults and keep it up-to-date. (A recently suggested basic collection[1] provides helpful suggestions for book titles, but it should be kept in mind that this is a minimal list.) Often no adequate provision has been made for the formation, development, and maintenance of such a collection. In addition supplementary materials--both historical and contemporary--must be made accessible for the research requirements of faculty and students.

No single pattern prevails for housing these collections in academic research libraries: Some items are in the rare book or special collections, while other not so rare materials may form a separate historical collection. Working collections frequently are part of a school or departmental library--usually connected with the library science or education studies--although some subject divisional libraries may also have related children's materials.

College libraries have, or should have, collections for children's literature and other courses. Historical or other special collections of children's literature, in some cases quite notable ones, can frequently be found in public, academic, state, museum, association, and other libraries that are not strictly classified as research libraries. Nor are school libraries to be totally ignored in this picture, for a few, at least, have some special collections or rare items.

In all the libraries mentioned above, examples can be found where the scope of materials in a collection is shaped by one or more factors. These factors include geographical origin of publication or production, language, time span or range, subject, and literary form (e.g., poetry, folklore, or textbooks). These collections are housed, arranged, and administered in a variety of ways. ("Memorial rooms" in libraries are not uncommon.)

Resources for Research

In building collections in research libraries there has been a tendency to consider acquisition of resources in children's literature in terms of rare materials, with rarity generally determined by age, uniqueness, condition, or monetary value of the item. In the total picture the strength of existing collections is historical in nature, with emphasis on eras prior to the twentieth century. Some areas important for research are poorly represented, if at all. (Since scarcity is surely one significant element determining rarity, many of these resources can be classified as rare!)

Those of us interested in the popular-culture facets of children's literature know the difficulty of finding in research libraries or on the market (with usually inflated prices when located) innumerable titles in the following categories: series books published before the middle of the twentieth century, comic books that are ten or more years old, early Disney items, books with movable parts of all vintages, McLoughlin books, and those of comparable mass market publishers.

Most of these and other works librarians customarily have never deigned to acquire, but such materials have been enormously popular with children. These materials represent fruitful and, in some instances, popular areas for research and should be included in the collections of research libraries.

In addition many titles become outmoded and are discarded or worn out and not replaced. Since a large number of children's books are not reviewed, they go out of print without ever reaching library shelves. Numerous titles, even well reviewed ones that have been published during the last two decades and earlier, go out of print for one reason or another and are difficult to locate. Finding these materials can be an arduous undertaking and often an unsuccessful one.

Developing historical collections of films, slides, filmstrips, and other audiovisual materials produced for children, or locating them for research purposes, presents problems that at best can be called challenging.

Any book, film, game, textbook, magazine, programmed instruction, advertisement, or other item designed for children carries within it the potential of being a resource for the scholar working now or in the future. The vast array of materials for children available today constantly attracts the attention of many inquirers interested in evaluating and analyzing these resources for their quality, usefulness, treatment of some theme, attitude, idea, or subject. Access to all these materials is not as easy as one might expect, a situation that needs rectifying.

Planning a Research Collection

The broad scope and range of materials, both retrospective and contemporary, make it evident that no single research library can or should attempt to build definitive collections of all types of children's literature; and that planning among these libraries is essential not only to avoid pointless duplication (and competition, too), but also to assure the systematic acquisition of resources for courses and research.

If a major objective of research libraries is to make available resources for study and research, then the whole spectrum of children's literature must be represented in some form of planned arrangement. This spectrum includes historical collections (all materials not now on the market), contemporary collections of materials currently available and published in the U.S., and such materials issued in other countries.

Making or assisting plans for the provision of children's collections for research and evaluation has been of concern and interest to many librarians over the years.

These include the American Association of School Librarians, with its recommendations for creating national and regional centers and a bibliographic apparatus for children's resources[2]; the Children's Services Division of ALA, through the activities of Carolyn Field[3] and the National Planning Committee for Special Collections describing and locating subject collections of children's literature; Ann Heidbreder and others involved in the Educational Media Selection Centers Project, directed toward the establishment of resource and evaluation centers; and James Fraser, with his study of collections of foreign language children's books[4] and his proposals for a national plan.[5]

Some Recommendations for Resource-Sharing

At this stage some recommendations for further planning relating to children's literature resources in research libraries are in order.

Academic libraries must provide an adequate collection of recommended resources for children's literature students and for teachers, social service specialists, psychologists, and any others working with children. Indeed it is difficult to think of any university department that would not have students or faculty members interested in exploring children's resources in their special field and who would not make use of this collection.

This working collection could be provided for the study of children's literature rather than for pure research, although its resources would be useful for some research purposes. Any academic library without an adequate collection of this type should take appropriate measures to acquire one. The study of children's literature represents an important and essential part of the university's disciplines, and materials must be available for its pursuit. Dependence on public and school library collections is not the answer to the university's obligation in this area.

For the requirements of research and the evaluation of resources, definitive collections of children's literature published and produced in the U.S. and currently available should be planned and made accessible in regional centers. (The number of current items published and produced in other countries that should be included in the centers requires careful planning, too.) These centers could also serve as depositories for materials that go out of print. In individual states smaller collections of current materials are needed so that librarians, teachers, parents, and others can examine them, see their uses demonstrated, and thereby get assistance in selecting resources. Pennsylvania has four centers of this type and is planning two more; examples can also be found in some other states. In both kinds of centers any equipment or technological apparatus required could also be available for examination and demonstration.

The many details connected with planning these proposed centers cannot be summarized briefly. Descriptions of their objectives, services, administration, plus bibliographic control, networking, and other features are presented in a publication originated and designed by the Educational Media Selection Centers Project.[6] Here, it is relevant to note that research librarians should be aware of the proposals for these centers and should participate in their future planning and implementation.

One or more regional centers could profitably be located in a university research library. The University of Chicago library, for example, with its Center for Children's Books and the resources of the Center for Research Libraries approaches this goal in the case of U.S. children's books. In any national plans LC would be a key resource for materials, bibliographic apparatus, and networking. Networking plans now being advanced, including those of the National Commission on Libraries and Information Science, must not ignore children's literature in any of its polymedia formats.

A Proposal for Cooperative Planning

It would seem desirable that representatives of research libraries having children's literature collections should meet to review the scope and status of existing collections, and to develop a plan or code of agreement. Such an agreement would reflect decisions about which libraries will specialize in which areas and actively build their collections in these areas. These plans would take into consideration the significant research collections in other than research libraries and in individual collectors' libraries that are open to researchers. The planning would cover not only existing collections, but areas of children's literature in all languages that are now treated inadequately, so that responsibilities for acquiring items in these areas could be allocated.

Some duplication among research library collections is inevitable and frequently desirable. Certainly no suggestion is being made that a library should reject gifts of alumni or other donors, or that libraries should turn parts of their collections over to other libraries. (Although in the case of some fragmentary or uncataloged collections, a suggestion of this nature might be supportable!) There are so many areas of children's literature that are poorly represented, or not represented at all, that a division of responsibility for the acquisition of these materials seems only sensible. In the case of collections that now overlap, as do numerous historical collections of English and American children's books, competition in acquiring expensive items might be avoided.

Specialization, Communication, Control

Even if this type of planning is not immediately forthcoming on a national scale, much benefit could be derived from comparable planning being undertaken soon on some regional basis. In many large cities and other localities, a wealth of children's literature resources for research can be found; but no agreement or understanding exists among institutions or individual collectors about areas for specialization. Thus resources are unnecessarily duplicated, with the result, frequently, that collection building is neglected in other areas. Similarly research libraries now having cooperative arrangements for acquiring and lending materials in designated fields should include areas of children's literature in their arrangements.

Other immediate actions that could well be taken in research libraries are the bringing together in one location of similar or closely related resources now in different parts of the institution and the cataloging of uncataloged items. (The number of uncataloged items in many research collections, including some very important ones, is amazingly large.)

Research libraries should plan, implement, and support effective channels of communication. Arrangements for an office to serve as a clearinghouse for resources, projects, and ongoing research and for publication of a newsletter would be useful. Communication could be further facilitated by regular meetings of the representatives of the research libraries, with attendance broadened to include those from other than research libraries that have noteworthy collections.

Ultimately part of the planning would deal with establishing some type of bibliographic control that would enable one library to obtain information about the contents of other libraries for interlibrary loan, or if materials cannot be loaned or photocopied, to make the necessary referral or location information available to the would-be users. This apparatus could also furnish information useful in making decisions about acquisitions. These simple forms of retrieval in due time could be expanded to cover more sophisticated computerized programs that would yield in-depth analyses of the contents of books and other materials for researchers.

Principles of Research Collections

Participating in some established plan, of course, would form a guiding principle for the research library in relation to its collections. Whether such a plan is in operation, certain policies and principles must be followed at the institutional level.

Knowledgeable staff is an essential. Many research libraries with large collections do not have a specialist in children's literature. Personnel with specialized competencies are needed for information, research, and advisory services; for building collections; for cataloging and classification; for identification and evaluation of items; for bibliographic activities; and, in many situations, for editing research publications. Academic research libraries need specialists in contemporary children's literature for the collection used in the study of children's literature, as well as specialists in the areas represented in their research collections.

Acquisitions for the collections cannot be left to chance gifts or spasmodic outlays of funds. An annual budget and an acquisition policy and plan are necessary. Research collections require files of desiderata and systematic searching by the staff in a wide range of publications and potential sources for purchases. An intuitive ability on the part of the staff to foresee future needs of scholars interested in interpreting themes, appeals, and attitudes in children's books as aspects of the cultural and social milieu of a period, assures preservation of many materials that would otherwise be lost (especially since many of these materials failed to meet the literary or other criteria for inclusion in children's and young adult collections in school and public libraries).

Related to the above principle is the obvious cautionary comment that those identified with research libraries mu not be elitist in their approach, either by placing children's literature in a submarginal category beneath the consideratio of the research library, or more specifically by thinking that "bad" books for children do not merit a place in the research collections. In many senses, these books more aptly mirror the culture of a period and the reading interests of children than do accepted works.

Children's literature collections must have the appropriate general and specialized reference and bibliographical tools, general and specialized historical accounts and commentaries, biographical materials, and research studies in the field. Here again, planning among libraries seems desirable. Currently a plethora of materials about children's books is being released--many of little value--that are obviously published with commercial profits the dominant motive.

Materials that enable those doing research to place children's literature in its proper context or perspective must be accessible. These include historical and sociological commentaries dealing with a given period or place, the status of youth in society, publishing, education, reading, and media. Newspapers and periodicals must be available, as well as such primary sources as letters or manuscripts.

With these principles as a starting point, those who are interested in, and committed to, children's literature in its many aspects can look forward to the day when its rich resources are easily available for research.

References

1. Weber, R. "Building a Children's Literature Collection: A Suggested Basic Collection of Children's Books." Choice, 11:1425-8+, December 1974.

2. American Association of School Librarians. Standards for School Programs. Chicago, American Library Association, 1960.
3. Field, Carolyn W., editor. Subject Collections in Children's Literature. New York, Bowker, 1969. This valuable resource is currently being updated and expanded.
4. Fraser, James H. Foreign Language Children's Literature in the United States. New York, 1972. Columbia University dissertation.
5. Fraser, James H. "Children's Literature as a Scholarly Resource: The Need for a National Plan." Library Journal, 94:4490-1, Dec. 15, 1969.
6. Bomar, Cora Paul, et al. Guide to the Development of Educational Media Selection Centers. Chicago, American Library Association, 1973.

CANADIAN BOOKS AND AMERICAN LIBRARIES*

Irene Martin

As a Canadian librarian now living in the U.S., I have been impressed by the quality of services offered in the libraries I have visited and with the friendliness of the librarians I have met. However, on several occasions I have been rather startled at the naivete of questions put to me as a Canadian librarian and disappointed at the representation of Canadian materials in libraries I have visited. In addition, I have had the opportunity to work with some American librarians in Canada, several of whom admitted the difficulties they had in dealing with Canadian materials, especially in acquisition, selection and reference work. This article, then, is written as a help to American librarians who may wish to acquire materials on Canada or by Canadians, and to those who may be considering working in Canada.

The first fact to keep in mind is that the Canadian publishing output is mainly in two languages, French and English. Canada is officially bilingual although many of her citizens, alas, remain fluently unilingual. This fact has caused a good deal of stress, and has also resulted in some high quality literature. Much as I would like to discuss this phenomenon in detail, I have decided to concentrate on Canadian literature in English, since this is the obvious "lingua franca" of the U.S. and Canada. For the curious reader, I would suggest that the chapter on Quebec in Read Canadian (to be described in more detail later) would serve as an introduction to French Canadian writing and lead to further exploration.

The second fact to be remembered is that of a recent upsurge in Canadian nationalism. I make no apology for this,

*Reprinted by permission of the author and publisher from PNLA Quarterly, Winter 1975, pp. 4-12.

as I am glad to see a growing awareness of what it means to be Canadian and how this affects one's life. Unfortunately, many Americans view the rising Canadian national feeling as anti-American feeling, which to some extent it is. I should give fair warning right now, that if this article is printed and the reference aids suggested are used to acquire Canadian materials, you will find some that you will consider prejudiced and unfair. I agree that some are so. But I also believe that if you yourself are fair then you will have to admit that the unflattering image of the U.S. portrayed at times may indeed reflect reality. You will find in our national magazines resentment at the economic domination of Canada by the U.S. and anger at the number of American professors teaching in our universities, and you will find that many of these articles will be well-documented and lead you to unavoidable and unpleasant conclusions. These are some of the problems that face the U.S. and Canada and there are many more.

The third and final fact to be discussed is the unique problem of publishing in Canada. With a population of approximately one-tenth of that of the U.S., the large press runs that are standard for U.S. publishers are not possible. As a result, much Canadian writing is published by small publishing houses. Most of the large publishing houses in Canada are subsidiaries of foreign firms, though many do publish works with Canadian content. Canadian publishers have been in financial straits recently, and the Ernst and Ernst report gave some rather unpleasant statistics on the effect of foreign domination on Canadian publishing. For example, in 1969, 52% of the books sold in Canada were foreign made.[1] If pure publishing, excluding publishers who are simply agents, is considered, "over 80% of the publishing done in Canada is done by foreign controlled firms."[2] "The Canadian book publishing industry's contribution to the national economy of 0.06% is significantly lower than the United States book publishing industry's value added which accounted for 0.22% of the United States G.N.P. in 1969."[3] The results of the above conditions are fewer books on Canadian topics, and distribution problems for the smaller publishers who must compete with large, foreign-dominated firms.

Why should American libraries bother about Canadian materials? In addition to the two countries' mutual problems already mentioned, which would seem to make information about Canada desirable in American libraries, there is also a substantial tourist trade between the two nations. For example, in 1970, 37,153,000 U.S. visitors entered Canada.[4] You probably have many travel books and histories of France, Germany and England on your shelves right now. Do you have any at all on Canada, and are they up-to-date?

Now that it has been established that there are books being published in Canada, and that there are valid reasons for U.S. citizens to become more familiar with them, how does the American librarian cope? I shall assume that we are discussing the acquisition of recently printed works of general interest, and shall exclude films and other non-print materials, since they would require an article of their own.

In general, the same basic kinds of tools that exist to aid in the acquisition of American works exist for Canadian works. Yes, there is a _Canadian Books in Print_, and there is, in addition, a national bibliography, _Canadiana_. The former does not, as yet, have a subject guide, while the latter lists not only books and periodicals, but also theses, films, pamphlets and many government publications, including those fugitive provincial government publications (more later on these). The two works form a comprehensive listing of current Canadian publications, and for a small or medium-sized library, the obvious choice of the two for acquisition purposes would be _Canadian Books in Print_, which contains a list of Canadian publishers and their addresses and is designed as an acquisitions tool.

For acquisition of periodicals, the standard directories such as _Ulrich's_, _Ayer's_, and the _Standard Periodicals Directory_ will help enormously, while a fairly recent publication, the _Canadian Serials Directory_, will provide detailed information on more periodicals than you will ever care to know about, let alone acquire.

There are several major reference tools which provide help for basic questions on Canada and please note, this is not the mythical well-rounded collection but a selection of titles belonging to basic types of reference works, such as almanacs, yearbooks and encyclopedias.

For reference work of a brief, factual nature, the _Canadian Almanac and Directory_ is a very good buy, being the Canadian equivalent to any good standard almanac. This should not be confused with the _Canada Yearbook_, also a very good buy, published by the Canadian federal government's publishing arm, Information Canada (formerly known as the Queen's Printer). The Canada Yearbook has vast quantities of information about the country and its government as well as current and retrospective statistics from Statistics Canada, formerly known as the Dominion Bureau of Statistics. By now it may be becoming apparent that Canadian government departments change their names with depressing frequency.

For fuller information, the Encyclopedia Canadiana will prove very useful though its statistics will usually need updating with some other reference source. It is a multi-volume work with maps and photographs, dealing with Canadian topics, and has recently undergone a major revision. The Canadian Annual Review is a unique annual publication which summarizes the year's happenings in a series of essays by noted public figures. Its closest U.S. equivalent would probably be an encyclopedia yearbook, though I hesitate to use the comparison, since the two are not really the same. It is connected with no encyclopedia, and is a collection of informed essays, opinions, and facts about national events and trends, rather than just a collection of facts. It has recently changed its scope and covers mainly politics, external affairs, defence, and the economy, whereas formerly it had a section called "Life and Leisure" as well.

Who's Who in Canada and the Canadian Who's Who are two works which often cause confusion at first. The latter is a general reference work, of use for figures of importance from all sectors of society, while the former lists mainly members of the business community and is not recommended for general usage. Finally, the work which indexes Canadian periodicals, the Canadian Periodical Index, published by the Canadian Library Association, would obviously only be useful to those libraries which have subscriptions to a substantial number of Canadian periodicals or have a continuing interest in a number of Canadian topics.

These, then, are a half-dozen or so of the most basic Canadian reference tools. As is evident by now, there quite often seems to be a U.S. equivalent for each major title. They may differ in format and style, but the concepts are generally quite similar. To illustrate this point, the following list contains several standard U.S. and Canadian titles which are roughly equivalent.

Dictionary of American Biography	Dictionary of Canadian Biography
Education Index	Canadian Education Index
Facts on File	Canadian News Facts
Statistical History of the U.S. ...	Historical Statistics of Canada
Oxford Companion to American Literature	Oxford Companion to Canadian History and Literature
Thomas Register	Fraser's Canadian Trade Directory

For the library interested in specialized reference works beyond the scope of this article, Winchell includes Canadian materials in her *Guide*, though now much of the material is out of date. There is also a recent work by Dorothy Ryder called *Canadian Reference Sources, A Selective Guide*, which is indispensable for any library wishing to acquire any substantial number of Canadian reference works. There is also an article by the same author which supplements this work for the year 1972 until a separate supplement can be printed. The article is "Canadian Reference Works 1972--a selection," published in the *Canadian Library Journal* for July-August 1973, pp. 346-351.

Tools for selecting books of general interest are next discussed, using the term "general interest" to mean both books specifically about Canada or some aspect of Canadian life, such as politics, art or music, and books written in Canada for a Canadian audience, which an American might read as a work of art in its own right, such as a book of poetry or a novel.

Americans have a number of good reviewing periodicals and newspapers, while Canadians have comparatively few. The only periodical devoted entirely to reviews of Canadian books of all subjects is *Books in Canada*. For children's books, the periodical *In Review* will be the desired tool. Whatever the good or bad points of these periodicals, there is one inescapable fact--they are there, and they are all that is there. There are, of course, book review sections in many specialized Canadian journals, such as *Canadian Literature* and *Canadian Historical Review*, and the Toronto newspaper, *The Globe and Mail*, has an excellent books review section on Saturdays, while many of the other newspapers have review sections of varying quality. MacLean's, which calls itself "Canada's National Magazine," also has a review section, dealing mainly with books of general interest. In addition, the University of Toronto Quarterly each July contains a section called "Letters in Canada" which reviews the year's output of Canadian books in all subject areas, and this gives an overview of each year's writing.

There are also some recent essays outlining exploratory readings in Canadian life, published in a book called Read Canadian. This is a fascinating collection of bibliographic essays, each of which describes the major works in an area such as foreign policy, women, art and architecture, labor history, and many others. A personal favourite is the essay on Canadian poetry, by Dennis Lee, and a library could do worse than follow the advice contained in this little volume, though it should by no means be looked upon as the definitive work on Canadian letters.

A selective list of children's literature can be found in the annotated catalogue, Notable Canadian Children's Books, which was prepared for an exhibition arranged by the National Library. It lists and describes books in both French and English, and also describes the difficulties and problems of publishing books for children in Canada. An earlier work by one of the compilers, Sheila Egoff, is called The Republic of Childhood. It deals with the entire range of Canadian children's books, and is the standard work in the field.

We come now to the question of periodicals. The few titles discussed illustrate the types of materials available, and I shall try to assuage the pangs of guilt at having omitted some fine magazines and journals which I am sure American readers would enjoy. MacLean's, published in both French and English, has already been mentioned, and it is a necessity for any kind of general readership. In the realm of women's magazines, Chatelaine is the major title, and I have found no women's magazine with its depth and breadth of coverage in the U.S. It carries the usual cooking and clothing items, as well as literary and historical articles and deals with social and political issues in Canada in addition. Published in both English and French, it makes stimulating reading. The Canadian Forum is another journal of exceptional merit, containing poems, reviews, and articles on many current social, economic, and political issues by leading writers. There are also learned journals such as Canadian Literature, Canadian Historical Review, business magazines such as The Business Quarterly, and the list of periodicals which appears at the beginning of the Canadian Periodical Index is an indication of the major standard Canadian titles, though it is not a complete listing of all Canadian magazines. Little magazines may be found by checking in The 'Alternative' Press in Canada, while the librarian wishing to purchase newspapers should consult Ayer's, which has a Canadian section.

Like governments everywhere, the Canadian government is in the publishing business. Briefly, there are three levels of government in Canada, federal, provincial, and municipal, corresponding to the federal, state and municipal governments in the U.S. All publish material. Not all, however, make it easy for you to get this material. Sound familiar? Let us leave aside the acquisition of municipal government documents, since the same problems of lack of indexing, lack of standard outlets, and lack of uniform procedures are ubiquitous (with one exception, to be discussed shortly), and concentrate on provincial and federal documents.

Each of the ten provinces has a publishing arm, known as the provincial Queen's Printer. So does the federal government, only in Ottawa it's called Information Canada. However, unlike the federal printer, the provincial Queen's Printers do not necessarily act as distribution agents for provincial publications. A recent study by Paul and Catherine Pross shows startling differences in practice among the various governments, so that, as a rule, systematic acquisition of provincial documents may be very difficult.[5] Many of these need to be acquired through the department responsible for their authorship. For an American librarian interested in a specific title published by a province, probably the best thing to do would be to write the department concerned. For a wider range of acquisitions, an arrangement may be attempted with the appropriate Queen's Printer. It should be noted, however, that a new microfiche service, called Profile, has begun, which hopes to provide documents from all provinces and territories, as well as major cities, and index them. In addition, portions of the service are available, so that a library need not buy the whole set to get the material it needs. The service received a very favorable review in the Canadian Library Journal[6] and appears to be the solution to many problems.

The federal government is much easier to deal with than the provincial governments (note, however, that I did not say easy, just easier). Depository accounts can be set up, and daily checklists, monthly catalogues and a yearly index are available. For details, write to Information Canada, Ottawa, Ontario, Canada. The Canadian government produces a great variety of materials, in both French and English, and since it and the U.S. government have many departments which perform similar functions, many publications will not be too unfamiliar. The above is, of course, a great simplification of the issues involved in acquiring Canadian government documents, but I hope it provides enough basic information to make a beginning.

Finally, for those Americans who may be considering emigrating to Canada, or who wish to know more about the Canadian library scene, there are several sources. Many libraries have the Bowker Annual, which contains an annual review of Canadian library trends. Unfortunately, the 1973 article is somewhat limited in scope, and those interested in libraries in the far north, maritimes, or the west, or in automation programmes or library schools outside of Ontario, will find nothing here. There is also no province-by-province reporting of significant achievements. There is, however, a book of essays, Librarianship in Canada, which may prove useful, and in addition a recent work, Canadian Library Progress, reprints a selection of articles from library-oriented periodicals published in Canada.

Doubtless, many Canadian librarians reading this article will feel that one or more of their favourite titles has been neglected or omitted. I apologize, but must point out that the space limitation has necessitated cutting out many titles I should like to have mentioned. In addition recent works may not have been available to me when I was last in Canada, or a favourite publication may have been too narrow in scope to be included. However, if there are any titles which you think I should know about, please let me know. As Dennis Lee said in his essay on Canadian poetry,[7]

> The first fact about Canadian poetry is that it is a living process; its most exciting feature is its messy, sprawling, gloriously various self-renewals. If you miss the chance to take part in that process, you miss one of the few civilized pleasures in the country.

I don't want to miss the poetry, the history, the music or any part of the process.

Notes

1. Ernst and Ernst Management Consulting Service. The Book Publishing and Manufacturing Industry in Canada (Ottawa: Information Canada, 1970), p. 21.
2. Op. cit., p. 36.
3. Op. cit., p. 22.
4. Canada Yearbook (Ottawa: Statistics Canada, 1972), p. 114.
5. Pross, A. Paul and Catherine A. Government Publishing in the Canadian Provinces (Toronto: University of Toronto Press, 1972), p. 35.
6. Dodson, Suzanne. "Review," Canadian Library Journal (Sept.-Oct. 1973), p. 437-438.
7. Lee, Dennis, "Modern Poetry," in Read Canadian, ed. by Robert Fulford, D. Godfrey, and A. Rotstein (Toronto: James Lewis and Samuel, 1972), p. 228-229.

BIBLIOGRAPHY OF CANADIAN TITLES MENTIONED

Books in Canada. Toronto: Canadian Review of Books, Ltd. Periodical. 15 pr yr. 1971-

The Business Quarterly. London: Univ. of Western Ontario, School of Business Administration. Periodical. 1934-

Canada Yearbook. Ottawa: Statistics Canada. Annual. 1867-

Canadian Almanac and Directory. Toronto: Copp Clark. Annual. 1847-

Canadian Annual Review of Politics and Public Affairs. Toronto: Univ. of Toronto Press. Annual. 1961-

Canadian Books in Print: Catalogue des livres canadiens en librairie. Toronto: Univ. of Toronto Press. Annual. 1967-

Canadian Education Index. Toronto: Canadian Education Ass'n. Quarterly. 1965-

The Canadian Forum. Toronto: Canadian Forum Ltd. Periodical. Monthly. 1920-

Canadian Government Publications du gouvernement canadien. Catalogue. Ottawa: Information Canada. Daily and monthly lists, annual cumulation. 1953-

Canadian Historical Review. Toronto: Univ. of Toronto Press. Periodical. Quarterly. 1920-

Canadian Library Progress: Progrès de la bibliothèque canadienne. Vancouver: Versatile Publishing Co., 1973.

Canadian Literature. Vancouver: Univ. of British Columbia Press. Periodical. Quarterly. 1959-

Canadian News Facts. Toronto: Marpep Pub. Co. Looseleaf. Semimonthly. 1967-

Canadian Periodical Index. Ottawa: Canadian Library Ass'n. Monthly, annual cum. 1938-

Canadian Serials Directory: Répertoire des publications seriées canadiennes, 1972. Toronto: Univ. of Toronto Press, 1972.

The Canadian Who's Who. Toronto: Who's Who Canadian Pubs. Triennial. 1910-

Canadiana. Ottawa: National Library of Canada. Monthly, with quarterly and annual cumulations. 1950-

Chatelaine. Toronto: MacLean Hunter Ltd. Periodical. Monthly. 1928-

Dictionary of Canadian Biography. Toronto: Univ. of Toronto Press, 1966-

Egoff, Sheila. *The Republic of Childhood*. Toronto: Oxford Univ. Press, 1967.

Encyclopedia Canadiana. Toronto: Grolier, 1966.

Fraser's Canadian Trade Directory. Toronto: MacLean Hunter. Annual. 1913-

Fulford, Robert, David Godfrey and Abraham Rotstein (eds.). Read Canadian. Toronto: James Lewis and Samuel, 1972.

The Globe and Mail. Toronto: Globe and Mail Ltd. Newspaper. Daily. 1944-

In Review. Toronto: Ontario Dept. of Education. Periodical. Quarterly. 1967-

MacLean's. Toronto: MacLean Hunter Ltd. Periodical. Monthly. 1905-

Notable Canadian Children's Books. Ottawa: National Library of Canada, 1973.

Peel, Bruce (ed.). Librarianship in Canada, 1946-1967; essays in honour of Elizabeth Homer Morton. Victoria, B.C.: Printed for the Canadian Library Ass'n. by the Morriss Print Co., 1968.

ProFile: Canadian provincial and municipal publications on microfiche. Toronto: Micromedia Ltd., 1973-

Ryder, Dorothy. Canadian Reference Sources: a selective guide. Ottawa: Canadian Library Ass'n., 1973.

Ryder, Dorothy. "Canadian Reference Works 1972--a selection," Canadian Library Journal, July-Aug. 1973, 346-351.

Story, Norah (ed.). Oxford Companion to Canadian History and Literature. Toronto: Oxford Univ. Press, 1967.

University of Toronto Quarterly. Toronto: Univ. of Toronto Press. Periodical. 1931-

Urquhart, M. C. (ed.). Historical Statistics of Canada. Cambridge: Univ. Press, 1965.

Who's Who in Canada. Toronto: International Press. Biennial. 1911-

Woodsworth, Anne (comp.). The 'Alternative' Press in Canada; a checklist of underground, revolutionary, radical and other alternative serials from 1960. Toronto: Univ. of Toronto Press, 1972.

THE WORLD AND THE RECORD*

James G. Olle

What right has a library journal to be dull?
--Arundell Esdaile

I. Past Imperfect

At first there were rumours, inevitably. Then came an official announcement: as from January 1975 the *Library Association Record* would appear in a new guise. (For various reasons, the transformation has been postponed for a year, until 1976).

Our professional journals seldom discuss themselves. Even less often do they comment on each other. In this respect the past year has been unusual. The decision by the LA to change the nature of its principal journal provoked comment not only in the LAR itself, but also in the pages of the *New Library World*.

The *NLW*'s reaction was hardly surprising. As the direct successor of the *Library World*, the *NLW* has every reason to be interested in the complexion of the *LAR*. The two journals have provided a steady flow of facts and opinions on librarianship, of more or less general interest (admittedly sometimes less than more), for over seventy years, and, except for one unfortunate lapse on the part of the *LAR*, they have done so monthly.

To describe these journals as rivals would be to suggest that each of them was striving to drive the other out of existence. In fact, they have always been complementary.

---

*Reprinted by permission of the author and publisher from *New Library World*, January 1975, pp. 13-15.

Over the years their fortunes have fluctuated, and at present they are both faced with major problems. But not all of these are quite new, as a brief comparative history of the two journals will show.

The LA, as we shall soon have reason to remember, was founded in 1877. It was born to troubles. One of the earliest and, as it turned out, one of the most difficult to solve, was the establishment of a permanent official periodical.

From November 1877 to June 1882 the LA was allowed to share the Library Journal with the American Library Association. As this was a dilatory way of publishing British library news, in 1880 the LA started a slim journal of its own called Monthly Notes of the Library Association, which continued until 1883. This was succeeded by the handsome Library Chronicle, 1884-1888, which in turn gave way to The Library, 1889-1898. Unfortunately, neither of these journals belonged to the association and apparently both of them depended upon financial help from their respective editors, Ernest Thomas and John MacAlister.

In the Autumn of 1898 the LA Council decided that the time had come for the association to publish its own journal and in January 1899 the LAR came into being.

The choice of editor was fortunate. Henry Guppy was enterprising and well-informed. Somehow he contrived to produce a monthly journal which was not only substantial in size but scholarly in tone. Nothing, it seemed, could have been more satisfactory. Unfortunately, in 1903 Guppy was obliged to resign, owing to pressure of work at the John Rylands Library. The council thereupon put the LAR directly under the control of the Publications Committee, and there it remained for twenty years.

Although this regrettable period in the LAR's history is usually glided over, it is by no means of minor interest, for it was then, more than at any time previous to 1974, that the purpose and policy of the LAR were hotly debated.

Then, as now, most of the members kept their views to themselves, but some were vehement in their denunciation of the council's action. The council was not to be budged. Indeed, it never revealed, in full, why it had chosen to put the LAR in chains. It eventually became apparent, nevertheless, that the council had not been entirely pleased with Guppy's editorship and that it was disinclined to appoint another personal editor with equivalent freedom, lest this freedom should be abused. The *LAR* must continue to be serious, but it must never give offence. If this seems unreasonable it must be remembered that the LA still had but few members and the council was not willing to risk losing any of them.

The result of this restrictive policy should have been anticipated. The *LAR* became increasingly dull. If any member felt inclined to be trenchant, satirical, or peevish, he had to contend with the blue pencils of the Publications Committee.

Inevitably, the livelier writers in the profession turned to the *Library World* when they wanted the freedom of expression which was denied them by the *LAR*. The *LW* was informative, lively and irreverent. It was also well produced and many of its articles were of practical value. In short, it was everything the *LAR* was not.

The *LW* had been founded in 1898 by James Duff Brown. As the self-appointed leader of the movement for better and brighter public libraries, Brown needed a crusading journal for himself and his supporters. To this end he not only founded the *LW*, he became its editor. In this capacity he worked unendingly, enjoyed himself hugely and wrote what he pleased. If the *LW* had had a motto, it might well have been

> With or without offence to friends or foes,
> We sketch your world exactly as it goes.

Brown also wanted a more vigorous LA and he did not shrink from publishing in the *LW* uncompromising criticisms of the association, notwithstanding that he was one of its best-known councillors. What is much less defensible is that he also published forthright criticisms of the *LAR*, whose only remediable defect was that it was published according to a formula which Brown had himself devised, in collaboration with Stanley Jast, when Brown was Chairman of the Publications Committee and Jast its Secretary.

In December 1907, for example, the *LW* described the *LAR* as "a costly, stodgy and bloated mass of journalistic twaddle." Nearly "half the association's annual income," it continued, "goes in support of a magazine which no one reads, or could read if he tried."

Undoubtedly the LAR was unsatisfactory. But its critics overreached themselves. Since 1898 the British library profession had been trying to support three monthly journals. (The third was the Library Assistant). It was too small to do so effectively.

Although the LAR was wary of publishing criticism of others, it did not entirely suppress criticism of itself. In March 1907 it published not only the text of a paper by G. T. Shaw on "How to improve the Library Association Record," but also a report on the discussion which followed it. One of the speakers was Wyndham Hulme, who said that "The Record represented the average intelligence and interests of the members," and that "It was impossible to raise permanently the existing standard until the standard of the association had been raised." If this observation was not the entire truth, at least there was some truth in it.

Brown became seriously ill in 1912. But when he died, two years later, it was the LAR, not the LW, which honoured him most. The LW survived Brown, but without him it soon lost its radicalism and its zest.

The exact nature of Berwick Sayers' involvement with the conduct of the LW is not clear, but apparently from about 1915 until his death, in 1960, he was its editor, except for a short period when he was advisory editor. In either capacity he continued to wear the editorial cloak of anonymity.

Sayers made his name as the indefatigable Secretary of the Library Assistants' Association. Under his direction the LAA expanded and flourished while the LA stood still. But when he took control of the LW, Sayers was a LA Councillor and well on the way to becoming the grave and respected member of the library "establishment" we remember.

Although there was something episcopal about Sayers, he had at least two things in common with Brown, namely, an unquenchable interest in librarianship and a fluent pen. Although he must have devoted thousands of hours to the LW, this part of his work is ignored by the Sayers Memorial Volume, perhaps rightly. Sayers kept the LW alive, but he did not keep it lively. Occasionally, as when Ernest Savage stormed into its pages, it regained part of its youthful vigour and from time to time it made other useful, but rather more solemn, contributions to the small literature of library economy. But it lacked strength of character and purpose.

Under Sayers the pattern of the LW hardly changed. For too many years space was taken up by an inadequate "Book selection guide" and an old-world feature called "Letters on our affairs," in which Callimachus reminisced with Eratosthenes, and Zenodotus spake peace unto Kallikrates. Every Summer one could expect an article on the literary and historical associations of the town where the LA was about to hold its annual conference. In 1938 this feature was written by Harry Sargeant, who was my chief. He told me grumpily that the LW had not paid him for it. As far as I know, hardly anybody was paid for writing for the LW when Grafton owned it.

While the LW was following this steady but unexciting course, the LAR had undergone a beneficial change. In 1923 "the dead hand of the Publications Committee" was removed. Once again there was a personal editor.

Arundell Esdaile, like Henry Guppy, was well-known, scholarly and respected. He knew what he wanted to do with the LAR, and with the council's blessing he did it. He transformed it overnight, not only in contents but in appearance. There was stylish typography, wide margins and paper of a quality we shall not see again. The journal was enshrined in covers of delicate pale green.

Naturally, not all the members were satisfied. Some unthankfully referred to Esdaile's creation as "the sea green monster." There was, in fact, one grave limitation. The LA was still, in the worlds of R. D. Hilton Smith, "poor in membership, money and in spirit." As an economy measure, the LAR was published quarterly.

The LA was rescued from its longstanding penury by the CUKT. In 1930 it amalgamated with the AAL. Thus it happened that, when many libraries and their staffs were suffering from the "slump," the LA was happy and solvent. One result of its new prosperity was that Esdaile was able to convert the LAR from a quarterly to a monthly publication in 1931. He continued as editor until 1935, by which time the LAR was in better shape than it had ever been.

The 1930's was perhaps the best time to be editor of the LAR. There were fewer interests to cater for then than there are now and production costs were relatively small. Such progress as there was in librarianship could be reported generously. (Compare, for example, the space given to the new Manchester Central Library in August 1934 with that given to the new Birmingham Central Library in March 1974.)

But looking back on this period one can see now that both the LAR and the LW presented a rather complacent view of the library scene. As far as public libraries were concerned, there was little in either journal which can be said to have paved the way for the startling frankness of the McColvin Report (1942). When that document was published, however, the LAR was suffering from war-time austerity, and by the time it had recovered from paper restrictions, librarianship had entered upon a period of change and expansion which still continues.

No longer was it a problem of how to fill the pages; rather it was a problem of what to leave out. Space was at a premium. Articles and book reviews had to be compressed. But the Liaison supplement, inaugurated in January 1957, and the expanded correspondence columns, seemed to find general favour; at least, no member could really say, with justification, that the LAR was altogether dull.

While the LAR was adapting its old formula to meet new conditions, the LW found an entirely new one, and not too soon. When Sayers fell ill, in 1958, the LW was near to eclipse. Happily, the smouldering embers were fanned into life by Roy McColvin, so that a major rescue operation became worthwhile. With a change of publisher, from Grafton to Deutsch, and shortly afterwards from Deutsch to W. H. Smith & Son, and the appointment of K. C. Harrison as substantive editor, the LW entered upon the most successful decade it had known since its Edwardian days.

As though anxious to make up for lost time, it swiftly established contacts throughout the entire world of librarianship. Suddenly it was eclectic and cosmopolitan. There were issues devoted to special topics. That for January 1967, the LW's 800th issue, was devoted to its own chequered history. (We still await a comparable history of the LAR, but who knows what 1977 may bring?)

Then, in July 1971, there was change again. The

Library World became the *New Library World*, under yet another editor. There were confused murmurs off-stage, but it was soon discovered that the best way to find out what the *NLW* was up to was to read it, and at least some of those who said, "This will never do" became, in due course, not only converts but contributors.

So much for the past. What of the future?

II. *Future Imperative?*

In February 1974 the *LAR* published a list of current British library periodicals. This shows that, since World War II, their number has markedly increased. But most of the new titles are specialised. The number of journals of general interest has remained small. In fact, there has been one loss.

Since the demise of *The Librarian and Book World*, the *LAR* and the *NLW* have become, once again, the only two monthly journals of general appeal. Both have had to grapple with the problem: What kind of journal should a general library journal be? Should it differ from the specialised journals in style as well as in scope?

It could be argued that the former is a natural corollary to the latter. Having reached the stage, common in other professions, where most of us are specialists, we use a different language in our areas of specialisation. We may feel that we should take some interest in what our colleagues are doing, but lose patience with them when, to borrow Stalky's phrase, they become "filthy technical."

If this is a fair assessment of the situation, it follows that, in our general journals, the accent should be on wide-ranging news and on brief articles, on topics of current interest, free from the paraphernalia of elaborate footnotes and bibliographical citations. In other words, we need library journalism. We already have it in the *NLW*. Do we want it in the *LAR*?

When the LA established the *Journal of Librarianship*, still more when it sanctioned the formation of many groups and sections, it relieved the pressure on the *LAR*, which was then able to devote more space to news and correspondence. The object of the *LAR*'s new policy, presumably, is to increase still further the percentage of its space devoted to features likely to be of general interest.

The first issue of the new style LAR is not now due for another year. But already some members of the association have set their hearts against it and others may follow suit. There is no point in condemning this attitude. There have always been members of the LA who felt that it would be inappropriate for its official journal to emulate the style of the independent journals.

The NLW is also dubious about the new policy of the LAR, but for reasons of its own. The independent library journals have always lived a precarious existence. Every profession has its independent journals, but in no other profession is it so difficult to keep an independent journal in existence. Not only is librarianship still a comparatively small profession; there is the awkward and inescapable fact that few of its members feel inclined to take out personal subscriptions to library journals, especially if they can see them without payment. It is hard to believe that there will ever be a library journal as flourishing as the Times Educational Supplement.

The library profession has had at least one independent journal for the whole of the past seventy-five years. If librarians only bother to think about it, they will realise why this situation should continue. It is possible, however, that they may reach the wrong conclusions, as the justification for the existence of the independent journals has never been satisfactorily explained.

The traditional reason given for their existence (it was recurrently cited in the editorials of the LW quite late in the Sayers' period) is that they are needed for freedom of speech. This is no longer valid. It is many years since the editors of the LAR were obliged to act as censors of anything other than the trivial, the libellous and the blasphemous. Apart from their standing obligation to report LA news they have not, in recent years, been unduly restricted. The correspondence columns alone bear witness to this.

The real reasons for the continued existence of the independent journals is that the profession needs more than one source of general information and more than one platform for voicing opinions. Small though it may be as a profession, librarianship itself is now so complex, and its boundaries are so rapidly expanding, that it must be looked at boldly, lucidly and centrally from as many angles as possible. No editor can hope to discover all the news that is worth publishing, all the ideas that are worth promulgating, or all the writing talent that needs encouraging.

A few years ago it seemed as though the future of book publishing in the field of librarianship lay only with the library associations. Do we want to return to that situation?

Unfortunately, the profession may appreciate these points too late. The rising costs of print, paper and postage are eroding the foundations of independent journals with much wider circulations than those of the NLW and the Library Review.

Every age has its idiosyncracies. One of ours is constantly to lament the loss of things we have made no particular effort to save. If the library profession really wants independent journals it had better consider what it may do to preserve and improve those it has got. It is too much to hope that they could readily be replaced.

To say that the independent journals are not good enough is true but not very helpful. Of course they could be better, but their quality depends on us. With more income and greater support of a literary kind they could be improved without difficulty.

It is no secret that some libraries do not subscribe to the independent journals, and others, with scattered branches, subscribe only to single copies. I know that when some of my students leave Loughborough they may never again see these journals regularly.

I am certain of two things. The first is that the NLW has greater difficulties to contend with than the changing image of the LAR. The two journals can never be like identical twins and I shall be surprised if they ever come to resemble each other very much. The second thing I am certain of is that the issue of the LAR for January 1976 will be scrutinised with unusual care.

It would be churlish, at this point, not to wish the members of the LA a journal nearer to their hearts' desires, although it is plain to see that there is no conceivable way of pleasing all of them.

I began with a quotation and I will end with one. "The essence of a virile magazine is its readiness to accept change--that every so often, if it seems to become sleepy or set in its ways, a shock or jolt should be administered to it, so that it is persuaded to reappraise its purpose and its place in the world." So wrote Clive Bingley in the *LW* for February 1967. I cannot forebear from quoting this passage here (if you will excuse the pun) for the record.

JOHN NEWBERY AND HIS SUCCESSORS*

Peter Opie

At long last, whether we looked forward to it or not, the collecting of children's books has come of age. For eighteen years now, or twenty-one years, or perhaps ever since the war, the collecting of children's books has been growing up, becoming in the process more earnest, more informed, more competitive, more prestigious, and, it must be added, more expensive. Under the influence of Harvey Darton, the gathering of little tomes in flowery Dutch paper covers has changed from being the childlike pursuit of pretty baubles, to the specialist's search for particular titles known to have significance in the history of a new branch of literature. Now, the inevitable has happened, the comprehensive bibliographer has appeared, he who is as detailed and meticulous in his description of a trifle from the chapman's tray as he is about the calf-bound classic. Recognition of a subject can go no further. Even the British Library Board, apparently, considers it essential that _Little Goody Two-Shoes_ and the Rosetta Stone should reside under the same roof.

To appreciate the change that has taken place during the past three decades it is necessary only to recollect how few and unsophisticated were the tools available to the student of early children's books in England before the Second World War. Other than Darton's incomparable history, and his lists in the old _C.B.E.L._, there was little to consult other than Thomas Hugo's _The Bewick Collector_, 1866-8; Mrs. Field's _The Child and his Book_, 1891; Tuer's _Forgotten Children's Books_, 1898, and _Old-Fashioned Children's Books_, 1899; Florence V. Barry's _A Century of Children's Books_, 1922; Gumuchian's catalogue, _Les Livres de l'Enfance du XVe au XIXe Siècle_, 1930; Philip James's exhibition memento _Children's Books of Yesterday_, 1933; and, that most prized

*Reprinted by permission of the author and publisher from _The Book Collector_, Summer 1975, pp. 259-269.

of reference books in its day, Charles Welsh's _A Bookseller of the Last Century: Being some Account of the Life of John Newbery, and of the Books he published, with a Notice of the later Newberys_, 1885.

The breakthrough, in my view, came in 1949 when Miss J. P. Weedon prepared for the Bibliographical Society her study of "Richard Johnson and the Successors to John Newbery." This was based on a close and perceptive examination of the personal account books of Richard Johnson, an active hack writer and proof reader, who kept a record of his literary transactions over a period of twenty-three years, 1770-1793. Miss Weedon showed, with the tact and clarity that comes from the full appreciation of a subject, exactly what could be achieved with such material; identifying and locating copies of the great majority of the hundred separately titled items in which Johnson had a hand; and revealing--since some sixty-five of the titles were for the young--the financial rewards for the authorship of mid-quality children's books in the late 18th century. Furthermore, since all but one of these little books had been published anonymously or pseudonymously, and the hand responsible for their production was being disclosed for the first time, the whole study of early juvenile literature was given a new dimension. By presenting us with the name and character of the man behind a shelfload of miscellaneous publications, many of which had hitherto seemed to be unrelated, she brought warmth, almost life itself, to the less exciting books we had been collecting; and she helped us appreciate that no matter how puerile or minute a publication might be, it must necessarily, once upon a time, have been the brainchild of some particular person, in a particular set of circumstances. Hitherto, for all our intellectual understanding that this was so (particularly if we ourselves had had a hand in such trivia for present-day children), it had been difficult to avoid the impression that the volumes produced for the little ones in the 18th century had required no authors; that they had merely needed to be printed; and that their chief interest lay in the name of the printer or bookseller appearing on their title-page. The discovery of Johnson's day books was as important in its way as had been the preservation of the John Newbery-Goldsmith accounts, used a century earlier by Prior and Foster, and subsequently quoted by Charles Welsh; and it is Welsh's work, in particular pp. 168-346 of Welsh's work, that has now after eighty-eight years been superseded in the grand manner.

John Newbery and his Successors 1740-1814, a 493-

page bibliography by S. Roscoe, is published by the Five Owls Press.[1] It is a record of some four hundred publications for children and some six hundred and fifty for adults issued by or advertised as being issued by John Newbery and his successors between--with six exceptions--1740 and 1801. They appear in two alphabetical lists, the children's and educational books being given pride of place, with a full or moderately full transcript of the title and imprint, a listing of every identified printing, a bibliographical description of all copies examined, the whereabouts of every copy located, and a fair number of notes about debatable authorship, uncertain dating, and suchlike eruditions. The adult books and almanacs are listed with short titles, partial imprints, and a census of editions and locations of copies. In total it appears Mr. Roscoe has identified some two thousand four hundred printings; and it must be said at once that this is a stupendous achievement, carried out with the zeal and conscientiousness that marked his bibliography of Thomas Bewick (1953), a work, incidentally, that has recently been reprinted.

It goes without saying that the collecting and studying of "Newberys," and hence the collecting and study of the incunabula of children's literature, is never going to be the same again. No longer will it be possible for a bookseller to describe every copy of an unassigned printing as a "first edition," or a seventh edition, hopefully, as "the earliest copy known," or some penny plaything as "unrecorded." The scientific bibliographer has not merely peeped into the nursery toy cupboard, he has emptied it, measured the size of each item, collated it, and assigned it a reference number. We now know the number of plates that should be inserted in a toddler's treasure of two centuries ago, whether or not advertisements were included at the end, and what was the probable material of its binding before it was abandoned to the extra-literary activities of sticky fingers or silver fish. The happy if haphazard days are over when, in making acquisitions, we relied on intuition, and the feel of the book, and our personal experience of its rarity. As a collector of such trifles, I confess to having more tenderness for the items Mr. Roscoe describes than for anything in this world that does not breathe; but I realize that personal appreciation of the layout of a John Newbery title-page or of the literary merit of a Carnan is, in the present text, out of place. The time has come to stop drooling over the condition of an individual copy of A Museum for Young Gentlemen and Ladies: or, A Private Tutor for Little Masters and Misses. The attempt must be made to see, through "Roscoe," what was the over-all Newbery achievement.

We already knew John Newbery as "the philanthropic bookseller of St. Paul's Churchyard," as the friend or befriender of Smart and Goldsmith (and, indeed, as "the friend of all mankind"), as Johnson's "Jack Whirler," as the projector of The Public Ledger if not of The London Chronicle, and as the successful promoter of Dr. James's Powders. Yet despite the charisma Newbery undoubtedly possessed--his advertisements immediately stood out in 1744 when he started making himself known in the London press--his contribution to general publishing during the twenty-four years that he hustled and bustled in the metropolis (he died in 1767), while creditable was not, but for one fact, outstanding. No bibliography of works bearing his imprint would be called for were it not for his association with the production of children's books and even in this department his story is curious.

Newbery was certainly not the originator of pleasure books for the young as has sometimes been asserted. He was, however, present in London in March 1744 when the widow Mary Cooper advertised for sale the first nursery rhyme book, Tommy Thumb's Song Book for all little Masters and Misses, by "Nurse Lovechild"; and although Mr. Roscoe is unwilling to commit himself there seems little reason for doubting that in May or June of that year he was one of those who followed suit, his offering being A Little Pretty Pocket-Book Intended for the Instruction and Amusement of Little Master Tommy and Pretty Miss Polly. What is surprising is that despite the ingenuity of A Little Pretty Pocket-Book, and its apparent success (a second edition was advertised in 1747 and a sixth in 1752), some six years were to elapse, or so it seems, before Newbery was to produce anything else that was for children's pleasure as well as enlightenment; and although the works he was then to publish, such as the penny booklet Nurse Truelove's Christmas-Box; or, The Golden Play-thing, advertised in January 1750, as being "given to all little good Boys and Girls ... they paying for the binding," and The Lilliputian Magazine: or the Young Gentleman & Lady's Golden Library, the first periodical for children, advertised in February 1751 as commencing publication, price 3d a number, show John Newbery to have been a man with an original turn of mind, the idea of producing little books for juvenile delight was, by this time, well established. During the second half of the 1740s his sole contribution to the juvenile field seems to have been his not very adventurous Circle of the Sciences, consisting probably of no more than nine volumes which essayed to make Arithmetic, Chronology, Geography, Rhetorick, and so on, "familiar and easy to every capacity."

Newbery was, indeed, to make up for his dilatoriness during the remaining years of his life, publishing some thirty titles for the juvenile market, amongst them A Pretty Book of Pictures for Little Masters and Misses, 1752; A Collection of Pretty Poems for the Amusement of Children Three Foot High, of which the undoubted first edition, 1756, was designated the "fifty-fourth edition"; The History of Little Goody Two-Shoes, 1765, the most notorious and oft-reprinted of his publications; The Important Pocket Book, or the Valentine's Ledger, c. 1766, the first account book or diary for children; and The Twelfth-Day Gift: or, The Grand Exhibition, 1767, the volume which Darton considered best expressed John Newbery's philosophy, with its frontispiece captioned "Trade and Plumb-cake for ever, Huzza!"

The importance of John Newbery thus lies in the zest with which he entered his undertakings and with which, fortunately for the young of the world in the 18th century, he infected his publications. He was also unusual in his persistence. He was not a man to let a good book go out of print, even if it was but a penny book, and he seems to have been the first man to have had a substantial list of children's books always available for purchase. Clearly, too, he was a man able to communicate his enthusiasm. His name would scarcely be so well known today if the publishing house he founded had not continued for more than a century after his death, so that not only were many of his own publications kept in print by his successors for a further thirty years or so, but his style and philosophy survived into the 19th century. It is by the publications of the house of Newbery that we judge all other publications for the young in the second half of the 18th century; and Mr. Roscoe has undoubtedly done right in continuing his studies through to 1801-2 when Elizabeth Newbery, the widow of John Newbery's nephew Francis, sold the business to her then manager John Harris.

While collectors of children's books everywhere are celebrating Sydney Roscoe's achievement--and a solid achievement it is, which places all of us in his debt--there will certainly be some people, whether their love of early children literature is for its own sake, or for the intimate contact it gives with the past, or for the unique place it has in the history of publishing, who will continue to feel concern about the new tools being provided for the study of children's books. They may feel, without quite knowing how it is happening, that children's books are coming to be separated from children's literature; and that children's literature is being separated from the times and conditions in which it was produced; in short that we are beginning not only to be unable to see the wood for the trees, but unable to see even the ground in which the trees have their roots. After my initial pleasure, even elation, at possessing a copy of Mr. Roscoe's bibliography, at having in my hand a record of virtually every edition of each publication of the House of Newbery (who would have imagined there to have been five printings of the undated edition of Don Stephano Bunyano's Prettiest Book for Children?), I have found myself experiencing a sense of disquiet. I cannot help feeling concern at the way children's books are at present being documented.

Although a reader of Sotheby's catalogue may not, until recently, have been aware of it, the children's-book scene over the past decade has been dominated by two publications: the 562-page catalogue of The Osborne Collection of Early Children's Books (1958), in Toronto Public Library, and the massive d'Alté A. Welch Bibliography of American Children's Books Printed Prior to 1821, which appeared in six parts in the Proceedings of the American Antiquarian Society, 1963-8. The direct influence of the Osborne catalogue, of which a further two volumes are in preparation, can be seen in the Catalogue of the Spencer Collection of Early Children's Books and Chapbooks (1967), in the Catalogue of the Hockliffe Collection of Early Children's Books (1969), and in the Wandsworth Collection of Early Children's Books (1972). The influence of d'Alté Welch can be seen in Roscoe, even to such a detail, alas, as the listing under locations of Xeroxes in the possession of the compiler; and the expectation must now be that the Roscoe bibliography, by its size, by its expertise, by its authority, and by the importance of its subject-matter, will--unless some fearsome nanny takes command--become the exemplar for all future bibliographers in the nursery. Indeed, the announcement has already been made that Roscoe is to be followed by a full-scale check-list of the publications of The Firm of John Harris; so we must waste no time, and ask ourselves what it is about John Newbery and his Successors that fails to give full satisfaction.

Certainly, we can assure ourselves, it is not the volume's physical appearance. It is a beautiful production. It handles well. It is the right size (23 x 15 cms) to stand on the shelf beside Darton. It is printed by C. U. P. It has 35 plates and a like number of figures in the text that convey a good impression of the range of Newbery publications (although a consortium reprint of a non-Newbery title seems a strange choice for the double-page spread on pp. 62-3); and it has as a pleasing bonus, a mounted five-colour frontispiece reproducing the glory of a piece of Dutch floral paper.

What will exercise some of us is the philosophy behind the enterprise. If the making of a good catalogue or bibliography is, in essentials, not very different from the making of a good collection, A. W. Pollard's dictum will be worth recollecting, that it is a collector's business "to illustrate his central idea by his choice of examples, by the care with which he describes them and the skill with which he arranges them." In Mr. Roscoe's bibliography the arrangement of the entries is not one which has called upon his skill. It is, as in many recent catalogues of children's books, simply in accordance with the dictates of the alphabet and whatever happens to be the initial letter of the author's surname, or of his pseudonym, or, if neither is known, of the first word of the title. This means, of course, that the need to refer to an index has been eliminated. It also means that the bibliography itself is formless; that it makes manifest no progression; that it tells no story; that we are unable to see by its continuity the relationship that any one entry has with another. Each title in the bibliography has, per force, to be looked at in isolation. Thus an early Newbery-Collins publication, The Royal Primer; or, An Easy and Pleasant Guide to the Art of Reading (J324), which was advertised for sale in 1751, is separated by almost two hundred pages from Alphabet Royal ou Guide Commode & agréable dan L'Art de Lire (J9), advertised in 1750, although one of these items must seemingly be a translation of the other. Further, in the 70 lines devoted to The Royal Primer no reference appears to Alphabet Royal; and in the Alphabet Royal entry no reference appears to The Royal Primer. Nor, unfortunately, are we certain of having the interest that might be expected to accrue from groupings under the names of individual authors. The Lives of the Fathers (J148) appears under Goldsmith, but not the companion volume The Life of Our Lord (J174) for which Goldsmith acknowledged the receipt of ten guineas, 11 October 1763. The productions of Richard Johnson are not brought together because, in Mr. Roscoe's view (J191) there is no single instance "in which one can feel certain, beyond all doubt, that Johnson was the real author." He cites, as an example, Juvenile Rambles through the Paths of Nature, 1786, as not being given under Johnson, despite the dedication signed "R. J.," since Johnson took his text from Mrs. Trimmer. But at J200 the volume appears under the first word of its title, with no mention of Mrs. Trimmer, although the volume must necessarily be by someone whether we like to give chief credit for it to Johnson as the producer of the Newbery edition (the book is an abridgement of Mrs. Trimmer's Introduction to the Knowledge of Nature), or to Mrs. Trimmer as the original begetter.

The point to be made here is that such difficulties would not have arisen, or would not have presented themselves in so intractable a manner, if all the Newbery productions--as also all related publications--had from the outset been looked upon as the integral parts of one great story: the rise and progress of the House of Newbery. And I would suggest that even if, in a compilation of this nature, it was decided for reference purposes that an alphabetical arrangement would be the most convenient when the work was published, the entries should be kept in chronological order while the work was being compiled. Such a procedure might possibly have given early warning that the fourth edition of Perrault's Histories or Tales of Past Times, noticed under J279 as advertised in 1752 printed for J. Hodges, could not have been one in the sequence of Salisbury printings, of which the third edition was dated 1763 (see New C. B. E. L.); and that Mrs. Trimmer is unlikely to have been responsible for The Ladder to Learning (J359), advertised for sale in 1772, when she herself stated she did not commence authorship until 1780. (Mrs. Trimmer does not seem to have had a hand in the work until it was "revised and corrected" for Harris, apparently in 1805.) Further if, for instance, the usual practices of a publishing house had been kept in mind, and Newbery's New Testament had been considered chronologically, a full transcription of the title of J35 (published 1755), which reads not only The New Testament Adapted to the Capacities of Children. To which is added, An Historical Account of the Lives, Actions, Travels, Sufferings, and Death of the Apostles and Evangelists, but continues With a Preface setting forth the Nature and Necessity of the Work, Adorned with Cuts, might have led to the suspicion that J32, advertised in 1770 as The New Testament adapted to the Capacities of Children: or, the Four Gospels Harmonized, and adorned with Copper Plate-Cuts. To which is prefixed a Preface, setting forth the Nature and Necessity of the Work, was simply a later edition, rather than a fresh compilation. And if the contents of J31, The New Testament ... Abridged and Harmonized in the Words of the Evangelists, and adorned with Cuts. For the Use of Children (dated 1764) had been examined, it might have been seen to be a slightly updated and abridged edition of J35. What publisher, after all, once he possesses his own text of the New Testament, is going repeatedly to commission further renderings?

It is to be wondered why the admirable examples set long ago by Rosenbach--or, rather, by Miss Sowerby--in Early American Children's Books, 1933, and by William Sloane in Children's Books in England & America in the Seventeenth Century, 1955, attract few followers today. Can it be that contemporary cataloguers are scared by the number of children's books which are undated, and are worried that, if they attempt chronological arrangement, some volumes may be placed in the wrong order? Or is it that the overriding desire today is to be scientific, to eliminate personal judgement by producing works to set formulas, preferably formulas of so simple a nature that the work can if necessary be delegated to underlings? Yet no work can be a great work, other than in bulk, that simply documents its subject, however precisely. Some insight must hold it together, some passion give it life; the value of the work as a whole must transcend the sum of its parts. Let the new generation of nursery archivists ask themselves why it is that Percy Muir's hasty exhibition catalogue, Children's Books of Yesterday (1946 and, miraculously, still obtainable at the N. B. L.), continues--for all its imperfections--to stimulate the mind each time we reread it, while the current procession of children's book catalogues at Sotheby's (A-Col, 1-2 July 1974; Com-F, 21-2 October 1974), which describe many of the identical volumes, already wearies the soul.

Of course the current Sotheby catalogues have not the benefit of Mr. Muir's informed enthusiasm; and of course our pleasure when looking at Children's Books of Yesterday stems in part from it being a pioneer work that showed, as no catalogue had done before, what the collecting of children's books is all about. But more went into the making of Mr. Muir's catalogue than enthusiasm and knowledge and novelty. There was also art. The little catalogue is so arranged that each entry seems to be related to the next. Each item is so placed or annotated that it seems part of a general conspiracy to add to the interest of its neighbours. Children's Books of Yesterday is one of those catalogues in which we propose to look up a single item and find ourselves delightedly reading an entire section. But whereas Sotheby's catalogues are to be commended for the chronological arrangement of entries under any one author, making for instance the assemblage of A. H. Forrester titles of considerable interest, the user of the catalogue (and an index is to be supplied when the series is complete), is, naturally enough, likely to have little idea of the contents of many of the items, or of their raison d'être, or, for that matter, of their desirableness in terms of the sale room.

On this count it could be argued that children's literature is not yet ready for the pure bibliographer. When we consult a bibliography of Cowper or Trollope or Graham Greene we are already familiar with the contents of the books described; we seek merely to know the format of a first edition, or the precedence of two issues, or the extent of the master's output in a particular period. But the situation with early children's books is different. Such is their general unavailability, if not rarity that, however well informed we may fancy ourselves, we can seldom, as I have suggested, glance at a check-list without seeing entries that refer to volumes of which we have not yet handled a single copy. Thus to read a catalogue of children's books which does not also give us an indication of their content can be as edifying as a reading of the telephone directory. Only occasionally will a name conjure up a face, or an address a house-front. Our only profit from perusing the telephone directory is to be reminded of the minuteness of our coterie in the vastness of the community.

The idea behind The Juvenile Library, published by O. U. P. under the general editorship of Brian W. Alderson, is thus a good one. Each volume (the series stated in 1966) contains a facsimile of one or more key publications in the history of children's book publishing; and the facsimile is surrounded with extensive descriptive and bibliographical material relating, very often, not only to the item or items reproduced, but to others of the genre. These volumes, it may be felt, fulfil each of my conditions: the children's book under examination can be read in its entirety; the preamble, which may amount to a hundred pages, gives the background to the publication; and the bibliography is always chronologically or progressively arranged--the volumes by Mrs. J. E. Grey on Sarah Fielding's The Governess, 1745; by Dr. J. H. P. Pafford on Watts's Divine Songs, 1715; and most recently by Mrs. M. Nancy Cutt on Mrs. Sherwood and her Books for Children, being particularly notable. So I am at a loss to know why--however much young students may appreciate these volumes--they have not received more critical acclaim, especially when works sometimes embodying considerably less original research have praises showered upon them. I can only surmise there is something unappealing about them in their format, or in the way they are organized, or in the balance between editorial and facsimile, or in the inclusiveness of what is attempted, or in the earnest non-literary style in which it is attempted; and that this inhibits their being recognized as the trail blazers they are, or should be, in the field of children's literature. Indeed, in the case of Mrs. Sherwood and Her Books (1974) the publisher or somebody does not seem to have appreciated he had the nucleus of an important book on his hands: one which could have been shown to be relevant to our intellectual situation today. But we have to acknowledge that while the collecting of children's books may have come of age, the recognition of children's literature as a subject of more than pedagogic interest is still only in its teething stage. The idea is as yet too novel to be accepted, probably, that light can be thrown on the world's problems by an examination of children's predilections and reading-matter.

Note

1. John Newbery and his Successors 1740-1814. A Bibliography. By S. Roscoe. (Wormley, Herts: Five Owls Press Ltd, 1973. £15.00.) Index of Publishers, Printers, Booksellers. Illus: colour frontis. + 35 plates + 35 figs.

PUBLISHING DETENTE IN THE TIME OF VAAP*

Alan U. Schwartz

The Soviet Union has had an internal domestic copyright law since 1918. However, since the Russian revolution and despite attempts by such statesmen as Franklin Roosevelt, Winston Churchill and Adlai Stevenson, the Soviets have refused to join in any international copyright association which would afford reciprocal copyright protection to works of Soviet and Western origin. It was therefore understandable that when the Russians joined the Universal Copyright Convention on May 27, 1973, a good deal of confusion and apprehension as to their intentions reigned in American and European publishing circles. Finally, the years of urging and behind-the-scenes work to get the Soviets into an international copyright body seemed to have reached fruition and most observers greeted the news with enthusiasm. However, because of the implications of a number of amendments to Soviet Copyright Law enacted shortly before they joined the U. C. C., this enthusiasm in most cases was tempered by a good deal of suspicion.

The dilemma which adherence by the Soviet Union to the Universal Copyright Convention poses for its dissident writers is clear when we realize that before such adherence there was nothing in the civil law to actually prevent a Soviet author from contracting to have his work translated and published in the West even if it had been banned in the Soviet Union. True, such publication might well subject the author to criminal penalties and other retribution under various provisions of the Soviet criminal law prohibiting the dissemination of anti-Soviet propaganda abroad (provisions, incidentally, under which the distinguished writers Sinyavsky and Daniel were tried and sentenced in the 1960s). But this was a risk

*Reprinted by permission of the author and publisher from Publishers Weekly, March 1975, pp. 28-31. Copyright © 1975 by Xerox Corporation.

an author could decide to run in order to get his works read in the free world. However, Soviet accession to the U. C. C. and the passage of amendments to its Copyright Law have presented two new potential obstacles toward dissident publication in the West. First, since copyright in translations is now recognized and protected by Soviet law (before 1973 all translation rights were in the public domain) and therefore a tangible asset of the individual, it has automatically become also an asset of the Soviet state and, like any other asset (such as machine tools, for example) its exportation is subject to state monopoly laws. Thus, any attempt to export or license any copyright or right of translation without permission of the authorities (even of a work innocuous in content) will subject the dissident writer to added penalties for violating laws against unlicensed exportations, or, to put it simply, smuggling. Second, and even more ominous, the Soviet Union could, through use of a compulsory licensing provision of its copyright law, theoretically at least, become the copyright owner of a dissident work, thereby depriving the author of his right of publication even if he were willing to risk the criminal penalties.

In the hope of clarifying Soviet policy about these and other matters the Soviet-American Publishing Committee of the Association of American Publishers (a distinguished group of American publishers headed by Robert L. Bernstein of Random House) prepared to meet with Soviet publishing leaders in Frankfurt in October of 1973 as part of the various meetings going on there in connection with the Frankfurt Book Fair.

Included in the Soviet delegation was a youngish man named Boris Pankin, the head of a new organization within the Soviet Union, referred to as the All-Union Copyright Agency, or VAAP, which had been set up to deal with the consequences of Soviet adherence to the Universal Copyright Convention and was to have precedence over most of the other agencies within Soviet publishing which had previously dealt with foreign rights. At the time of the meeting the Soviets were vague about the nature and precise details of their new copyright agency. However, although they chose to delay public announcement of the enactment of the law establishing the All-Union Copyright Agency until January, 1974, the preamble to the law itself made clear that it had actually been passed on September 20, 1973. In other words, the Soviets knew precisely all the terms of the law establishing VAAP before Frankfurt but chose not to discuss them in detail with the American delegates. The reason for this decision was porbably a lack of clarity within the Soviet system itself as to exactly how the provisions would be put into effect rather than any conscious attempt by the Soviets to withhold information from the Americans. However, the fact that knowledge of the actual statute was denied the Americans at Frankfurt points up once again the difficulties of conducting negotiations between, on the one hand, a group of private individuals representing separate publishing houses, and on the other, representatives of a monolithic governmental publications system. Obviously this difference in structure reflects a great difference in attitudes and has resulted, at least to date, in a serious problem in communications and in the evaluation of the intentions of the parties.

While a number of governments have established seemingly all-embracing copyright organizations to deal with the transaction of publishing business abroad, VAAP is the only one in a major "civilized" country which requires that all contracts for foreign licensing of rights in and out of that country must be approved by the organization. If such approval is bypassed or not granted, the affected foreign license is considered by Soviet law to be invalid and the author's copyright in the work itself is voidable. Although VAAP is strictly speaking a non-governmental agency, the penalties for ignoring its requirements can be severe. Briefly, writers who violate them are subject to the forfeiture of all royalties on the work in question and the invalidation of their copyright on the work, as well as severe criminal penalties for violation of the state monopoly on foreign trade (three to ten years in prison, confiscation of property and five years' exile). And it should be noted that those writers who bypass VAAP are guilty of this crime regardless of the content of the work they are licensing for foreign publication. Thus, even in connection with the most inoffensive and non-political work a violation of the All-Union Copyright legislation can produce severe criminal penalties.

The disclosure of the terms under which authors are required to deal with contracts for foreign rights under VAAP has done nothing to dispel the fears of those concerned with the fate of dissident writers in the Soviet Union. While copyright has generally been considered to be a monopoly granted by a particular government to its citizenry, the Universal Copyright Convention establishes certain basic copyright protections for all authors of all member states, protections of which the authors cannot be deprived simply by the unilateral national action. When VAAP was announced, Western commentators were afraid that its provisions might _per se_ violate these basic protections of the U.C.C. The unhappy conclusion is that they probably do.

First of all, what is the intention of the Universal Copyright Convention of 1952? It is made clear in the preamble, which reads in part: To "insure respect for the rights of the individual and encourage the development of literature, the sciences, and the arts ..." and, further, "Persuaded that such a universal copyright system will facilitate a wider dissemination of works of the human mind and increase international understanding...."

Article I unequivocally establishes that the purpose of the Convention is to protect the rights of the creator:

> Each contracting State undertakes to provide the adequate and effective protection of the rights of authors and other copyright proprietors....

The basic method of achieving this protection is set forth in Article II, which states that works of nationals of any contracting state and works first published in that state "shall enjoy in each other Contracting State the same protection as that other State accords to works of its nationals first published in its own territory."

For their part, the Russians have claimed at Frankfurt and elsewhere that the U.C.C. does not prohibit the continued application of their own, seemingly antithetical, laws because Article III, Clause 2 of the U.C.C. provides that contracting states will not be precluded from requiring "formalities or other conditions for the acquisition and enjoyment of copyright." However, it is generally maintained by commentators that the conditions referred to are simply formal conditions and do not permit a contracting state to require conditions for copyright protection in its own state which would effectively deprive an author of his right to freedom of contract.

The right of a creator to deal with foreign rights in his work is established by the U.C.C. (Article V, Clause 1) as follows:

> Copyright shall include the exclusive right of the author to make, publish, and authorize the making

> and publication of translations of works protected under this Convention.

It is obviously impossible to reconcile the requirements of VAAP and the Soviet penalties for an individual freely contracting for the publication for his work abroad with this clear statement of rights under the Universal Copyright Convention. Since VAAP requires state approval of all foreign agreements between Soviet writers and foreign publishers, it is difficult to maintain that the author has the "exclusive right to ... authorize the ... publication of translations...." Indeed, the form license agreement submitted by VAAP to foreign publishers who wish to license rights in Soviet works is made with VAAP rather than the author, and approval of all changes in the text are the province of VAAP and not the author. In addition, the agreement contains the following clauses, which indicate rather conclusively that VAAP does not intend to be overly influenced by the U. C. C.:

Paragraph 8 of the VAAP agreement (in part):

> All the financial and other questions in the relations with the author of the WORK shall be regulated by the AGENCY (VAAP) directly on their own behalf.

And then, the "final solution" (Paragraph 11):

> All the differences and disputes which may arise from the present Agreement or in connection therewith shall be settled by direct discussions between the parties.
>
> Should such discussions give no result, the dispute shall be submitted to the Foreign Trade Arbitration Commission at the USSR Chamber of Commerce and Industry in Moscow for settlement in accordance with the rules of procedure of this Commission.
>
> The decisions of the arbitration are final and binding upon both parties.
>
> Reference to courts is excluded.

Actually, it is fairly obvious that the requirements of VAAP violate the Universal Copyright Convention. Technically this circumstance should subject the Soviet Union to stringent penalties and even expulsion from the U. C. C.

However, matters of this kind concerning international politics are very rarely settled by legalisms or courts of justice. In order to establish such a violation and thereby to pressure the Soviet Union into modifying the repressive nature of VAAP, the matter of Soviet violations would have to come before the Inter-Governmental Copyright Committee (IGCC) of the U. C. C. This group consists of 12 member states. Apparently, the Soviets attempted to become one of the 12 as soon as they joined the Universal Copyright Convention last year but in this they were rebuffed, at least for the time being.

There are, of course, imposing problems involved in attempting to bring an issue as politically sensitive as this one before the IGCC. First of all, the issue could be raised only by a governmental member and not by individuals or private organizations such as the Author's League, P. E. N. or the Association of American Publishers. Thus far, our State Department has refused to raise this issue in Geneva, primarily because of its interest in economic détente with the Soviet Union. And the various publishing and authors' groups which have attempted to urge our government to greater heights in this regard have been met with resistance and in some cases, actual hostility. Secondly, one must remember that the U. C. C. is basically a child of UNESCO and that therefore matters of overall United Nations policies are also involved. The delicacy with which UNESCO, and indeed the United Nations in general, has approached matters involving dissidents within the Soviet Union may be seen in all its glory (or rather lack of it) in the recent action of the United Nations banning from its bookstore in Geneva copies of Solzhenitsyn's _The Gulag Archipelago_ for fear of offending the Soviet Union (a position later--much later--reversed after pressure from P. E. N. , the AAP and others). In view of this persistent attitude of appeasement by most members, it is difficult to see how the question of Soviet violations of the U. C. C. could actually come before the Inter-Governmental Copyright Committee.

Representatives of the Soviet Union have, formally and informally, repeatedly expressed their surprise that author and publishing interests in the West should view with suspicion their various actions since joining the U. C. C. They have stated often, and with vigor, that they did not join in order to strengthen their repression of dissident writers. They point out that they had enough legal weaponry before adherence to the U. C. C. to deal with these writers. In fact, the available evidence is inconclusive as to their primary intent. The probabilities are very strong that their emergence as a copyright nation in the international community is part of the price they had to pay for trying to improve trade relations with the West, especially the United States, and not a calculated thrust against their own literary outcasts. Nevertheless, once having joined the U.C.C., the actions they have taken since and their attitude towards American and other Western publishers indicate clearly that the Soviets do not intend to relinquish any of the new weapons which the creation of this asset of state monopoly has provided in their fight against the publication abroad of the works of dissident authors. Before evaluating the effect of present Soviet policy on the dissident writers, it is well to examine these weapons and the likelihood of their successful application by the Soviet government.

Let us assume that a relatively well-known but not terribly powerful Soviet dissident writer wishes to make a contract with a Western publisher for the publication of a work critical of the Soviet Union. Obviously such an arrangement would not be approved by VAAP. Therefore the author decides to make the arrangement directly with the American publisher and somehow gets his manuscript out and signs a contract. By so doing, the author immediately becomes subject to prosecution for violation of sections of the Soviet Criminal Code which prohibit the spreading of anti-Soviet propaganda. In addition, by virtue of his having bypassed VAAP, the author is now automatically in violation of the Soviet trade monopoly laws. Moreover, under the rules of VAAP the author's copyright is voidable and the contract he has made with the American publisher is void and of no effect. If the publisher ignores all of this and continues with his publication plans, it is theoretically possible for the Soviets to try to force the author to take action in an American court to prohibit publication. If the author refuses, the Soviets could use the compulsory transfer of copyright provisions (Article 106) of the Russian Copyright Law and assign the author's copyright directly to the government. Then, as copyright owner, the Soviet government could enter an American court and attempt to prevent publication.

It is precisely to avoid such a possibility that legislation has been proposed by the Authors League and others prohibiting foreign governments from using American courts to enforce copyrights obtained by compulsion. But even without such law it is unlikely that an American court would grant the Soviet Union an injunction against publication. It is certainly doubtful that given the political climate of the times in our country, a court of law here would be in a position psychologically and practically to participate in such an obvious deprivation of rights.

Indeed, it is most unlikely that the Soviets themselves will attempt to use our courts to protect their objectives in dealing with dissident writers. Despite the publishing activities of such men as Solzhenitsyn and Sakharov, the Soviets have not as yet, to the best of Western knowledge, tried to use the newly formed provisions of VAAP in the manner described above. It is more likely (as they have stated in conversations with members of the International Publishers' Association in Moscow recently) that the Soviets will attempt to use economic sanctions against Western publishers who continue to publish dissident works. In other words, they will give, and are giving, concessions to so-called "friendly" publishers and refusing, at least in practice to do business with those they consider less friendly. (The recent whirlwind business trip conducted by Mr. Pankin and others in the U.S. clearly showed the "blacklist" to be in operation.) But since there is probably relatively little profit to be made in publishing relations with the Soviet Union, it is unlikely that this kind of behavior by the Soviets will effectively deter the continued publication of dissident works in the West. Nevertheless, the existence of the requirements of VAAP will inevitably produce a collision between the transfer of works of dissident writers from the Soviet Union abroad and the requirements of Soviet law. Unless the Soviets are prepared to close their eyes completely to the activities of those authors who do not go through VAAP (and it is very doubtful that they will do so), there are bound to be violations of law which the Soviets will have to act upon if they wish their law to have both viability and credibility with their own people.

On another front, the inability of the Soviets thus far to wrest concessions from American and other Western publishers regarding highly valued scientific and technical journals (at this writing I understand that some agreements have been made but these do not cover the major journals which are published in the United States) might well lead them to publish these journals in forms similar to photocopying under which they can claim that copyright permission and royalties are not required, on the theory that protection for such reproduction is not covered under the Universal Copyright

Convention of 1952. As most readers know, this is a point of some confusion under our own law at present. Perhaps clarification will come when the Supreme Court decides the Williams & Wilkins case later this year.

The Vonnegut Piracy

While we can only speculate at this time whether the Russians are actually reproducing our journals contrary to U. C. C. policy (they have denied that they are), we have already had evidence of a Soviet publishing practice which, if it continues, raises grave doubts about the possibility of accommodating the Soviet attitude to copyright with the requirements of the U. C. C. On October 3, 1974, at a press conference in New York called by the AAP, it was revealed that the Literary Gazette of Moscow, the leading Russian literary journal, had published in Russian sections of both Marilyn by Norman Mailer (with pictures) and Breakfast of Champions by Kurt Vonnegut, Jr. without authorization and without compensation. Since both these works were first published in the West subsequent to the date of Soviet adherence to the Universal Copyright Convention they were clearly protected by copyright within the Soviet Union. However, in rejecting complaints from both publishers involved, the Russians invoked the provisions of a newly enacted amendment to their Copyright Law which provides that "reproduction in newspapers of the speeches and reports publicly delivered as well as the published works of literature, the sciences and the arts in the original and in the translation is permitted without the author's consent and without the payment of the royalty to the author."

The Soviet position in this matter led many Western commentators to question whether there is in fact any real meaning left to Soviet adherence to the U. C. C. For if the Soviets continue to invoke the provisions of this amendment, there would be nothing to prevent them from publishing entire books rather than excerpts and, of course, since the authors and publishers have no control over what is published there is no way of assuming the accuracy, let alone stylistic fidelity, of the published Russian translations. As must be obvious, it is simply impossible to square this view of copyright with the provisions of the U. C. C. as set forth in Article V, Clause 1 cited above.

It remains to be seen how the Soviets will finally

react to pressure from the West to repeal, or at least modify this incredible provision of their law. At this writing, they seem to have backed down, at least somewhat, in the case of Breakfast of Champions and have, in fact, contracted to publish all of Breakfast of Champions for a flat fee, without royalty. The sum involved was modest, but the principle is, of course, significant. One hopes they will now be encouraged to refrain from repeating these slight but nonetheless disconcerting adventures in literary piracy. It is difficult to see how the Western publishing community can long continue to tolerate such an obvious method of avoiding international copyright law without losing its own credibility in this field. I don't believe it will.

In the course of discussions between various Soviet publishing leaders and members of the AAP, the Russians argued with great insistence that their activities on behalf of Soviet publishing are in no way connected with the condition of dissident writers within the Soviet Union. Quite recently, Boris Pankin made very specific his position that since the All-Union Copyright Agency is technically not a governmental agency he should not be asked to engage in questions involving Soviet literary censorship or the right of Soviet dissident writers to publish abroad. At another meeting with the Soviet-American Publishing Committee of AAP, Boris Stukalin, chairman of the State Committee of the U. S. S. R. Council of Ministers on Publishing, Printing and Book Trade, recently made the same point. However, Mr. Stukalin, being a government official in a more powerful position, added that if the Americans wished to meet again with the Soviets it would have to be on condition that nothing dealing with "political" rather than "business" matters would be included in the discussions. This position is understandable. Bluntly, Soviet publishing leaders have been told by their superiors to get on with the business of working out publishing arrangements with countries which are also members of U. C. C. and have obviously been given certain priorities as to what they are to acquire (such as the technical journals). Naturally, any discussion of Soviet censorship or persecution of dissident writers is a source of irritation and an obstacle to their general objectives. Moreover, the Soviet publishers are probably right when they say that they have no power or control over the fate of Soviet dissident writers and that complaints regarding the treatment of such writers are best directed to persons with authority in those areas.

All of this is quite logical, and one may view with a

certain sympathy the plight of Soviet publishing representatives, from Mr. Stukalin on down, who are clearly not themselves in a position to do anything about dissident writers even if they wished to. Nevertheless, to construe the issue so narrowly is, it seems to me, to miss the main point. The undeniable fact is that Soviet censorship and the persecution of dissident writers (whether through criminal prosecution, exile and/or involuntary psychiatric incarceration) is extensive.

In fact, since joining the U. C. C., the Soviet government has engaged in a "mopping-up" campaign against its dissidents. The chilling effect of this systematic repression of dissident writers upon the hundreds of other writers within the Soviet Union whose works circulate through Samizdat only (and sometimes not at all) because of the ever-watchful eyes of the censors, is great indeed. As has been stated by many commentators on the literary scene in the Soviet Union, the self-censorship which such a system of repression has imposed upon the Soviet literary community has had a stifling effect upon the creative output of the society, a circumstance for which we will all, including the Soviets, be the worse.

Soviet adherence to U. C. C. has not changed Soviet policy with regard to its dissident writers but has merely provided the Soviets with additional potential tools of repression to be used against the communication of the ideas of these writers abroad. In order to neutralize this potential, the dialogue which has been instituted with the Soviets as a result of their adherence to U. C. C. must be a dialogue which deals with the rights of authors and publishers to contract freely and without fear for the communication of ideas. Any system of any government which interposes, either through punishment or legislation, obstacles which effectively prevent this intercourse must constantly be reminded that publishing, at least, is not like the distribution of Pepsi-Cola and that the communication of ideas, unlike the consumption of soft drinks, is not and cannot be the subject of state monopoly legislation. Therefore it is not only right but necessary that in their discussions with Soviet publishers, American publishers' and authors' representatives continually remind their Soviet counterparts that the object of the exercise is the free communication of words and ideas and that the various structures which have been set up to deal with publishing, such as U. C. C. and others, have and must continue to have as their primary purpose the attainment of this object. Anything less cannot be acceptable. And while it is true that the Soviet publishing representatives may themselves be unable to institute changes which would affect the objectives and principles stated in U. C. C. and elsewhere, they must be persuaded that if their spperiors or other branches of their governments are desirous of establishing détente in other areas of trade, they must also begin to produce an atmosphere which will make true publishing détente possible. This is not done by sentencing Soviet writers such as Vladimir Bukovsky or Gabriel Superfin to long terms in labor camps or prisons for expressing their ideas. Nor is détente furthered by depriving men like Valery Chalidze and Pavel Litvinov of their citizenship because of activities in furtherance of human rights, or by sentencing Alexander Solzhenitsyn to the severe penalty of involuntary exile as a result of the publication of "The Gulag Archipelago."

Search for a True Détente

At best, commercial publishing business with the Soviet Union will represent a minimal part of all publishing business in the United States and certainly a very minimal part of the developing trade relations to which Secretary Kissinger and others are committed. American publishers in general are already finding that there is really not a great market in the Soviet Union at present for their wares (although certain publishers, especially in the scientific fields, are being given special, positive treatment by the Soviet Union). Thus, even from a purely commercial point of view the business of dealing with the Soviet Union in the publishing field is really the business of trying to establish a structure under which détente--a true détente--can flourish. We must, in fact, help the Soviets over their own schizophrenia and confusion caused by the abrupt decision of their leaders to enter the field of international copyright.

The role played thus far by the United States government in this international publishing chess game, while understandable, is nevertheless difficult to justify. In commenting recently about the strong push of our government towards a trade détente with the Soviet Union while downplaying the need for cultural détente, the distinguished playwright Arthur Miller, who has had his own bouts with repression in this country, has commended:

> Exactly because the exchange of goods and technology tends to unify the world, the conditions of

> liberty in the world become a crucial issue. One cannot stand silent before the likelihood that our friendship is to be used to imprison and persecute yet more people, that our products and scientific ideas are to be used as insurance by Mr. Brezhnev, as the imprimatur of the United States upon his treatment of dissidents....

In the face of this "stonewalling" attitude of our government thus far, it is certainly a tribute to the American publishers' and authors' organizations, such as the Authors League and P.E.N., that they have raised their voices and brought to bear whatever financial leverage they may have against continued Soviet repression of dissident writers. Although the Soviet-American Publishing Committee of the AAP, having done its limited job, has disbanded, it is encouraging to report that in recognition of the need for increased vigilance in this area, the AAP has just formed a new, permanent committee (the Committee on International Freedom to Publish) which intends to deal vigorously with violations of freedom of contract between authors and publishers not only in the Soviet Union but throughout the world. The principle is clear: if governments will not or cannot enforce the principles of the U.C.C. then the authors and publishers will have to get the job done.

The archipelago of Soviet repression and censorship is not impassable. Men like Solzhenitsyn and Sakharov and their colleagues have proved that not only to us but also to the Soviet leaders. These leaders are beginning to realize that they can no longer avoid international commitments in the field of freedom of expression and that membership in U.C.C. is more than just a technical way of fulfilling other commercial trade obligations or of securing certain protective rights for themselves. Rather it requires, as does our own First Amendment, a certain basic commitment to individual creativity and freedom of expression. By continuing to show a willingness to engage the Soviets in discourse on these subjects and continuing to do business with them, while at the same time remaining firm in their commitment to principles of freedom of contract and expression, American publishers' and authors' groups are basically helping the Soviets to understand the true meaning of international copyright and the full extent of international détente. If they persist--and I feel they will--and if they are given at least some support by our government, the effects of their endeavors will endure long after equally vital but perhaps less far-reaching matters such as Soviet immigration policy have been dealt with and forgotten.

LIBRARIES AND PUBLISHERS: THE UNEASY PARTNERSHIP*

Thomas M. Schmid

Frank Wardlaw, when director of the University of Texas Press, used to liken the editor-author relationship to a porcupine that backed into a prickly pear and murmured, "Is that you, honey?" I'd like to borrow that characterization and extend it to the uneasy connection between publisher and librarian. As one who spent a goodly number of years in publishing before becoming a librarian, I am thoroughly persuaded that a strong symbiotic tie exists. It seems equally evident, unhappily, that this tie is frequently strained by both parties.

Libraries represent the overwhelming market for scholarly books. I wonder how many university presses have a librarian from their institution serving on the press committee or board of governors. It seems possible he/she could be of more than ornamental value, if only to question occasionally that well-loved assessment of a manuscript as one "which every library will have to buy." More positively, the librarian could help in certain policy decisions faced by most presses today. One of these involves the format in which information is to be published. I get the distinct impression that publishers decide on format--e.g., microfilm or microfiche, positive or negative, high or low reduction ratio, filmstrips or slides, phonodisc or audiotape, A-V materials bound into the book or offered separately--without regard for the technological trends and capabilities of libraries; without regard, in brief, for the preferences of the greatest single segment of their market. The presence of a librarian, either formally on the press committee, or informally as a consultant, might prevent the scholarly

*Reprinted by permission of the author and publisher from Scholarly Publishing, October 1974, pp. 3-7.

publisher from making some of the more egregiously wrong choices.

Another benefit resulting from such association would be the education of the librarian to the harsh realities of publishing. In such an event, his/her attitude toward publishers might change from focused dislike to vague compassion. The basic aim should be to establish communication at the level of workaday concerns, rather than relying on high-level inter-professional committees such as ALA and AAP, whose great goodwill has traditionally been exceeded only by their ineffectiveness.

Co-operation between librarian and publisher is crucial, moreover, if we are ever to come to grips with a set of problems which will yield only to a willingness on both sides to abandon dearly held concepts in favour of real change. I mean no less than a basic alteration in the economics underlying the publication of information, the distribution of information, and the compensation of its authors. This alteration was not planned, nor were plans made to cope with it. However, it is upon us and must be dealt with.

Traditionally, the economics of publishing has rested upon the physical number of copies sold--of a book, of subscriptions to a journal, of recordings, of microfiche sets, or whatever. A well-defined compensation scheme has been in force, involving purchase price, royalties, extra rights. This traditional scheme, which, with variations, has worked quite well since the time of Gutenberg, has now been badly upset by technological and societal changes. Among these changes are: scarcity and consequent high prices of paper, ink, and binding materials; cheap, convenient photocopying; computer storage and manipulation of information; relatively cheap, convenient electronic transmission of information; and increasing eagerness of libraries to form consortia, networks, and other constructs to further the sharing of resources.

All these factors are interrelated; all tend to work against the sale to libraries of large numbers of physical information packages (all right, books). As materials become scarcer and prices of books go up, libraries avail themselves of technological and co-operative means to share them, which means the price per copy goes up still further, and so on. The spiral ends when the price of books exceeds the willingness of taxpayers or boards of trustees to carry the burden.

We have seen this point reached at more than one institution, which has then had to make even greater use of photocopying, interlibrary loans, etc.

Quite apart from considerations of economy, there is the temptation, posed by the photocopying machines in libraries, to substitute wholesale copying for tedious note-taking. In the process, the copyright law takes a fearful beating. Articles, diagrams, poems, and even entire books are duplicated. To be sure, such duplication often violates copyright, but when the technology becomes irresistible, can it be stopped? An old legal tag applies here: A right without a remedy is no right at all.

There are still some librarians around who are parochial enough to think that this is mainly the publishers' problem. In a vague sort of way, they believe that the high calling of service to research and scholarship carries with it a dispensation from certain laws of the land, and they regard it as a "victory" for libraries when a ruling goes against a publisher in favour of a library: "[The Williams & Wilkins decision] is a victory for NLM and NIH and for libraries generally." (The quotation is from the ARL Newsletter of 10 January 1974). It does not require a great deal of reflection to determine just how hollow such a victory is. Given enough such victories, in the courts or in the more relevant arena of day-to-day practice, the sources of publication will surely wither. They won't disappear entirely, given people's apparently inherent drive to communicate, plus the Diktat to "publish or perish," but quantity and quality will inexorably tend to decrease.

This cannot be in the interests of libraries. We are the preservers and disseminators of information, not the originators. If our sources dry up, we will become museums, fascinating ones to be sure, but hardly places where the action is. Let me illustrate. A year or so ago, a respected reprint house announced a major project which would make widely available in microfiche an important research collection encompassing several thousands of volumes. The price was high but not exorbitant, reflecting, I assume, the publisher's break-even point if a reasonable number of research libraries were to buy the set.

What happened then? If one may extrapolate from the experience of a library at the foot of the Wasatch Mountains, my guess is that telephones were picked up all through the little universe of the Association of Research Libraries (the logical marketing target for the set), and groups of libraries--ad hoc congeries as well as established consortia--informally decided that perhaps a dozen institutions purchasing this set would be sufficient to serve the needs of their patrons. In the particular instance cited the copyright law does not even play a role, since the overwhelming bulk of the material is old enough for the copyright term to have expired. Since the format was to be microfiche, and since fiche can be reproduced at a cost of about four cents apiece, access to individual titles would be both cheap and fast for a library unwilling to incur the hefty purchase price for the whole set but prepared to go to the designated repository to fill its needs. Score one for libraries. But really? At this point, the publisher may well decide that there is no possibility for profit, and abandon the project. If that should be the case, everybody loses: the publisher, the library, and the researcher, who after all is what the whole thing is about.

So far, this discussion has been a bit hard on librarians. It is time to point out that publishers have done their ample share to contribute to the problem. What other industry would rely so trustingly on a law passed in 1909 to protect it from all the advances in technology since that date? This reliance creates a wonderland where what ought to be (according to law and statute, right and precedent) becomes what is flying in the face of experience and reason. It is perfectly possible to be comforted by counsel and upheld in every legal test, and yet be vanquished by what happens in real life. There are no winners in a struggle in which the protagonists try to ignore the twin powers of economics and technology.

After writing the previous paragraph, I was struck by the fact that I seem to have fallen into the prevailing rhetoric almost without being aware of it--using words like "struggle" and "protagonist" to describe what should essentially be a partnership between librarians and publishers. To restore that sense of partnership, I suspect that some traditional attitudes will have to be abandoned by publishers as well as librarians. I do not mean to suggest that we have already arrived at some sort of technological millennium. It was very much the fashion, ten or fifteen years ago, to predict that books and journals would soon be published in a single copy. That copy would, according to the futurists, be keypunched into a national computer, from which it could be called up on a cathode ray tube anywhere in the country (or indeed the world), and reproduced in hard copy or microform. There is no question that the technology to do this is present in full measure. The only reason that particular prophecy has not been fulfilled is that the cost would be prohibitive.

What we are dealing with, therefore, is a much more subtle problem, involving not a technological breakthrough, but a sort of technological creepthrough. The book has surely not been replaced, but the number of physical copies sold is not keeping pace with the increase in costs. It thus seems inevitable that publishers must abandon "number of copies sold" as the index of profitability. This, however, requires also that libraries in their turn abandon the concept of unrestricted access--by circulation, copying, interlibrary loan, microfilming, computerization--to the published product.

At this point, my cloven hoof will have become apparent to any librarian who might be reading this paper. It's true: the logic of the situation as perceived from at least one university library seems to dictate some form of per-use fee, a prospect that has been singularly unpalatable to librarians ever since the idea of "free access to information" gained wide currency in the nineteenth century. What's worse, I believe that librarians themselves must volunteer to make this change, for publishers do not have the power to impose it, either politically through legislation or economically through sanctions. It seems passing strange for a librarian to regard the powerful publishing establishment as something of a helpless giant. But if libraries continue to lend to each other, and their patrons continue to copy, so that one book does the work formerly performed by many, what can the publisher ultimately do? He can win the quintessentially Pyrrhic victory of going out of business, and I don't think that's what anybody has in mind.

RACE RECORDS: VICTIMS OF BENIGN NEGLECT IN LIBRARIES*

Gordon Stevenson

> The blues is an impulse to keep the painful details and episodes of a brutal experience alive in one's aching consciousness, to finger its jagged grain, and to transcend it, not by the consolation of philosophy but by squeezing from it a near-tragic, near-comic lyricism. As a form, the blues is an autobiographical chronicle of personal catastrophe expressed lyrically.
>
> --Ralph Ellison

> You may bury my body
>   down by the highway side
> So my old evil spirit
>   can get a Greyhound Bus
>   and ride
>
> --Robert Johnson

> NOTICE. STOP. Help Save The Youth of America. DON'T BUY NEGRO RECORDS. (If you don't want to serve negroes in your place of business, then do not have negro records on your juke box or listen to negro records on the radio.) The screaming idiotic words, and savage music of these records are undermining the morals of our white youth in America. Call the advertisers of the radio stations that play this type of music and complain to them! DON'T Let Your Children BUY, or LISTEN To These Negro Records. [1]

I went to the crossroads, fell down on my knees
I went to the crossroads, fell down on my knees.
Asked the Lord above: Have mercy, save poor
  Bob, if You please.

Standin' at the crossroads, I tried to flag a ride
Standin' at the crossroads, I tried to flag a ride.
Ain't nobody seem to know me. Everybody pass
  me by.

And the sun goin' down, boys. Dark's gonna catch
  me here,
Oh dark's gonna catch me here.
I haven't got no lovin' sweet woman left. Love did
  steal my gal.

You can run, you can run: tell my friend poor
  Willie Brown,
You can run: tell my friend poor Willie Brown,
Lord, that I'm standin' at the crossroads.
  Babe, I believe I'm sinking down.[2]

The above poem is one half of the "Crossroad Blues": that is, words without music. It was recorded in a cheap hotel room in San Antonio, Texas, in 1936, by a young man named Robert Johnson. Johnson was a complex, driven man with an uncommon talent for poetic imagery and musical expression. His extant works suggest that he was something of a genius, but by all standards of our society he was a loser. From the shattered fragments of a life that seems to have been continually on the verge of disaster, he created a kind of art. He confronted his world, not with poems or literature in any printed form, but with songs, and the best of his work is lost when transferred to the visual medium of print. His medium was sound, and his legacy is a small stack of old 78-rpm phonograph records. The people who manufactured and sold recordings of this sort in the 1920s and 1930s called them "race records."

Robert Johnson was a black man, and everything else proceeded from that single fact of his life. He was born on a plantation near Robinsville, Mississippi, worked as an

---

*Reprinted by permission of the author and publisher from Wilson Library Bulletin, November 1975, pp. 224-232.

itinerant musician, recorded 29 sides in Dallas and San Antonio (for which he was paid a total of around $600), and died violently in his early or mid-twenties. But for his singing, his life may not have been substantially different from the lives of many other young men who came out of the Mississippi Delta area in the 1920s and 1930s--except, perhaps, that he was more disconnected, more sensitive to his own condition, and more confused by the alien world in which he found himself. He was, in any case, one of the thousands of musicians who worked in a musical-cultural genre which is today categorized as the country blues.

The Musician as Communicator

Johnson's work has already been subjected to considerable scrutiny, as he is widely recognized as one of the most important artists in the development of certain musical styles. But beyond any consideration of the man and his work as purely musical phenomena lie the complex questions of messages, media, meanings, and the role of the library in the communications process. To say only of Johnson that he was a musician is to miss the point; he was part of a complex system of social communications. Consider for a moment the nature of communications in a culture (rather, a subculture) which, in the midst of a growing nationwide network of communications, was largely cut off from the mass media (and such was the case in Johnson's time, as it still is today to a lesser degree). What was left? Only whatever communications systems were beyond external control or did not threaten the existing relationship between the black and the white cultures. In such a dichotomous social structure, race records emerged as an important ingredient of cultural dynamics.

Librarians are interested less in Johnson (or even in music) than in the interaction between technology and culture in the communications process, in the relationship between cultural values of two different social systems, and in finding out something about our past. If one of the foundations of librarianship is an understanding of the role of communications and media in society, then we will not find a more useful or a more neglected area of investigation. We need to consider some of the hidden dimensions of this innocent diversion, the phonograph record. Like many other artifacts of popular culture, it seems so innocuous that we have tended to assume that we know all there is to know about it. In fact we hardly understand it at all.

> The blues are fantastically paradoxical and, by all logical and historical odds, they ought not to have come into being.
>
> --Richard Wright

The 35-cent Blues

Long before Johnson briefly interrupted his wanderings to record in Dallas and San Antonio, the recording companies had discovered that there were markets for the music of ethnic minorities and regional cultural groups. By present standards the southern Negro market would not have been a large one, and most of its members were poor. But they were not so poor they could not occasionally afford whatever it cost (35 to 75 cents) to buy a phonograph record. Thus in the early 1920s the manufacture of blues and gospel records was found to be a feasible business venture. Originally "race entertainment" included a broad range of material directed to special audiences (e.g., "hillbilly music" and many diverse ethnic and local styles, including much material in languages other than English),[3] but eventually the term "race record" was associated almost exclusively with music for blacks. It remained in use through the early 1940s and was used to identify audiences or markets, not musical styles. If the term sounds racist, that's because it was racist.

And so began, almost by accident, the documentation of a musical culture in such detail as had never been done before. The idea, of course, was to make money by exploiting new markets for the relatively new disc recordings, but in the process the manufacturers put us in everlasting debt to them by recording a tremendous quantity of material which would otherwise have been lost forever. Once recorded, it became a fragile resource and one in which few whites were interested. If the survival of these early recordings had depended on the interest of the library profession, the result would have been a near-total loss. Nor is it likely that more than a few libraries used them as expendable material for circulation--I should, in fact, be surprised to learn that even one public library purchased and circulated race records when they still were race records. The extent of our monumental self-deception ("serving the needs of all the people") emerges as one begins to grasp the full social and artistic significance of the material preserved on these records.

The era of the classic race record lasted in all less than 20 years, but the traditions it documented had existed decades before the rise of the phonograph and continued to exist long after the race record was identified as a marketable product. The most extensive recording activity took place between 1926 and 1930. Major record companies had their special series, which included a special "race line": RCA's race records were on the Bluebird label, Columbia Records acquired the OKeh label in 1926, and the Paramount Company purchased the Black Swan label in 1924. Other historic labels were Gennett and Brunswick-Vocalion; besides these, there were many, many more.

A wide variety of material was recorded: blues, gospel music, jazz, folk music, humorous novelties, country band music, and sermons. In the search for talent the net was cast wide, and sometimes one gets the impression that anyone who could carry a tune eventually found his or her way to a microphone. Much of the recording was done on field trips which took mobile recording units into such cities as Atlanta, Dallas, and Birmingham, and even as far afield as Kansas City, Kansas; Hot Springs, Arkansas; and Indianapolis, Indiana. The only mistake the recording companies made was in not going into Southern prisons and prison farms, where they surely would have found some first-rate musicians. (It remained for John Lomax to begin to document some of these sources in his Southern field trips in 1932.)

No Way to Fame and Fortune

At best the career of a recording artist lasted only a few years, and for most of them it was not exactly a lucrative arrangement. They were generally paid a flat rate of from $6 to $15 or $20 for each 78-rpm side. Though some singers achieved considerable fame and large, devoted followings, in the end most of them disappeared into their former milieu or found their way to the urban ghettos of the North. Some were rather ordinary in their musical abilities; others were clearly endowed with more than a touch of genius. But they all had something to say, and most said it with real style: Blind Lemon Jefferson, Charley Patton, Lonnie Johnson, Leroy Carr, Gus Cannon, Willie Johnson, Texas Alexander, Son House, Sleepy John Estes, Roosevelt Sykes, Luke Jordan, Turner Parrish, Jack Dupree--a complete list in the area of blues and gospel music would run to more than a thousand names. Some of these artists were "rediscovered" in the 1950s and had a profound impact on the subsequent course of popular music.

The discs were issued, for the most part, in small editions that ranged from the hundreds to a few thousand; though at the height of their popularity some discs were pressed in quantities as large as 7,000 or more. Recordings by very popular artists were sometimes issued in quantities running as high as 100,000. Some of these artists also were paid royalties. Discs were sold through the mails, but most were sold at such outlets as country stores, barber shops, and music stores. The number of titles issued was considerable, probably running into the tens of thousands. RCA Victor issued 2,000 titles on its Bluebird label alone. Paul Oliver wrote that "in examining the situation in the middle of the twenties when the recording of Negro artists was still young, the sociologists Odum and Johnson assessed the combined annual sales of records made by and for Negros at a figure between 5 and 6 million. At this time examples of folk musicians had scarcely appeared."[4] During the peak years around 500 titles were issued annually on race record labels. The total commercial output listed in Dixon and Godrich's Blues and Gospel Records: 1902-1942, runs to around 15,000 titles.[5]

Black Music from a White Perspective

Unlike jazz, spirituals, and urban blues (e.g., the blues of Bessie Smith), the race record did not find much of an audience with white people. There are several explanations for this: Most people outside of the black culture would have found the music neither entertaining nor enlightening, for it was not very "nice" compared with styles which then prevailed in white urban music. The texts of the secular songs were often coarse and at times vulgar, with innumerable references to sex; and the music, with its black melodic-rhythmic style, sounded primitive. It was often impossible to understand the singers, and they seemed unmusical or uneducated at best. Even when the texts were intelligible, they were filled with references and allusions which would have been meaningless to white urban audiences. In other words the idiom, the message, and the style were all wrong.

Another possibility for their lack of popularity is that rather than de facto musical segregation, there was a deliberate and systematic attempt to keep white culture free of the influences of black music. Evidence to support this theory may be found in the reaction to jazz by the white establishment, which has often been irrational (especially between 1920 and 1940) and at times has verged on hysteria. In any case most of the channels for the dissemination of the discs (including radio) were controlled by white business interests; and apparently they were under pressure from the antiblack music forces whose avowed aim was to "protect the youth of America from corruption."

This theory is not without complications. For one thing, I find it hard to believe that the ethics of the American businessman could not be made to accommodate any situation which was likely to increase profits (they have, after all, accommodated war, ecological suicide, and a sort of cultural rape). I doubt that anyone really gave a damn about the youth of America, white or black. What was wanted was a continued belief in the myths and superstitutions that supported the racial system of white supremacy. Thus the aim was to denigrate all aspects of black culture. For example, advertisements for race records pictured blacks as rakes, fools, or simple-minded but happy and harmless wards of white society. It is very possible that pious, self-righteous attempts by some whites to "protect the youth of America" were in fact shrewd tactics to postpone the day when the youth of America would respond to the substantive content of the race records. This theory, then, would suggest that race records were thought to be a potential threat to some sectors of the white community, not because they might corcupt the value systems of young people, but because they might break down cultural barriers and open up lines of communication and understanding.

"The Fabric of Cultural Identity"

Even today, more than 30 years after the end of the era of the race record, what is considered one of the great musical accomplishments of the twentieth century is surrounded by a pall of irrespectability and locked into grotesque stereotypes. But a thorough study of the material on race records will reveal that some forms (e.g., the blues and gospel music) were as perfect as any art forms ever invented. Furthermore, the system as a whole was a remarkably efficient means of sharing a set of cultural values.

The milieu into which the records were introduced was described by Charles Edward Smith as a society in which music "was the binding fabric of cultural identity, entering into every phase of life, not merely in terms of spiritual and secular but in terms of work and play, love and loneliness, good and bad, and the world of waiting and the wall of color."[6]

The uniquely authentic tone of the race record material, its undiluted honesty and stark realism were the result of circumstances surrounding its manufacture and dissemination. In the 1920s and 1930s, when providing material for black audiences (and, for that matter, for rural whites and urban ethnic audiences), the manufacturers simply plugged into and expanded existing channels of communication. The industry had not yet begun to think in terms of manipulating audiences, manufacturing images, and influencing styles. This is not to say that the interaction between the medium and the music did not have important ramifications for the music. On the contrary, the introduction of the record affected the whole structure of the black music system.

It seems to me that because of the wide currency of the disc recordings, the culture we are talking about was nonliterate in only a very narrow sense. It created a literature, but its form of publication was the ten-inch 78-rpm shellac disc, not the printed word. The music was communication, entertainment, art, and education within a culture. This appears to be the unique feature of race records. To dismiss them as mere entertainment would be absurd; it would be equally absurd to study them exclusively in terms of musical or esthetic values (in any case, whose esthetics would be used?). These are uncompromisingly faithful documents, primary sources which touch on facets of the structure and meaning of life, and as such can contribute something to our understanding of the Afro-American experience which can probably not be gained from any other source. Imamu Amiri Baraka put it this way: "If the music of the Negro in America, in all its permutations, is subjected to a socioanthropological as well as musical scrutiny, something about the essential nature of the Negro's existence in this country ought to be revealed, as well as something about the essential nature of this country, i.e., society as a whole."[7]

Putting Down Musical Roots

Of what value are the race records today; to whom,

if anyone, are they valuable? To most whites they are of no value whatsoever, and will remain forever remote and alien. In terms of music the race records are indeed the source, the roots of jazz and the roots of the quintessential music of the twentieth century--and here I agree with Henry Pleasants, the music critic who believes that our musical epoch is the Afro-American epoch. [8]

What the race-record repertoire means to blacks, I do not know; though I think of something that Harold Cruse wrote: "The Black man's one great and present hope is to know and understand his Afro-American history in the United States more profoundly."[9] Much of that history has only been preserved in the grooves of thousands of those old recordings. Black studies programs in history, sociology, music, literature, religion, and education should be enhanced by at least some use of these resources. One might turn to them for such reasons as these: to learn to appreciate Afro-American culture and its art; to understand something of the origins of the great stylistic changes in twentieth-century music; to understand, at least in part, the life and times of black people in the United States; to enrich our repertoire of American poetry and folk literature; and to experience an art which at its best transcends time and place and deals with the constants of humanity.

To approach the music of the race records in search of those more illusive and subjective (and certainly more important) experiences--that is, to somehow get involved in it, rather than merely observe it as an outsider--requires for many of us a complete reorientation, including some deschooling in the area of music appreciation. Music is human behavior; it is created through a complex interaction of persons and their environment. Creating it, performing it, and listening to it are activities which are learned within a culture. Songs mean something to somebody within a specific context. Now if this is true, who is to say that Robert Johnson's "Crossroad Blues" is any less a masterpiece than, say, Schubert's "Erlkoenig"? Perhaps the "Crossroad Blues" is the better work--does it not depend on who we are, on our points of reference? And if Johnson does not speak to us, we may well ask where the fault lies.

Some of us have learned to understand and to enjoy the music of Schubert; with considerably more effort we might be able to understand and even enjoy the music of Robert Johnson. Just how difficult this may be is clear when we realize that some of us have closer cultural and musical ties with the early nineteenth-century European romanticism which produced Schubert than we do with the black culture of the southern United States in the twenties and thirties which shaped the idiom, the message, and the style of the likes of a Robert Johnson.

Private Hands or Public Access?

How librarians respond emotionally or intellectually to this material is beside the point. As a profession committed to dealing with socially useful systems of communication, our responsibilities are clear. We need to build up archival and reference collections of the original 78-rpm recordings, assist in the bibliographical organization of their contents, make them accessible, and encourage their use.

What progress have libraries made to date? This is not an easy question to answer, for whatever is being done is not reported in the library literature. To most students and collectors of the various genres of music preserved on race records, libraries are a complete anathema. As far as I can tell, the library profession's treatment of these resources is a disgrace, and prospects for change seem quite remote. Most of what has been preserved is in the hands of private collectors. Until more librarians learn how to organize and administer collections of early sound recordings it is probably just as well that they remain there.

Some of our large general archives of recorded sound, though not specializing in race records, do contain some resources. Few of them have the money or the staff to organize and expand their collections. In this situation the Library of Congress comes through magnificently. Their interest in this material dates back at least to the 1930s, and LC now has substantial holdings of commercially issued material along with invaluable field recordings never issued in the trade. Collections serving graduate studies in folk music and ethnomusicology usually include race records (the Archives of Traditional Music at Indiana University, for example). Some universities with a commitment to the documentation of black culture or to formal programs of black studies are interested in them. Of course, the Schomburg Center for Research in Black Culture (NYPL) holds material in this area. Collections specifically documenting the history of jazz inevitably include at least some blues and gospel music. Any library that started to assemble a race record collection as late as the early 1950s could still have picked up a lot of material at bargain prices. But the days when these discs sold for a dime or a quarter are long since past; prices are much higher today, although it is difficult to estimate just how much higher because most of the discs are sold through mail-order auctions. (Some specialty stores that stock 78 rpm's also sell them.)

How to Find Race Records

To find out what is going on, librarians have to make use of the "invisible college" that ties together a worldwide network of blues and jazz collectors and specialists. One begins by subscribing to such periodicals as *Record Finder*, *Vintage Jazz Mart*, *Blues Unlimited*, and *Living Blues* for discographies, auction lists, reviews, and list of reissues. An up-to-date and detailed list of dealers and periodicals can be found in the second edition (1975) of Paul Jackson's *Collectors' Contact Guide*.[10]

Back in the Groove

For libraries less interested in preservation than in developing current programs, the prospects are much brighter. The extent of the popularity of early blues and the economics of the record manufacturing industry are such that there are a dozen or more companies reissuing material. As one would expect, Folkways Records was active in this field quite early (some 25 years ago) and has an excellent catalog of basic materials. Most of the reissuing companies are relatively small independent firms. One thinks of such labels as: Yazoo, Milestone, Library of Congress, Biograph, Arhoolie.

The monster companies, Victor and Columbia, have also reissued some historical material from the vast holdings in their vaults (including a virtually complete reissue of the works of Robert Johnson on Columbia CL 1654 and C 30034). There is also a large literature about certain types of race records, particularly the blues. Paul Oliver, Samuel B. Charters, Eric Sackheim, Pete Welding, Imamu Amiri Baraka, Robert Dixon, John Godrich, Charles Keil, and Frank Driggs, among others, have all made substantial contributions to our understanding of the blues and other race-record material.

The secondary sources, then, are at hand for those librarians who want to use them. The larger issue of the responsibility of the profession in preservation, restoration, organization, and access, however, remains unresolved. The reasons for this are not just cultural, for it is a simple fact that librarians have never learned to cope with sound recordings as historical research or reference materials. When we do learn, though, we will discover--through such musical genres as the race record--a richness that can only enhance our library collections.

References

1. From an undated broadside reproduced in Paul Oliver's The Story of the Blues. New York, Chilton, 1969, p. 167.
2. Transcribed from Robert Johnson's recording as issued on Columbia CL 1654. The transcription of the last line of the third verse is conjectural.
3. The production of foreign language material was an established part of the industry by 1910. For clarifying this and many other points, I am indebted to Dick Spotswood.
4. Oliver, Paul. The Meaning of the Blues. New York, Collier Books, 1963, p. 2.
5. Godrich, John, and Robert M. W. Dixon. Blues & Gospel Records: 1902-1942. (Rev. ed.) New York, Int. Publications Service, 1969.
6. Notes to Down Home: A Portrait of a People. Folkways FA 2691.
7. Baraka, Imamu Amiri. Blues People. New York, Morrow, 1963, p. ix-x.
8. Pleasants, Henry. Serious Music and All That Jazz. New York, Simon and Schuster, 1969.
9. Cruse, Harold. The Crisis of the Negro Intellectual. New York, Morrow, 1971.
10. Jackson, Paul T. Collectors' Contact Guide, No. 2. Recorded Sound Research (1506 W. Barker, Peoria, IL 61608), 1975.

PART IV

THE SOCIAL PREROGATIVE

THE RIGHTS OF THE YOUNG*

Dorothy Broderick

Librarians have been quick to recognize that the passage of state obscenity laws dealing with the protection of the young can directly and seriously affect library service to children and adolescents. However, what is only just emerging is that the traditional library policy of ducking the issue of the rights of youth by saying that it is up to parents to control their children's reading materials may become an equally explosive issue.

When a situation like the West Virginia textbook controversy arises, we see clearly that more is at issue than parental rights to control their children's knowledge exposure. Those children must grow up to live in a world broader than that of their parents and much as dedicated individualists may not like it, there is a concept in most democratic governments that there are issues which transcend an individual's rights and on which the general welfare of the "state" takes precedence. When education became compulsory, it removed from parents the right to have their children grow up ignorant, but only in the broadest definition of the term. When compulsory vaccination was introduced, it removed from individuals the right to infect others--and the right of parents to determine whether their children would or would not be vaccinated. In our present era, we see these events as representing nothing more than common sense, forgetting the struggle it took to achieve them.

Perhaps some of us will live long enough to see a society that takes for granted the rights of youth, but in our present society, we are a long way from that goal. It seems vital that we begin talking frankly among ourselves about how

*Reprinted by permission of the author and publisher from Young Adult Alternative Newsletter, Vol. 3, No. 2, March 15, 1975.

we feel about the rights of youth. Does the public library turn its back on the young and say, sorry, it's not our fault you were born to restrictive parents? Or do we have the courage to assume an advocacy position in our communities and say that young people have rights, including the right to make their own mistakes. The key word is mistakes. Adults who advocate restrictions upon youth do so out of the very best intentions. All of us want for the young a better world than we had.

The problem is that we want to keep the young from making the mistakes of our generation without recognizing that our environment no longer exists. Most of us, if we were honest, would have to admit that the world in which today's youth live has little resemblance to the one in which we grew up. Thus, none of our experiences are particularly helpful to us or the young in dealing with today's world.

Librarians who express horror at the separate school systems being developed in West Virginia--one for those students whose parents are willing to risk having ideas presented in the educational process--are going to have to accept the fact that, if they continue to cling to the idea that parents have the right to control their children's reading, they (the librarians) are equally guilty of restricting youth's right to know. Most of us rejected the efforts of white parents to set up separate schools following the _Brown vs. Board of Education_ decision. Is segregation of the young because of parental attitudes inside the library any different?

Do we understand that, when a school system sets up a sex education course and says that only those students whose parents give approval may take it, we are seeing an erosion of youth's right to know? Do we recognize that all of us will eventually be forced to pay for the ignorance imposed upon those young people? Do we lose any sleep over the fact that such ignorance may ruin the lives of those young people? Do we CARE?

Whether we like it or not, it is time to recognize that the traditional stance of the public library in relationship to the non-rights of the young is the same as all other institutions in our society. Our attitude is firmly based upon the idea that children are the property of the people who biologically reproduce them. They aren't. And we are never going to have a truly human society until we recognize that the young are a _bona fide_ part of the human race.

In The Battered Child in Canada*, there is this plea:

> So let us become more sensitive to the needs of children, both others' and our own. Let us accept the notion that they, too, ought to have human rights, which their parents ought to recognize.... Not only can we help specific children by becoming pillars of emotional support and perhaps in nitty-gritty ways, too; but we can also by our sensitivity and good sense help improve the general atmosphere in our neighbourhoods, so that respect for the rights of children to be children, secure and free, becomes the 'in' thing.

Can we as librarians working with children and young adults take that statement and make it our commitment to the youth we serve?

Sure, it will be hard work and tough sledding, but who ever promised us a rose garden?

POLITICS AND THE NEW BRITANNICA*

Harvey Einbinder

The creation and distribution of a major adult encyclopedia is an international enterprise. Scholarly contributors are recruited from all over the world, and a sales force is organized to market the set in foreign countries where English is used as a vehicle of information and education.

In the past, encyclopedias were identified with particular countries. The famous eleventh edition of the *Britannica* of 1910-11 was the work of British scholarship. The fourteenth edition of 1929 was a product of American and English learning. The new Britannica 3 employs contributors from many countries, although its inspiration and guiding force is American. The international emphasis is accentuated because more than a third of the sales of adult American encyclopedias are now generated overseas.

The preceding edition of the *Britannica* was a monument to the marketing genius of its principal owner, the late William Benton. He obtained a two-thirds interest in the set in 1943, and successfully transformed an aging, mediocre reference work possessing a famous name into a financial bonanza. He fixed the *Britannica* in the public mind as a symbol of accuracy and authority by means of skillful promotion and aggressive advertising, and convinced middle-class parents that the set was an indispensable educational aid for their children. Thanks to his brilliant salesmanship, Benton realized almost $100 million from an initial investment of $100, 000, and provided an additional $45 million in royalties for the University of Chicago.

This financial success occurred despite a host of biased, outmoded and inaccurate entries in the *Encyclopaedia*.

*Reprinted by permission of the author and publisher from *The Nation*, March 22, 1975, pp. 342-344.

These editorial failings were documented in my articles in Columbia University Forum in 1960 and in Encounter in 1961, and in my book The Myth of the Britannica in 1964. The Britannica's publisher ignored these findings and my proposal for a completely new edition. Instead, it continued to promote the old set, which was brought up-to-date by means of piecemeal revision. This process culminated in the 200th anniversary edition of 1968, which was celebrated with an exuberant display of humbug and hullabaloo.

At the same time that this edition was being touted as the last word in scholarship, editorial work was started to create a totally new Britannica, the first complete overhaul in its 200-year history. The new EB, which appeared in the spring of 1974, contains many innovations. Instead of a single alphabetic arrangement, its thirty volumes consist of two essentially independent encyclopedias. Ten volumes are devoted to an alphabetic array of short factual entries; nineteen volumes to an alphabetic sequence of long essay-articles; and one volume to a systematic topical outline of the subjects covered in the set.

The new edition is dedicated to Queen Elizabeth II and the President of the United States, who is not named. A year earlier, the Britannica's dedication identified the President as Richard Milhous Nixon. In the new edition, he is not named--a wise precaution, since Mr. Nixon resigned a few months after this dedication appeared.

The new EB contains a wide range of geographical and historical articles because it is intended for readers in many countries. Subjects are treated from an international perspective, rather than a narrow American (and British) viewpoint. As a result, the Encyclopaedia possesses a broader perspective than works such as World Book, designed primarily for American schoolchildren. To accommodate this wider audience, the EB frequently employs foreign experts, who sometimes present points of view characteristic of their native countries rather than American scholarship.

Dr. Pangloss is alive and well in the new edition. Foreign countries are portrayed in glowing terms. An insistent optimism that is reminiscent of the National Geographic infuses the pages of the Encyclopaedia. Positive developments are emphasized; negative factors are slighted. Growth and progress are stressed; inertia and stagnation are minimized. No matter how impoverished a nation may be, hope is held out for a brighter, better future. Even when the facts presented are bleak and forbidding, contributors manage to find something hopeful to say about the future.

A striking instance is the essay on Liberia, which notes that malaria afflicts nearly 100 per cent of the population. It records that dysentery and diarrhea are important causes of infant mortality. Influenza, intestinal worms, sleeping sickness and elephantiasis are also prevalent. Nevertheless, the article asserts, "Living conditions throughout Liberia, while poor, are improving."

Political and social problems are treated cautiously. Controversial topics are covered superficially to avoid antagonizing national prejudices. This is natural because foreign schools and libraries are major overseas prospects for the Britannica. The purchasing policies of many of these institutions are controlled by officials who expect their country to be presented in a flattering light. Thus the essay on South Africa, which is an important English-speaking market, employs the term "separate development" in discussing the government's racial policies. The word "apartheid" is not used because South African officials now frown upon this term. (A brief entry on apartheid, however, appears elsewhere in the set.) The essay observes that at the beginning of 1970 more than 800 people were serving sentences under various security laws, but does not describe those laws, which permit authorities to imprison suspects for months without trial. The essay also records that the prison population has risen sharply to more than 90,000 with 750,000 admissions a year, the majority being for violations of the pass laws that define the right of Africans to live and work in "white" areas. The essay, however, does not explain how these laws are used to control the life and movement of the black majority, and to insure the continued supremacy of the white minority.

Distortions and omissions are inevitable when articles are prepared by citizens of authoritarian regimes. The article on Spain disregards the existence of censorship, the secret police, and a large category of political offenses. Instead it claims that Spain has fewer prisoners than any other country in Europe. One section describes the structure of the government without describing the role of Francisco Franco, who has dominated the political life of Spain for nearly forty years. This is hardly an oversight, since the article was prepared jointly by a professor at the University of Madrid and the Secretary General of Tourism of the Spanish Government.

When articles on Communist and Fascist states are written by native authors, they inevitably contain government propaganda. Objectivity is impossible, since articles must follow the party line and portray the regime in power in a favorable light. An example is the EB's rosy survey of Soviet cultural life prepared by the editor of a Moscow publishing house. He offers a glowing description of creative activity under communism, and points with pride to the current five-year plan that will raise the cultural standards of the Russian people. His survey hails the 80,000 book titles published each year in the Soviet Union, and singles out the novels of Sholokhov and Fadeyev as major works of Socialist Realism. But he does not hint at the repressive efforts of the Communist Party and the Soviet State to control the creative output of authors, artists and composers. Characteristically, the editor praises the poetry of Boris Pasternak, but says nothing about Dr. Zhivago. His party-line account treats Isaac Babel, Osip Mandelstam and Alexander Solzhenitsyn as nonpersons since it disregards their literary achievements.

Presumably Britannica editors commissioned and accepted this apologia by a Soviet bureaucrat, and others like it, in order to secure the cooperation and approval of the Soviet Government in recruiting Russian scholars to prepare articles on other subjects.

Perhaps the spirit of détente explains why the long essay on Soviet legal systems by a Columbia University law professor disguises the crimes committed in the name of law against millions of Russian citizens. The professor fails to cite Article 58 of the Criminal Code, used as a legal instrument by Stalin and the secret police to imprison a generation of victims. The professor disposes of the millions who were condemned and who perished in Soviet labor camps by simply asserting that in punishing "attempts to subvert state authority, the definitions and practice under Stalin exceeded the norms of liberal Western democracies in vagueness and severity of penalties prescribed."

In dealing with backward countries, the Encyclopaedia usually does not attempt to convey social and political realities. Instead it supplies a neutral account buttressed with statistics that allow conditions to be inferred, rather than made manifest. In addition, political oppression is often treated in gingerly fashion. Thus the EB reports: "Haiti under Duvalier was, in effect, a police state ruled as a dictatorship.... The Tontons Macoutes, Duvalier's private police force, became less brutal and arbitrary, because its earlier conduct had disturbed tourists." The article, however, does not portray the fear and terror generated by the Duvalier dictatorship. Similarly, the entry on Paraguay claims, "The future of Paraguayan political life depends on the maintenance of the principles of free enterprise ... and on free elections." Yet since 1954, Paraguay has been ruled by General Stroessner, who has abrogated constitutional guarantees and employed the secret police and political terror to stamp out opposition to his dictatorial regime.

Occasionally the Britannica speaks frankly about foreign tyrants, particularly in articles written by American scholars who are not hobbled by the caution and restrictions that inhibit some foreign contributors. An example is the essay on the history of the Dominican Republic which bluntly states, "The dictatorship of Rafael Trujillo was one of the longest, cruelest, most absolute dictatorships the world has ever known. For over three decades Trujillo ruled his country with an iron hand; virtually everything in the country he touched belonged to him.... In 1965 the Dominican Republic exploded in a popularly based and democratic social revolution. Fearing a second Cuba, however, the United States again occupied the country militarily and snuffed out the revolution."

Such outspoken essays are the exception rather than the rule. Britannica 3 maintains a low profile in dealing with recent history, seeking to serve as a repository for facts and information, rather than ideas and controversy. Thus it devotes only a page to the war in Vietnam, restricting itself to a dry, factual summary in the entry on Vietnam, but does not attempt to analyze the impact of this traumatic conflict on American political life.

Although the treatment of political topics in the new edition is very cautious, many of the taboos of earlier editions have been discarded. Victorian prudery no longer prevents sexual subjects from being discussed freely and frankly. Religious articles are no longer exercises in special pleading. Again and again, the new edition has benefited from its origin as a completely fresh work and from advances in contemporary learning. Although the EB's defective handling of certain political issues is significant, this flaw affects only a small proportion of the set because of the wide range of subjects covered. Therefore, despite such imperfections, the new Britannica represents a major advance in encyclopedia construction; its contents and organization are far superior to competing adult works, such as the _Americana_ and _Collier's_.

The new _EB_ has been published a decade too late for the company to readily recoup its multimillion-dollar investment. Had the new edition appeared in 1964, it would have benefited from rising college enrollments, teen-age population growth and the years of prosperity. Today the company is faced with an unfavorable economic and educational climate. Declining school enrollments, limited library budgets, a falling birth rate, and the prospect of "hard times" make it difficult to market an encyclopedia that costs more than $500. Faced with this forbidding future, executives may be tempted to utilize the hard-sell techniques exploited so profitably in the past.

Aggressive salesmanship rather than editorial innovation has always been the driving force behind reference book publishing. Unlike the publishers of trade books, the content of which largely determines their sale, encyclopedia publishers rely on an army of door-to-door salesmen armed with "special offers" and glib sales pitches to entice parents to sign on the dotted line. Since sales managers are paid according to the number of sets sold in their territory, they have often encouraged salesmen to engage in deception and deceit. The resulting unethical practices have been repeatedly censured by the Federal Trade Commission, and have led to substantial fines levied against major reference book publishers. This record has been documented by _The Nation_, the _National Observer_ and _The Wall Street Journal_. Despite this adverse publicity, dubious sales methods are still employed because of their success.

Evidence that fraudulent practices persist in the encyclopedia industry is furnished by the recent ruling of an FTC judge who found that the _Britannica_ has been recruiting employees by promising them middle-management training, when they were actually being hired as encyclopedia salesmen. The judge also found that salesmen were entering the homes of consumers under false pretenses by claiming to be conducting a market survey, when they were actually selling the _Britannica_, and by offering fictitious discounts. These deceptive techniques may cast a pall over the genuine achievements of the editors of _Britannica 3_, as executives convert a major new reference work into a commodity to be marketed by means of the high-pressure huckstering endemic in the encyclopedia trade.

THE ZOIA HORN CONTROVERSY: A STUDY OF GROUP INTERACTION*

Joan Foster

On March 3, 1972, Zoia Horn, a graduate of Brooklyn College and Pratt Institute, and a reference librarian, was led from a courthouse in Harrisburg, Pennsylvania and imprisoned. This was one scene in a drama that began to unfold in 1968 when draft records were burned in protest in Catonsville, Maryland, and the brothers Daniel and Philip Berrigan first achieved front-page notoriety as anti-war radicals. For the purposes of this case study, the drama ended on the floor of the 1973 Midwinter American Library Association Convention where an important resolution concerning governmental intimidation was passed by the ALA Council. Briefly, the aspect of this controversy which most affected the library community and its major professional organization was the refusal of Zoia Horn to testify at the trial of the "Harrisburg 7," as the defendants were known, in a case growing out of the Catonsville affair. Her refusal was a matter of conscience because "as a private citizen and librarian," she could not lend herself to "a legal process that was destructive of our freedoms."[1]

The pressures which led to this "outraged act of resistance by a quiet, gentle woman who had never before made a comparable political gesture,"[2] must be examined in their social and political context so that we may fully comprehend the effect of the action on the American Library Association. Zoia Horn acted as a catalyst which polarized groups within the ALA and led to a reexamination of relevant social issues within that body. This paper employs an approach similar to that used by Ruth Aaronson,[3] in which pressures and counter-pressures of various groups are examined within the atmosphere of the total community.

---

*Reprinted by permission of the author and publisher from Pratt Portfolio, Fall 1975, pp. 17-39.

The pressure groups involved here were both formal and informal. The informal were more general, sometimes amorphous groups representing many different factions motivated by a broad idea or direction. Various manifestations of this emerged in the anti-war movement and among the dissident forces within the ALA. Growing out of the climate and attitudes spawned by these general groups were more formalized, structured groups with specific names and objectives. However, one of the important distinctions in this study is that Zoia Horn as an individual was a prime motivating force. She was clearly affected by the pressures exerted upon her by various groups, as described in part one of this study; but the efforts to mobilize these groups within the library profession, discussed in the second part of this paper, occurred largely because of Zoia Horn's moving description of her experiences before the membership of the ALA at Dallas in 1971.

Part 1

The earliest significant protest against the Vietnam war was a "declaration of conscience" made public in February of 1965, just shortly after the United States began non-retaliatory air attacks against North Vietnam. The declaration was endorsed by hundreds including Martin Luther King, Bayard Rustin, Lewis Mumford, Linus Pauling, Benjamin Spock, and two Catholic priests--Daniel Berrigan and Philip Berrigan. One study characterized this anti-war movement as unprecedented in the United States, for historically, "the wars most closely resembling the current one did not generate a comparable reaction."[4] This protest movement constituted a group in the broadest sense which emerged from a combination of unusual factors: extensive communications and documentary coverage of the events of war, a long knowledge of its course and history on the part of the American people, and misleading governmental promises and arguments. While the anti-war movement consisted of a number of small groups with differing principles, their techniques--demonstrations, mass marches, and picketing--were often similar, and certain generalizations can be made. It was a basically unstructured group nurtured by events rather than ideology, and consisting of a fluid membership with very limited national control. Basically, membership derived from the middle-class and consisted largely of teachers, students and clergy. Each of these smaller groups made their unique contributions to the whole with the students providing the masses needed for demonstrations, the teachers engaging in debate with opposing interests, and the clergy raising moral issues and performing dramatic acts to focus attention on the movement. Despite these elements, the anti-war movement was primarily a response to events that occurred in the war--it generally did not create events. Thus, any analysis of the motives and actions of the so-called leadership, like Dr. Spock or the Berrigans, must be predicated on the fact that their actions were a sympathetic and often dramatic response to the dissent and resistance of their young followers. Usually, their arrest and conviction generated greater support for their positions. And, aware of this, the leadership willingly entered into acts of illegal protest.

The events at Catonsville, Maryland on May 17, 1968 can be viewed as a natural outgrowth of thie kind of group movement. It was in Catonsville that Daniel and Philip Berrigan along with seven other Catholic radicals burned local draft records with napalm, then joined hands and recited the Lord's Prayer as they awaited arrest. As expected, they were arrested, tried and convicted, and the stage was set for the activities at Bucknell University which were eventually to lead to the Harrisburg trial and Zoia Horn's protest.

After the Catonsville trial, Philip Berrigan was jailed in the federal prison at Lewisburg, the same town in which Bucknell University is located. Daniel Berrigan, whose arrest was also ordered after the trial, successfully eluded the FBI for several months, staying in thirty-seven different homes in ten cities in the east and midwest. He was finally arrested on Block Island.

Either out of vindictiveness for Daniel Berrigan's successful avoidance of the FBI or in an effort to increase FBI appropriations, Director J. Edgar Hoover made a startling announcement to a Senate Appropriations Subcommittee in November of 1970, just a few months after Daniel had been arrested. He announced that a group called the "East Coast Conspiracy to Save Lives" had conspired to blow up the heating system in federal buildings in Washington and kidnap Henry Kissinger. The plot, seemingly irrational and unlikely, was treated generally as a joke, and Hoover was roundly criticized for making a "grand-stand play designed only to help him win funds for 1, 000 extra FBI agents."[5] Representative William Anderson (D. -Tenn.) was particularly vocal, accusing Hoover of resorting to "tactics reminiscent of McCarthyism, using newspaper headlines and scare dramatics rather than the due process of law he has so proudly upheld..."[6]

Perhaps in response to this criticism, the case was quickly brought to the grand jury convened in Harrisburg, Pennsylvania, which in turn handed up indictments on January 12, naming Philip Berrigan, the Rev. Joseph R. Wenderoth, the Rev. Neil R. McLaughlin, Anthony Schoblick, Eqbal Ahmad, and Sister Elizabeth McAlister as defendants. Daniel Berrigan and six others were named as co-conspirators.

The chief government witness at both the grand jury investigation and the "Harrisburg 7" trial a year later was Boyd Douglas. Douglas had been an inmate at the Lewisburg prison during the time that Philip Berrigan was imprisoned there. Through a special program with Bucknell, Douglas was allowed to attend classes at the University, where he also worked as a student assistant in the processing department of Bucknell University Library during the spring and fall semester of 1970. (Douglas was the only one of 1400 prisoners who participated in this "program" during this period.) It was as a result of this activity at the library that Douglas became friendly with Zoia Horn and Patricia Rom, another librarian. Douglas also became involved with anti-war activists, developed outside contacts, and arranged meetings with various people later named in the indictments. He carried letters from Philip Berrigan inside the prison to the Berrigan circle outside; en route, he made copies of these letters and dispatched them to the FBI. It was later revealed that Douglas did all this while actually in the employ of the FBI. Zoia Horn was called to testify because she knew Douglas and because one of the "arrangements" made by him was for Father Neil McLaughlin and Father Joseph Wenderoth to stay at her home in the fall of 1970.

This was a major case, but not an isolated one, for in the late sixties and early seventies the anti-war movement and the Government's efforts to control it were major opposing forces in the nation. As the anti-war groups became more effective, there was a corresponding increase in governmental controls. On June 19, 1968, one month after the Catonsville protest, Congress passed the Omnibus Crime Control and Safe Streets Act which in President Johnson's words sanctioned "eavesdropping and wiretapping by Federal, state and local officials in an almost unlimited variety of situations."[7] As a result, electronic surveillance and wiretapping were freely employed against domestic anti-war groups. Other devices like interrogation of leaders, high bail and paid informers like Boyd Douglas were also used. Many of these factors disturbed Zoia Horn and Patricia Rom. Although they both testified at the grand jury investigation, they had serious misgivings. The influence of the anti-war movement and the nature of the governmental action in this case generated a reaction within them and moved the two librarians to initiate action on their own in the most productive manner they could. Zoia Horn and Patricia Rom elected to describe their experiences to the gathered membership of the American Library Association and introduce a resolution on the floor of the American Library Association convention in Dallas in 1971. An examination of the effects of this action on various groups within the American Library Association is the subject of the second part of this study.

Part 2

Since its establishment almost one hundred years ago, the American Library Association has developed an influence beyond the confines of the library profession, extending to scores of organizations and institutions interested in its recommendations and decisions. These include national and local governments, publishers, students, and international groups. But as it has grown larger and more influential, the ALA seems to have followed the pattern of large corporations. As analyzed by Eli Oboler, [8] corporations undergo "a long period of slow growth and development, a relatively short period of reformulation both of basic structure and underlying beliefs, a short period of rapid expansion, and a period of varying lengths of time of relative dominance." Oboler would place ALA today in the "short period of rapid expansion," but he wonders how long the periods of "relative dominance" will last when there are strong indications of "great difficulties" and "irreconcilable tensions" within the organization. As early as 1949, Garceau described ALA as "a maze of overlapping, ill-defined groups, some very active and eager, some rather confused."[9] Other criticism has included charges of unresponsiveness, lack of relevance, bureaucratism, and lack of democracy. Since most of the recent criticism of the organization stems from its structure, it would be useful to briefly review that structure.

The membership is divided into thirteen Divisions, each with its own governing board and an unspecified number of special committees within them. A Division has the authority to act on matters within its area of responsibility (e.g., school libraries, reference and adult services, library education, etc.). There are ten Round Tables which are largely discussion units with power only to recommend policy. The Council is the governing body with a large voting membership that makes all the decisions of the Association, while an Executive Board serves as the administrative arm of the Council. General membership actions have no authority but are construed as recommendations to the Council. In recent years, the Council has been accused of unresponsiveness to wishes of the membership; the late Executive Director of ALA, David H. Clift, has observed, "the result could be loosely characterized by saying that the membership often goes overboard in its recommendations while the Council often reacts in a conservative manner."[10]

Throughout its history, ALA has gone through various critical periods of self-examination. One of these began about 1968 and is particularly pertinent to the Zoia Horn controversy. It must be recalled that during this period, rebellion and protest were commonplace and "relevance" was a very popular word. Criticism of ALA, particularly by new librarians, became strong and vocal. On the petition of 300 members, the idea of a "social responsibilities of libraries" Round Table was presented and approved by the membership in June of 1968. The membership requested immediate action by the Executive Board and Council but it was not until the 1969 Midwinter meeting that the Social Responsibilities Round Table--SRRT--was approved. Its purposes were

> to provide a forum for the discussion of the responsibilities of libraries in relation to the important problems of social change which face institutions and librarians; to provide for exchange of information among all ALA units about library activities, with the goal of increasing understanding of current social problems; to act as a stimulus to the Association and its various units in making libraries more responsive to current social needs;...[11]

Once approved, SRRT immediately set about organizing task forces and action groups based on the work of "aggressive volunteers" while simultaneously providing a voice for "activists" and a forum for "letting off steam" on many issues on which the official voice of ALA could not be heard.

SRRT was one of the major groups prodding and pushing the ALA to take a stand on the Zoia Horn issue. SRRT's involvement in the matter began during the grand jury hearings when a request for documentation by the Harrisburg

Defense Committee brought about the creation of the "Task Force to Document the East Coast Conspiracy Trial." Because of the manner in which SRRT is organized, it was relatively simple to establish this Task Force and by March of 1971, about 70 periodicals were being scanned, clipped and photocopied by librarians. Anything relating to the Harrisburg trial or "conspiracy" was sent on to the lawyers and investigators in the case.

Another ALA group of major importance here was the Intellectual Freedom Committee, which is a standing committee of the Council established to

> ... recommend such steps as may be necessary to safeguard the rights of library users, libraries and librarians, in accordance with the First Amendment to the United States Constitution and the Library Bill of Rights as adopted by ALA Council; to work closely with the Office of Intellectual Freedom and with other units and officers of the association in matters touching intellectual freedom and censorship.[12]

The Office of Intellectual Freedom, established in 1967, serves as liaison to the Committee and administers the Freedom to Read Foundation and the LeRoy C. Merritt Humanitarian Fund.

This organizational structure was established in 1948 with the adoption of the Library Bill of Rights, which has served as the basis for all future efforts in the area of intellectual freedom. The "Freedom to Read" statement was adopted in 1953 and remains an ALA landmark against suppression and censorship. By 1969, the Freedom to Read Foundation was established as a device to expand ALA activities in this area. The Foundation was set up as a separate corporation to avoid jeopardizing the entire ALA program in the eyes of the Internal Revenue Service; but, it does, nevertheless, have a tax-exempt status and requires lengthy investigations before taking action. To answer the demands for immediate response without careful scrutiny, the LeRoy C. Merritt Humanitarian Fund was created. It has no tax exemption, is unconcerned with the tax laws, and can, therefore, provide quick support to a librarian in need who is threatened by problems relating to intellectual freedom.

The resolution against governmental intimidation

introduced by Zoia Horn and Patricia Rom at the ALA Convention in 1971 can be compared with the Freedom to Read Statement in that it responds to governmental attempts at restricting traditional American freedoms. It said, in part:

> ...What has happened to us is of extreme importance to our profession. We move: (1) that ALA Membership meeting at Dallas recognizes the danger to intellectual freedom presented by the use of spying in libraries by governmental agencies; (2) that ALA go on record against the use of the grand jury procedure to intimidate anti-Vietnam War activists and people seeking justice for minority communities; (3) that ALA deplore and go on record against the use of the Conspiracy Act of 1968 as a weapon against the citizens of this country who are being indicted for such overt acts as meeting, telephoning, discussing alternative methods of bringing about change, and writing letters; (4) that ALA ... assert the confidentiality of the professional relationships of librarians to the people they serve ... ; (5) that ALA assert that it is expected that no librarian would lend himself to a role as informant, whether of voluntarily revealing circulation records or identifying patrons and their reading habits.[13]

Thus with the issue clearly defined as one of intellectual freedom, the resolution was approved by the membership at Dallas and sent on to the Council. The Council debate which followed revealed the group conflicts within the ALA. Some were concerned about the form of the resolution and so the preamble was revised; others felt that further investigation was needed; and some, including Zoia Horn, were opposed to further investigation because it was simply a policy statement which did not require any action. The resolution, with slight revision, was finally passed by the Council. The Executive Board, functioning as the administrative arm of the Council, then requested an interpretation from the Intellectual Freedom Committee (IFC). And, there the newly-passed Resolution remained for some time.

In Harrisburg, the judicial procedure ground slowly forward and in January 1972, the trial of the "Harrisburg 7" finally began. Boyd Douglas testified again as the chief Government witness, while Ramsey Clark and Leonard Boudin, representing the defense, argued that the Justice Department had prosecuted the case in an effort to protect the reputation of J. Edgar Hoover. Zoia Horn was called as a witness and tried to make a statement to the Court explaining why she refused to testify; but, she was allowed to read only a few lines before the judge silenced her and ordered her to jail. According to the New York Times:

> Her imprisonment as a dangerous criminal came before the hearing was even over and before various milder options could be explored legally. She was branded in contempt of court for the duration of the trial and held up as a warning to future witnesses. Although defense counsel had offered to stipulate her previous testimony before a Grand Jury, the government prosecutor and judge were adamant... [14]

The statement she was not allowed to read in court said in part:

> It is because I respect the function of this court to protect the rights of the individual that I must refuse to testify. I cannot in my conscience lend myself to this black charade. I love and respect this country too much to see a farce made of the tenets upon which it stands. To me it stands on freedom of thought, but government spying in homes, in libraries and universities inhibits and destroys this freedom. It stands on freedom of association--yet in this case gatherings of friends, picnics, parties have been given sinister implications, made suspect. It stands on freedom of speech--yet general discussions have been interpreted by the government as advocacies of conspiracy... [15]

Within the ALA, issues of intellectual freedom and governmental intimidation now become complicated with the question of civil disobedience; and requests for financial support were introduced as a result of Zoia Horn's actions and their consequences. The Council Resolution was still being "interpreted" by the IFC when SRRT requested that ALA publicize the Association's policy as expressed in the Dallas Resolution and provide financial support in the form of bail money for Zoia Horn. The Executive Board's response was negative, for as the voice of ALA, it felt it could not support her action in challenging a duly constituted court of law. The Board took this stand even though it was aware that the LeRoy C. Merritt Humanitarian Fund had made a contribution of $500 to Mrs. Horn "to help defray hardship occasioned by her opposition to threats of intellectual freedom," and that the SRRT Action Council had also granted an equal sum to her.[16]

The Merritt Fund trustees could act without the delay of consulting the entire board of the Fund and, in this instance, they at first refused financial support but within two days reconsidered their action via telephone conference. Apparently some trustees had serious doubts about the propriety of Zoia Horn's actions, but other considerations prevailed and the financial aid was granted. Obviously, there was dissension within this group, but the Merritt Fund is a unique ALA creation. It is not open to public scrutiny and its decisions are not easily reversed by other ALA groups. The SRRT donation came from membership dues and did not require the approval of ALA Council or the Executive Board.

Other groups associated with ALA now became involved, exerting pressures which were eventually to reverse the stand of the Executive Board. On March 28, 1972, the Executive Board of the New Jersey Library Association sent a letter to the Attorney General of the United States protesting the treatment of Zoia Horn during the trial and questioning the right of the government to interfere with activities in libraries. The letter was, of course, duly publicized within professional associations. The ALA Executive Board was also faced with the necessity of responding to a resolution passed by the California Library Association urging it to reverse its earlier action and support Zoia Horn. The Bay Area Social Responsibilities Round Table requested both public and monetary support. On the surface this would appear to be a clear instance of the Executive Board refusing to act on membership wishes and official policy as expressed in the 1971 Dallas Resolution. As indicated, however, the issue had become more complex, and for many, whether or not this was still a question of intellectual freedom could be and was disputed.

During the ALA Chicago Convention in 1972, the IFC conducted some twelve hours of meetings during which there were angry exchanges about secret sessions and charges of undemocratic procedures, demonstrating once again some of the structural problems and schisms within ALA. After considerable agonized discussion, a new and revised statement was prepared by the IFC, sent on to the Council, and endorsed by the Executive Board as a substitute for the earlier one. The statement of support declared:

> ... The Library Bill of Rights, Article IV, explicitly encourages librarians to actively support and cooperate with those individuals and groups who are engaged in resisting censorship and the abridgements of the freedom of expression and of access to information. It is obvious from Mrs. Horn's published statement, which she had attempted to present to the court at the time of her refusal to testify, that the above principles were the basis for her actions in protest. Therefore, the American Library Association commends Mrs. Horn's commitment and courage in defense of the principles of intellectual freedom.[17]

ALA had reconciled the many issues involved sufficiently to agree on a policy statement. No further financial support was forthcoming, however. But once this commitment had been made, the Association went further in protesting governmental intimidation. The IFC broadened the original Dallas Resolution and substituted a new resolution at the 1973 Midwinter ALA Conference. It was considerably stronger than the original and put the Association squarely on record in this issue. It is another important milestone in the interpretation of intellectual freedom and represents a coalescence of "radical" and "traditional" thinking within ALA.

It seems likely that ALA has reached a stage in its growth that will lead it inevitably into the political and social arena of contemporary concerns. Many, like Zoia Horn, believe that librarians should take action on vital issues because they are both knowledgeable and vulnerable. Others are fearful of this extension of interests. Simmering beneath the surface for some time, this problem was aired in the recent "Berninghausen debate" and will certainly engage the library profession for years to come. It will engender debate and discussion that may increase the tensions and pressures within the ALA before it is resolved. In any event, we have been how the actions and interactions of groups can generate change in a complex organization and how an individual act or event can catalyze issues around which group processes are defined and carried out. Such group activities, long recognized as a fundamental feature of the social environment, will appear more significant to librarians as the issues in our society which affect them become more demanding and complex.

Notes

1. From Zoia Horn's response to a Statement by the ALA Executive Board, in John Berry, "Documenting Zoia Horn's Protest," Library Journal 97 (June 15, 1972), p. 2153.
2. Paul Cowan, "Bearing Witness: Some Thoughts on Zoia Horn," Library Journal 97 (June 15, 1972), p. 2150.
3. "The Role of Interest Groups in the Formation of a Library," in Social and Political Aspects of Librarianship, edited by Mary Lee Bundy and Ruth Aaronson (Albany: State University of New York, School of Library Science, 1965).
4. Jerome H. Skolnick, The Politics of Protest. A Task Force Report submitted to the National Commission on the Causes and Prevention of Violence." (New York: Simon and Schuster, 1969), p. 28.
5. "The Berrigans: Conspiracy and Conscience," Time, 97 (January 25, 1971), p. 12.
6. Paul Cowan, "Anderson on Hoover; a Populist Congressman: North Pole to Danbury," The Village Voice, 15 (December 17, 1970), p. 18.
7. "Transcript of Johnson's Statement on Signing Crime and Safety Bill," New York Times, CXVII (June 20, 1968), p. 23.
8. Eli Oboler, "A Constitutional Crisis in the ALA?" American Library Association Bulletin 60 (April 1966), p. 384-386.
9. Oliver Garceau, The Public Library in the Political Process (New York: Columbia University Press, 1949), p. 169.
10. David H. Clift, "The Organizational Environment," in The Changing Environment of Libraries, edited by John T. Eastlick, (Chicago: American Library Association, 1971), p. 41.
11. Ibid., p. 45.
12. "ALA Handbook of Organization, 1972-73," American Libraries 3 (November 1972), p. 1048.
13. American Library Association, Annual Conference Proceedings, 1971 (Chicago: ALA, 1972), p. 83.
14. "Handcuffs in Harrisburg" (an editorial), The New York Times CXXI (March 8, 1972), p. 42.
15. John Berry, op. cit.
16. "Memo to Members," American Libraries, 3 (May 1972), p. 511.
17. "Intellectual Freedom Committee Report to Council," Newsletter on Intellectual Freedom VXXI (September 1972), p. 139.

NOTES ON CONTRIBUTORS

Laura ARKSEY is the humanities bibliographer at Seattle Pacific College Seattle, Washington.

L. BELL is with the Paper Records Office, London, England.

Curtis G. BENJAMIN is the former president and chairman of the McGraw-Hill Book Company.

Edmund and Dorothy BERKELEY are the authors of John Beckley: Zealous Partisan in a Nation Divided (Philadelphia: The American Philosophical Society, 1973).

Walter BRAHM recently retired as the Connecticut State Librarian.

Dorothy BRODERICK is on the faculty of the School of Library Service, Dalhousie University, Halifax, Nova Scotia.

Richard DE GENNARO is Director of Libraries, University of Pennsylvania, Philadelphia.

Antonia DOBI is Periodicals Librarian, De Paul University, Chicago.

Harvey EINBINDER is a well-known encyclopedia critic.

Rudolph C. ELLSWORTH is Head of the Bibliographic Research Services, Douglas Library, Queens University, Kingston, Ontario.

Paul J. FASANA is Chief of Preparation Services for the New York Public Library.

Joan FOSTER is a student at the Graduate School of Library and Information Science, Pratt Institute, Brooklyn, N. Y.

David GERARD is on the faculty at the College of Librarianship, Aberystwyth, Wales.

Michael GORMAN is Head of the Bibliographic Standards Office of the British Library and Associate Editor of the Anglo/American Cataloging Rules revision.

Patricia Kennedy GRIMSTED is a research associate at the Russian Research Center and Ukranian Research Institute, Harvard University.

Gerald F. HAM is with the State Historical Society of Wisconsin.

Francis HENNE is a Professor at Columbia University, School of Library Service.

Irene MARTIN, formerly a Canadian librarian, is now residing in Skamokawa, Washington.

Ellsworth MASON is Director of Libraries, University of Colorado, Boulder, Colorado.

Cavan MC CARTHY is a Teaching Assistant, School of Library and Information Science, SUNY at Albany, Albany, New York.

James G. OLLE is a lecturer at the Department of Library and Information Studies, Loughborough College, England.

Peter OPIE is co-author of The Oxford Dictionary of Nursery Rhymes, among other works.

David PEELE is Head of Technical Services at Staten Island Community College, New York.

Robert J. RUBANOWICE is an Associate Professor in the Department of History, Florida State University, Tallahassee.

Thomas M. SCHMID is Acquisitions Librarian at Marriot Library, University of Utah, Salt Lake City.

Jeanne SCHRAMM is Reference Librarian at West Liberty State College, West Liberty, West Virginia.

Alan U. SCHWARTZ is a lawyer with Greenbaum, Wolff and Ernst, New York City.

Kenneth SHAFFER is a Professor at the School of Library Science, Simmons College, Boston.

Gordon STEVENSON is an Associate Professor at the School of Library and Information Science, SUNY Albany, Albany, New York.

I. R. WILLISON, at the time of his visit to the U. S., was in charge of the United States Collection and Superintendent of the North Library in the British Library's Reference Division.